ENDORSEMENTS

End Times Made Easy has been a wonderful reminder for me on how end times and Judaism coexist and, subsequently, the special bond between Christians and Jews.

RAANAN (RANI) LEVY
Former Advisor to the Prime Minister of Israel
on World Jewish and Christian Affairs

Joe Morris has such a clear understanding of the times in which we live. I've never heard or read after anyone who could make end-time teaching more biblically accurate and positive. This is a book everyone needs to read.

MARK BRAZEE
Pastor, World Outreach Church of Tulsa
Founder, Domata Bible Schools

Joe Morris is one of the most prolific teachers on end-time events in the body of Christ today. He always brings such insight and light into an area that is often shadowed and obscure. You will love the simplicity and illumination that comes as he unfolds these revelations as only he can do.

RAY GENE WILSON
Pastor, West Coast Life Church
Recording artist

END
TIMES
MADE
EASY

END TIMES MADE EASY

THERE IS NO BAD NEWS FOR THE CHRISTIAN!

JOSEPH MORRIS

"
DEFINITIVE FACTS PROVE JESUS IS COMING IN *THIS* GENERATION.
"

Charts and graphs by Clarence Larkin used with permission from the Rev. Clarence Larkin Estate, P.O. Box 334, Glenside, PA 19038, U.S.A., 215-576-5590, www.larkinestate.com.

Published by Harrison House Publishers
Shippensburg, PA 17257

ISBN 13 TP: 978-1-6803-1699-5
ISBN 13 eBook: 978-1-6803-1700-8
ISBN 13 HC: 978-1-6803-1702-2
ISBN 13 LP: 978-1-6803-1701-5

For Worldwide Distribution, Printed in the U.S.A.
1 2 3 4 5 6 7 8 / 26 25 24 23 22

CONTENTS

INTRODUCTION

WHO AMONG US has not noticed how volatile the world around us has become—threats of war, rampant viruses, natural disasters of every kind, and hatred and violence spilling into the streets? Many people feel like they live in an alternate universe because the culture around us is a classic example of people calling evil good and good evil. In fact, many people wonder, *Is the end near?*

Yes, the end of the age is very near. But it's wonderful news!

Jesus is coming soon, but it's nothing but good news for the Christian. Sure, there is plenty of bad news on the horizon—but not for you. Jesus' end-time agenda is to give you great hope and great joy about His return. Jesus wants to bless you and prepare you for your destiny in these last days.

For a lot of people, end-time teaching over the years has either been confusing or downright scary, but it should not be either one. When you look at the plan of God, everything about His end-time plan makes absolutely flawless and perfect sense. We should be filled with blessing, joy, and strength when we talk about the end times—not sorrow, fear, and confusion. When the Lord called me to teach on end times, He really stressed to me, "I want My kids to be happy and expectant." The whole thing about end-time preaching is expectation because Jesus cannot wait to see you!

Throughout this book, we will connect the dots between Bible prophecy and current events. We will look at easy-to-understand scriptural evidence that lays a foundation of Bible prophecy along with 75+ signs (and counting) of Jesus' soon return. We'll answer tough questions about the Tribulation and look at amazing, mind-boggling biblical descriptions of the glorious life Jesus has planned for us during the millennial reign. We will take a look at charts and pictures that lay out the end times one, two, three.

When Jesus taught on this earth, He always made things easy to understand, and He wants His return explained the same way. A study of the end times does not have to be complicated. Once you get your questions answered and understand what happens why and when, you will be empowered to run your race and be so excited to see Jesus face to face that you can hardly wait!

Joe Morris

CHAPTER 1

JESUS APPEARED TO ME WITH AN END-TIME MANDATE

EVERYWHERE YOU TURN there are signs that Jesus is coming soon. You can easily look around today and picture your future because blatant signs are found in Bible prophecy and news headlines. It's very intentional. Jesus is trying to show you how near we are to His return. He does not want these signs to frighten you, but He does want them to wake you up. He wants you to recognize the hour you are living in.

Jesus wants these signs to make you bold and motivate you to pick up your pace and accelerate doing the will of God. The more intimately you get to know Jesus and what His Word says about His return, the freer and more excited you will be.

But there is something else Jesus wants you to know more than anything else: He wants you to know how much He loves you and how excited He is to see you face to face.

On more than one occasion, Jesus has appeared to me with a mandate to preach on His return. In 1987, Jesus appeared to me and told me to preach on end times. Respectfully, I explained that I did not want to preach on that topic.

"But, Lord," I said, "I don't want to be weird. People equate end times with weirdness. You know, it's right up there with locust burgers and weird hair—just strange."

"This is what I want you to do," Jesus said. "It's what you're supposed to do."

Four years later in 1990, Jesus appeared to me again. At first, He just looked at me because I had not preached on end times like He told me to do. At the time, I was staying in Michigan at Tom and Judy Hicks' house preparing for a service that night. I was praying in their really cool office. The den had walnut walls and an amazing fireplace. Sandi Patti music was playing, and I was praying in tongues, getting ready to go preach.

All of a sudden, the presence of God filled the room, and I began to cry. I thought, *Lord, You* are *so good to me! Why are You so good to me?* I looked up, and there was Jesus, leaning against the desk in front of me. He was wearing a white robe with an olive-green sash, and His hands were folded behind His back.

I was no longer crying at that point; I was outright bawling. Jesus just looked at me. I was overcome by His presence and crying uncontrollably because of the goodness coming out of Him.

Jesus continued looking at me. I knew He was there because I hadn't preached what He wanted me to preach. He could have said, "Hey, you're a loser. You haven't done what you're supposed to do." But He just sat there and looked at me, and His goodness led me to repentance (2 Pet. 3:15).

I realize now the urgency of His end-time mandate. Why is it so urgent? Because Jesus wants you prepared and loved. The number-one thing Jesus really instructed me to tell you is how much He loves you. Friend, no matter how much you already believe Jesus loves you, you can magnify that number by a billion trillion. In fact, you could not magnify it enough to show you just how much He adores you. Jesus cares deeply for you and wants you nourished, instructed, and strengthened. He only wants good things for you, and He gave His life to prove it.

> No matter how much you already believe Jesus loves you, you can magnify that number by a billion trillion.

God has gotten blamed for so many evil things the devil does, but the Bible says every good gift and every perfect gift is from above, and that never changes (James 1:17). Your Father loves you and wants you excited, hopeful, and happy when Jesus raptures the Church. He wants you so happy that you are almost giddy. People may even think there's something wrong with you and ask, "Why are you so happy anyway?"

You will answer, "Because I'm about to see Jesus Christ, my Savior and Lord, face to face!"

I absolutely light up when my phone rings and I see a picture of my only daughter calling who lives several states away. I drop everything to talk to my little girl. She is a married woman now with a child of her own, but she will always still be my little girl. And, if I think like that, imagine how Jesus thinks about you.

He can't wait to see you in person, and we should have a radical joy about seeing Him face to face.

Jesus wants us to finish our courses on earth with joy because joy is our strength (Neh. 8:10), and He knows we need strength to finish strong. He wants the message of His soon return pumped into us, enabling us to run faster and get more accomplished in a shorter period of time. We have been destined to close off the Church Age, and we have more to get done than any generation before us.

Think about it. You are about to be caught up to meet Jesus in the air. How cool is that? This King we worship and serve will go from faith to sight. You will see His eyes that are flames of fire and His feet of fine brass. You will see the love in His eyes and the nail prints in His hands. And in heaven, you will see the fountain filled with blood, drawn from Emmanuel's veins.

> You are about to be caught up to meet Jesus in the air. How cool is that? This King we worship and serve will go from faith to sight.

Yet before that day, we have a lot of inheritance to walk in. We have a lot of important things to do in this hour to accomplish the will of God and prepare for His coming. God's agenda in this hour is to love you, inform you, bless you, strengthen you, and help you because there's destiny on you just as there is on America and every nation.

From the very beginning of this nation more than 245 years ago, I believe Christians walked this continent praying and decreeing God's will over this nation and what would happen right before the coming of the Lord. We are all walking out those prayers even now, so let's be faithful to fulfill them and get the message of Jesus to everyone—next door and from coast to coast. You and I need to daily demonstrate that Jesus came out of the grave.

There's just so much happening right now. You are living when all of the prophetic verses in the Bible are coming to pass. I remember end-time preachers 20 to 30 years ago who would lay out everything that had to happen—all the pieces of the puzzle that would need to fall in place and come together before Jesus could return. But, my friend, we are there! Last week something happened that was a sign of His coming. The week before that something happened. Yesterday something happened. Literally, the dots are connecting before your eyes with Bible verses coming to pass click, click, click. It's an exciting time, a rejoicing time!

TIME TO ACCELERATE

As you begin to recognize the timing of Jesus' return and the signs all around, it will propel you in your race. It will fuel you to run faster. After all, when you're running a race, you don't slow down when you can see the finish line. You run faster—a whole lot faster! That what Jesus wants you to do now.

My daughter ran cross country in high school, and I remember how she practiced hard for every race. Every day she ran miles and miles, and I did my best to cheer her on. I would get on my motorcycle and ride beside her, shouting, "You're doing good, Lauren! You're doing great! Keep going!" She would run four or five miles and not even be tired while I got tired just riding my motorcycle. On the weekends, Lauren would train even more intensely for her cross-country events.

I'm so glad I got to attend almost every single race because I loved cheering for her. I would be right there at the first mile marker waiting for her, and she would come running by yelling out, "Daddy, how far? How far?"

"Lauren, you've got two more miles. Pace yourself!" I would answer. She asked about the distance because she was calculating how much energy she should exert at that point.

I didn't want her to give it all out at the beginning, so I'd say, "Pace yourself, Lauren! Two more miles!"

Then I would cut across the field to beat her to the next mile marker. The first thing she would say when she would run up is, "Daddy, how far? How far now?"

"Lauren, you've got another mile," I would answer. "Pace yourself! You've got plenty of time!"

Eventually, there would come a point in the race where I would cut over to the last place, and as she would come running up to reach that marker, she would see the finish line. She would see me but not say a word to me at that point. She no longer asked, "Hey, Daddy, how far? How far?" No, she could see the finish line for herself.

Her countenance would change. Joy would come all over her. All that practice, all that training, all that hard work every day meant nothing until, all of a sudden, right there I could see determination all over her face.

She was saying to herself, "I'm not going to come to the end of this race and slow down now. Let's blow it out!"

I would scream, *"RUN!"* And everything about her changed. I could see it on her face and in her movement. She picked up her pace, resolute to finish the race.

Words were not necessary, but I would scream just the same, "RUN! RUN, LAUREN, *RUN!* The finish line is just ahead! *GO!"* And she would cross that line and finish with her hand in the air—victory all over her!

My friend, *you* are also in a race—the race of your life! We all are. Can you see the finish line just ahead? It's the finish line for the Church Age. And it's time to RUN! RUN, CHURCH, *RUN!* The finish line is just ahead! *Go!* It's time to finish with your hand in the air—victory all over you!

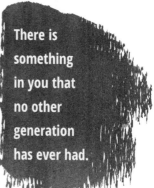

In a relay race, the fastest guys always run at the end. That means the Lord looked down through the corridors of time and picked you to run fast at the end. He is right now giving you a heightened awareness about these last of the last days.

There is something in you that no other generation has ever had.

Everything we've been taught until now has been an investment of the Word for our generation, and it's time to accelerate. Jesus is calling on those investments now. He's tapping all those spiritual deposits right now. Greater is He that is in you than he that is in this world (John 4:4). Whatsoever is born of God overcomes the world. This is the victory that overcomes the world, even our faith (1 John 5:4). Come on now!

PROPHECY TO THIS GENERATION

There is something in you that no other generation has ever had. Daniel saw you and prophesied about you. He said you would be strong. He said you would know your God and do exploits! (Daniel 11:32.) Okay, it's time. That day has come.

A lot of people know the Word of God, but not the God of the Word. I believe God is getting us acquainted with the God of the Word so we can step into our end-time destiny.

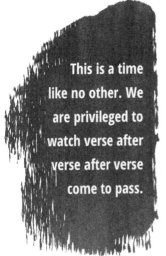

> This is a time like no other. We are privileged to watch verse after verse after verse come to pass.

This is a time like no other. We are privileged to watch verse after verse after verse come to pass. There are more verses about the time we live in right now and the Tribulation period than any other topic in the Bible. In fact, the Bible is one-third prophecy, so, clearly, this topic is on God's heart, and there's more documentation right in front of us than ever before.

So, let's get into what the Bible has to say about end times. These verses will comfort us, excite us, strengthen us, and help us pick up the pace so we can run our race and cross the finish line.

CHAPTER 2

THE CULTURE OF THE LAST DAYS

THE APOSTLE PETER had a lot to say about the culture of the last days—how society would be thinking, acting, and going about their lives. In Peter's day— some two thousand years ago—the early church would have been excited about Jesus' return. They would have thought, *Wow! Jesus is coming! I can hardly wait to see Him again!* But clearly, that is not the case today. With spiritual insight, Peter looked ahead to the culture of the day when Jesus was about to return and described a fleshly people who scoffed at the return of Jesus. Truer words were never spoken.

2 PETER 3:1-3 (NKJV)

Beloved, I now write to you this second epistle (in both of which I stir up your pure minds by way of reminder), that you may be mindful of the words which were spoken before by the holy prophets, and of the commandment of

us, the apostles of the Lord and Savior, knowing this first:
that scoffers will come in the last days, walking according
to their own lusts.

Notice the tone of Peter's writing. He calls you His beloved in verse 1, which is an intimate description. In the Gospels, Peter instructed us to pray that we might be counted worthy to stand before the Son of Man, but here in 2 Peter, he no longer tells us to pray to be counted worthy. He says we are His beloved because we are *in Him.* As we read in the Epistles, we are reading about "as He is, so are we in this world" (1 John 4:17).

Then in verses 2 and 3, Peter goes on to talk about the end times and tells us what to expect. He nailed it in the next verse when he quoted what people would be asking.

2 PETER 3:4 (NLT)

What happened to the promise that Jesus is coming again?
From before the times of our ancestors, everything has
remained the same since the world was first created.

In other words, Peter prophesied that in our day—just before Jesus comes—people would be saying, "Enough already. I don't believe Jesus is coming back. It's been 2,000 years, and He hasn't come yet."

That same thinking has even crept into the Church. I'm sure you have heard Christians flippantly say, "Nah, I've heard that Jesus is coming soon all my life." Well, yes! That's exactly right. You have heard all your life that Jesus is coming back because He *is* coming back.

Before I would go to bed at night at as a little kid, my mother would tell me, "The Rapture could happen tonight!" As the lights went out, I would say, "Lord, I love You!" because I didn't want to miss the Rapture. You also have a choice when you hear the message of Jesus' return. You can respond haughtily or humbly. You can say, "Yeah, whatever, I've heard it all before," or you can say, "Lord, I love You."

The whole purpose of the Tribulation is to catch all those people who are haughty or hardheaded and who don't know whether to believe in Jesus' return or not. During the Tribulation, there will be fireworks of every kind going off for seven years—judgments, seals, vials, and undeniable signs that cannot be ignored. The Lord loves people—the whole world past, present, and future—so much that all sorts of events will transpire to turn their hearts to Him that they would be saved from eternal hell.

God tells us through Peter precisely what the cultural climate will be like before the Church leaves this earth in the Rapture.

2 PETER 3:5-7 (NLT)

They deliberately forget that God made the heavens long ago by the word of his command, and he brought the earth out from the water and surrounded it with water. Then he used the water to destroy the ancient world with a mighty flood. And by the same word, the present heavens and earth have been stored up for fire. They are being kept for the day of judgment, when ungodly people will be destroyed.

Peter says people will have forgotten about the flood that occurred during the days of Noah. Scoffing, they will ask, "Hey, where is the promise of the coming?" They did not realize that change came when no one believed change was coming. Imagine that.

Can you also imagine what it was like for Noah to be called to preach something no one had ever seen before? That would be kind of a bummer. The Lord told Noah, "Oh, by the way, you're going to preach about rain."

"What's rain?" Noah asked. Up until then, the earth was watered by the dew.

God explained, and Noah responded, "Oh, great! I get to preach on something people have never heard of and won't understand." Sure enough, when Noah began to preach, people mocked him. Hebrews 11:7 (NLT) says:

> It was by faith that Noah built a large boat to save his family from the flood. He obeyed God, who warned him about things that had never happened before. By his faith Noah condemned the rest of the world, and he received the righteousness that comes by faith.

The word *warned* in the Greek is the word *krimatasio*, which means to be divinely instructed. Noah was divinely instructed that the flood was coming, and so he preached. You would think people in Noah's time would have paid attention to the signs around them, especially after the animals started coming in together. You would think they would have been like, "Hmmm, something is up. As crazy as Noah is, he's got a pretty good caravan of animals arriving in pairs." I'm sure they asked themselves a few questions when signs started appearing. Nevertheless, it is amazing that he preached and preached, and people only mocked him.

The truth is, the Bible says the climate today would be just like that. And it is. We encounter scoffing, mocking, and disbelief all around us. At the same time, signs abound, and the day of Jesus' return quickly approaches.

It's weird, but even Hollywood movies sense and convey what's ahead better than the Church does. There are so many movies about vampires and zombies because even unbelievers feel an ominous change and a resurrection coming, and that's their way to interpret it. There *is* a change coming! The Church will depart and seven years later, the King of Kings and the Lord of Lords will return to earth with a scepter of righteousness to set up His kingdom. We Christians will be right there with Him riding on white horses. What a view that will be! We who call Jesus Lord will return to planet Earth and see firsthand the brightness of His glory. These events even now are lining up before our eyes.

A CLUE ABOUT TIMING

We are living at a time when the gospel is being preached all over the world, and nations are moving into position for the Tribulation that happens after the Church is raptured. We are privileged to be alive and witness these prophetic events unfold. Look at the clue Peter gives us about timing.

2 PETER 3:8

But, beloved, do not forget this one thing, that with the Lord one day is as a thousand years, and a thousand years as one day.

If you do the math, your 80-year life is like a two-hour movie to the Lord. So, squeeze in all you can! There are 2,000 years from Adam to Abraham, 2,000 years from Abraham to Jesus' coming, and 2,000 years from the First Coming to the Second Coming. That totals 6,000 years, and everything you and I do revolves around that format. Our week follows that format. We have six days in our week, on the seventh day we rest, and then we start over again. The Earth itself follows the same pattern. Peter's point to believers by the Holy Ghost is that there is only a small window of time before Jesus returns.

The Bible gives us many more time clues. For example, Jesus told the story of the Good Samaritan in Luke 10:27-35. Most Christians enjoy the parable as a lesson about helping those who are down and out, but in this simple parable, Jesus also paints a dispensational picture about the timing of His return. After caring for the injured man, the Good Samaritan took him to a local inn. Luke 10:35 says, "And on the morrow when he departed, he took out two pence, and gave them to the host, and said unto him, Take care of him; and whatsoever thou spendest more, when I come again, I will repay thee." The amount of two pence is significant.

In Matthew 20:1-16, we are told that a pence, or a penny, was a full day's wage. That means the Good Samaritan—representing Jesus—gave the host enough money for two days. Jesus was giving us insight about the timing of the Church Age.

In Luke 13:31, Jesus gives us another clue. We read how Jesus was teaching along and certain Pharisees told him to get out of town before Herod heard about Him and killed Him. Jesus said, "Go tell that fox that I will keep on casting out demons and healing people today and tomorrow; and the third day I will accomplish my purpose" (Luke 13:32 NLT). Jesus is still casting out demons and healing people today through His body, and on the third day He *will* accomplish His purpose and return.

There are several more examples in the Bible of Jesus talking of His own return, but here's the bottom line. We are at the end of 6,000 years of human history, and change is coming. Planet Earth itself has been getting ready in the past 100 years. Even today's technology has surpassed all expectations. Everything has sped up to get the message out that Jesus is alive and well and coming soon.

A FALL FROM STEADFASTNESS

A few verses further on in 2 Peter 3, the Lord tells us to beware as we recognize the hour we're in. He says there's something important we must do! Peter already prepared us that we would live in a time of scoffing and mocking. He prepared us that we would be surrounded by people who were lovers of self and not paying attention to Jesus' return. He realized that even Christians would become callous, so what advice did Peter give?

2 PETER 3:17 (NKJV)

You therefore, beloved, since you know this beforehand, beware lest you also fall from your own steadfastness, being led away with the error of the wicked.

Peter cautions us to beware when we see signs of Jesus' return. Anytime you see *beware* in the Bible or anywhere else for that matter, you need to pay attention. Peter said beware or watch out that you're not led away by the error of the wicked and fall from your own steadfastness. What is the "error of the wicked"? Their error is that they think life will just keep right on going as it always has. *But beware!* Change is coming—big change.

Some 2,000 years ago—beforehand—God inspired Peter to warn us that if we don't watch it, the error of the wicked will creep into the Church. How right on was that message?

In these last days, the Church needs to think like an athletic team with a two-minute warning. When you are playing sports—football, soccer, basketball, or whatever—you know when the clock is ticking down. You don't think, *Hey, let's chill!* You think, *I've got to work harder! I've got to do whatever it takes to score and do it fast!* Everything changes when you're running out of time.

> In these last days, the Church needs to think like an athletic team with a two-minute warning.

At the two-minute mark in American football, teams have special plays they have rehearsed so the quarterback can come to the huddle or to the line to call audibles. At that point, the team members don't worry about how tired they are. There's no complaining or murmuring. Could you imagine a team needing to score a goal in the final seconds of a game and one of the guys saying, "Can we slow down a little? My knees hurt!"

The rest of the team would say, "Hello? Seriously? Quit whining about your knees! We've only got seconds left to score!"

An athlete's mentality changes when he or she is trying to cross the finish line and running out of time. The thought pattern becomes all about making every second count to finish and win.

Church, it's time to watch the clock.

"Where is the clock and how do we read it?" somebody might ask.

Israel is the timepiece, and the clock is ticking down!

That's why Peter said not to "fall from your own steadfastness." Think about it. A person cannot fall from something if he or she was not already there in the first place. You have been steadfast because you are in the body of Christ, and you know who you are in Him.

That's why the teaching revival of the past 45 to 50 years has taught the Church the message of faith, so we're not moved by how we feel in these last days. God has sown the Word so strong in our generation that we are not moved by anything.

You've no doubt heard 20th-century apostle of faith Smith Wigglesworth quoted saying, "I'm not moved by what I see. I'm not moved by what I feel. I'm moved by the Word of God that's real." That has been deposited in you and me, and that *is* the steadfastness Peter told us about. That is how strong and solid Peter said we need to be as we walk out these last of the last days.

Six times in the Bible we are told the condition we need to be in before the Rapture:

1 Corinthians 15:58 (NKJV)

My beloved brethren, be steadfast, immovable, always abounding in the work of the Lord, knowing that your labor is not in vain in the Lord.

Why is that a big deal? Noah was preacher of righteousness, and in righteousness you will be established or made to stand. That's why, right before the Rapture of the Church, Peter instructed us to be steadfast and immovable. He was saying that as you live in the time all these verses are coming to pass, don't you dare be casual about the will of God.

> The Bible admonishes us to preach to one and another about Jesus' return because we are warned that in the very climate people don't believe, Jesus will return!

We all know people who say, "Jesus is coming soon? Yeah, whatever. I've heard it all before." Forcibly reject that sort of thinking! We must say, "No! I am steadfast. My King is coming back." The Bible admonishes us to preach to one and another about Jesus' return because we are warned that in the very climate people don't believe, *Jesus will return!*

CHAPTER 3

THE FUTURE BEFORE IT HAPPENS

END-TIME PREACHING IS such an opportunity to highlight just how flawless the Word of God is because it proves the Scriptures through and through. I love how cool the Scriptures are and how God watches over His Word to perform it and bring it to pass. It is nothing less than amazing. No one but God Himself could tell us the future thousands of years before it happens.

To see just how shockingly perfect God's Word is, look with me at Isaiah 46, where we see the *moeds*[1] or set times in the Bible.

ISAIAH 46:9-10 (NLT)

Remember the things I have done in the past. For I alone am God! I am God, and there is none like me. Only I can tell you the future before it even happens. Everything I plan will come to pass, for I do whatever I wish.

Here's why you can be at rest and relax about end-time prophecy: God promised to tell you what's going to happen before it happens. How amazing is that? No other religion can do that. Your Bible is the only book that can accurately tell you the future because it is one amazingly supernatural book.

God promised to tell you what's going to happen before it happens.

God said you can know that I am God because I tell you the future before it happens—thousands and thousands of years before it happens. For example, Ezekiel prophesied the very year that Israel would be made a nation, and it was so. Gabriel prophesied the exact year that Jesus would come the first time, and it was so. Isaiah prophetically described Calvary for us. And John has given us a revelation of thousands of years yet to come. I'm telling you the Bible is flawless.

In fact, God gave us the entire plan of redemption in the Hebrew meanings of the first 10 names of the Bible:

- Adam means *man*.
- Seth means *appointed*.
- Enus means *mortal.*
- Canaan means *sorrows.*
- Mahilia means *blessed God.*
- Jared means *shall come down.*
- Enoch means *teaching.*
- Methuselah means *his death brings.*
- Lameck means *to despair.*
- Noah means *rest.*

Do you see it? The first 10 names lay out God's plan for the ages: Man is appointed mortal with sorrow. The blessed God shall come down teaching. His death brings a despairing rest.

FLAWLESS PREDICTIONS

The entire book of Revelation is one huge word of wisdom—one of the nine gifts of the Spirit. The first part of Revelation is a word of knowledge that outlines the present-tense conditions of the churches. After that, it outlines their future. As I said earlier, the Bible itself is one-half prophecy. Why did God do that? He is showing you that it is outside of man's realm and capability to write the Bible. God is the Author, and He proves it by telling you the future.

Let me show you what I mean. Paul talked about baptism 12 times, but he talked about the coming of the Lord 52 times. For every verse about the first coming of the Lord, there are eight times more verses about the Second Coming of the Lord. There are 300 prophecies about the first coming of the Lord but almost 2,500 prophecies about the Second Coming of the Lord. Why? God wants to make sure you recognize the appointed time.

He did it so you would read His Word and say, "Wow! I've got to hustle because this is the very end." Folks, right now you are writing your resume for what you will do during the millennium. You are deciding now whether you will rule over two cities or ten.

Listen to how perfect the Bible is and the flawlessness of the first coming. Here are just 17 of many more verses that predict and prophesy the first coming of the Lord:

1. Jesus would be born in Bethlehem—Micah 5:2.

2. Jesus' lineage is of the tribe of Judah—Numbers 24:17.

3. Jesus would be preceded by a messenger—Isaiah 40:3-5.

4. Jesus would be betrayed by His friends—Psalm 41:9, Zechariah 11:12-13.

5. Jesus would be quiet before His accusers—Isaiah 53:7.

6. Jesus would be given away for 30 pieces of silver—Zechariah 11:12-13.

7. Jesus' betrayal money would be used by Judas to buy a potter's field—Zechariah 11:12-13.

8. Jesus would ride into Jerusalem on a colt—Zechariah 9:9.

9. Jesus would be crucified among thieves—Isaiah 53:12.

10. Jesus' side, hands, and feet would be pierced on the cross—Psalm 22:16, Zechariah 12:10.

11. Jesus would wear a crown of thorns—Isaiah 53:5.

12. While Jesus was on the cross, the sky would darken midday—Amos 8:9.

13. Jesus' bones would not be broken—Exodus 12:46, Psalm 34:20.

14. Jesus would be buried in a rich man's tomb—Isaiah 53:9.

15. Soldiers would gamble over Jesus' robe after He was crucified—Psalm 22:18.

16. Jesus' body would not decay—Psalm 16:10.

17. Jesus would be raised from the dead (who but God could pull that one off?)—Isaiah 26:19.

A STATISTICAL MIRACLE

Do you realize the odds statistically of every one of those Bible prophecies coming to pass from one generation to another? There are some 300 prophecies, and I only gave you 17 of them. Yet the odds of 17 coming to pass from one generation is 400,000,000,000,000,000,000,000,000,000,000,000.

That's 480 with 33 zeros after it, or in other words, 480 billion times a trillion and a billion.

Some people think, *Well, these prophecies all just happened by chance.* Are you kidding me? Even in the scientific world, it's acknowledged that after so many zeros, an occurrence is no longer by chance. Then how did it happen that all these prophecies came true? God. Period.

This book we call the Bible is one supernatural book from beginning to end. God moved on some 40 different authors to write down 66 books over 16 centuries or 1,800 years. These men and women came from all walks of life, never knew each other, and were from various countries over three continents. And yet, *not one* of its prophecies has ever failed to come to pass.

God Himself is the author of the Bible. Therefore, when you recognize how flawlessly the Bible told of the first coming, what does that tell you about Bible prophecies forecasting the Second Coming? Actually, there is eight times more flawlessness at the Second Coming.

> The veracity of Bible prophecies should preach to us as we watch events in the news line up right before Jesus comes back to planet Earth.

The veracity of Bible prophecies should preach to us as we watch events in the news line up right before Jesus comes back to planet Earth. We need to watch Russia, Syria, Crimea, and Libya because all these nations prepare for what will happen right after the Church is raptured. How do we know this? We have flawless prophecies in hand that show us the way, and we will look at them along with prophetic signs being fulfilled right before our eyes.

CHAPTER 4

75+ SIGNS OF JESUS' RETURN . . . AND COUNTING

CAN YOU REMEMBER a time you were driving down a freeway and felt like you were starving? Suddenly, you see a McDonald's billboard that says: *Hot and Juicy Burgers 8 Miles Straight Ahead.* The next sign says seven miles to McDonald's. Then the next sign says six miles, then five miles. But let me ask, as you see sign after sign, do you think, *Man, I'm never going to get my burger?* No. Your mouth begins to water as you move toward your Big Mac because the signs keep you alerted that your burger is coming soon. The signs were intentional—put there to guide you and fire up your taste buds.

In the same way, Jesus has given us signs that show us He is coming soon. We will look at 75+ signs that alert us to Jesus' soon return. You may already be aware of some of these signs, but my friend, stamp them in your heart because they will change your life.

I've heard some people say, "I believe the Lord is coming back but that doesn't change anything." Are you kidding me? If you *really believe* the Lord is returning soon to the planet, it changes everything. You live differently. You are kinder, gentler, and more merciful. You get rid of bitterness and animosity. You determine without a doubt what God wants you to do in life, and you get busy doing it. All the "Mickey-Mouse" stuff that used to bother you drops off because you know you are about to see the King. Come on!

> Jesus has said you will see and know of His return, and here are 75+ ways He's showing you.

New signs are added often in this hour of the last-days Church, and each sign is remarkably distinctive for our generation, our lifetime. Jesus has said you will see and know of His return, and here are 75+ ways He's showing you. Jesus isn't hiding anything. He wants you to notice these signs! As we've said before, they are very intentional. So much had already happened, and even more is unfolding right before our eyes. Get a clue! Jesus is coming soon!

#1 ISRAEL MADE A NATION IN **1948**—LUKE 21:29-33 // JEREMIAH 30:1-31 // JEREMIAH 40

Israel's declaration of independence, proclaiming the State of Israel, was delivered on May 14, 1948. It came just under the wire—one day before the expiration of the British Mandate, which formalized British administration of territory conceded by the Ottoman Empire in a peace treaty ending World War I.

Centuries before, God declared this day would come.

JEREMIAH 30:1-3 (NKJV)

The word that came to Jeremiah from the Lord, saying, "Thus speaks the Lord God of Israel, saying: '...For behold, the days are coming,' says the Lord, 'that I will bring back from captivity My people Israel and Judah,' says the Lord. 'And I will cause them to return to the land that I gave to their fathers, and they shall possess it.'"

In Luke 21, Jesus pointed out that Israel being made a nation is a timepiece central to Bible prophecy.

LUKE 21:29-33 (NLT)

Then he gave them this illustration: "Notice the fig tree, or any other tree. When the leaves come out, you know without being told that summer is near. In the same way, when you see all these things taking place, you can know that the Kingdom of God is near. I tell you the truth, this generation will not pass from the scene until all these things have taken place. Heaven and earth will disappear, but my words will never disappear."

Let me explain the importance of these verses by asking this question: Do you wear a watch? Why? You wear it to know what time it is. If you don't have an appointment, you don't have need of a watch. But if you don't want to miss an appointment or be late, you better keep track of the time. Likewise, Jesus said to look at Israel to keep track of time because you have an appointment.

In Acts 8, we read how a great wave of persecution began and swept over the church in Jerusalem. All the believers except the apostles were scattered. This certainly was true of the Jews. But in 1948, God regathered Israel—the fig tree—as He said He would do. What a miracle!

God moved the Jews back to their land so He could court them. We know from Bible prophecy that right after the Rapture of the Church, the spirit of supplication will come upon that land. The Jews will turn to Jesus, and we see the setup for that now. God is smart enough to work with them as a nation and bring them back by courting them.

JERUSALEM WON BACK IN **1967**— LUKE 21:24 // AMOS 9:14-15

History tells us that in AD 70, Jerusalem was overthrown and remained overthrown until 1967, when Jerusalem was won back in the Six-Day War. Boom. The war was fought between Israel and the neighboring states of Egypt, Jordan, and Syria. A ceasefire was signed June 11, leaving Israel in control of the Gaza Strip and the Sinai Peninsula, the West Bank, East Jerusalem, and the Golan Heights.

Notice what Jesus said about this.

LUKE 21:24

And they [the Jews] *will fall by the edge of the sword, and be led away captive into all nations. And Jerusalem will be trampled by Gentiles until the times of the Gentiles are fulfilled.*

In other words, Jesus was saying, "Hey, when you see Jerusalem won back, time is up. Buckle up." What a bold and radical statement!

From beginning to end, it's incredible to hear how God supernaturally helped during this war. You can Google amazing miracles that occurred during the six-day period. The media has interviewed many of the Israeli soldiers in that war. Most of them didn't even believe in miracles but testified to them anyway. Several of these interviews can be found on YouTube.

I heard a couple of soldiers tell this story. One guy said, "Against all odds we won. I don't know what happened, but something happened that day!"

Another guy said 88 Egyptian tanks were coming down on his one Israeli tank, and he began firing with all he had. "If I'm going out, then I'm going out with a bang!" he said.

The Israeli tank fired shells all night until eventually the Egyptian commander came out waving a white flag and yelling, "Where is your commander? I surrender to the highest-ranking officer."

"It's just me here," the lone soldier said who had been firing all night. "There's nobody else!"

"There have to be more soldiers!" the Egyptian commander answered. "The whole night the countryside was filled with tanks and men dressed in white. You fired at us all night, and we can't take anymore!"

Another miracle during the Six-Day War involved a regiment of Jewish soldiers who each only had three or four bullets left as the Syrian army bore down on them. The Jewish soldiers talked among themselves. "I got three bullets. How many you got?"

"I got four bullets."

"Well, it's been great serving with you guys, but it's all over now. We're about to die. No big deal, I guess."

All of a sudden, the Syrian army stopped in their tracks. They looked up and screamed, "Father Abraham." I think they saw Jesus. They just didn't know who they were looking at. Then they shrieked and took off running.

Later, the media interviewed the soldier who screamed, and it was pretty cool to see and hear from the actual soldier in battle. He said, "It wasn't Father Abraham that scared me so bad. It was all those angels with flaming swords. We knew we couldn't defeat them."

I recall yet another story about the Six-Day War where a division of the Israeli army was completely surrounded by a minefield on one side and the enemy on the other. The troops looked at each other and said, "There's nowhere we can go. We're outnumbered a hundred to one. What do we do?"

There was no way through the minefield. It was a pure deathtrap. Suddenly, a huge wind blew through exposing all the mines. The Israeli soldiers walked right down through the middle of the minefield, easily avoiding every explosive. It was such a miracle—like you read about all through the Old Testament. God did some amazing things during the Six-Day War because the times of the Gentiles are pretty much up, and the dispensations are bumping up against each other.

God helped the Israelis fight that battle during the Six-Day War to fulfill His Word. It was divine intervention in the ordinary course of nature for Jerusalem to be won back, and it was right on time—exactly one Jubilee,[1] or 50-year period, from 1917 to 1967.

Remember, everything points to that prime and pivotal piece of real estate called Jerusalem. For the most part, if you live west of Jerusalem, you read left to right. If you live east of Jerusalem, you read right to left. Everything comes back to that one location, and no wonder. Jesus will return to the Mount of Olives where He was beaten, mocked, and crucified. But He will come back as the King of Kings to reign forever, and the earth is getting ready for His arrival.

Both end-time signs #1 and #2 powerfully tell time for us. Read a little further in Luke 21.

LUKE 21:30

When they now shoot forth, ye see and know of your own selves that summer [harvest] *is now nigh at hand.*

This scripture is telling us that when Israel was made a nation and Jerusalem was won back, we can see and know. In other words, we won't have to be told what's coming next because it will be obvious. Likewise, in the spring of every year, we don't have to be told that summer is coming—we know it because trees bud and grass turns green. This past year, did anyone say to you, "Hey, I wonder if summer will come this year?" Of course, not. It would be crazy to ask something so obvious, which is the whole point here.

Jesus said in the same way that you are bold about seasonal temperature changes you've experienced year after year, you can be bold about what will happen when you see Israel made a nation and Jerusalem won back. Jesus summarizes His point in the next verse.

Luke 21:31 (NLT)

In the same way, when you see all these things taking place, you can know that the Kingdom of God is near.

I hear people say all the time, "You cannot tell when Jesus will return." You can if you can read. Jesus has given us sign after sign after sign. The next verse is the real kicker.

Luke 21:32

Verily I say unto you, This generation shall not pass away, till all be fulfilled.

Wow! That's pretty amazing! Jesus said "this generation." What generation is that? The one that sees Israel made a nation. That's *your* generation.

I don't see how Jesus could have been any clearer. He said when you see Jerusalem won back, buckle up. Time is up. Israel became a nation in 1948, and Jerusalem was won back in 1967. Jesus said when you see these things come to pass, you will know that this generation will not pass away until all is fulfilled.

People often ask me, "How can you be so bold about Jesus' soon return?" Because you and I can do the math and add up the generations from then until now. A generation in the Bible is how long man's life span was at the time. In those days, it was 40 years; today it's 70 to 80 years. So, when we figure this up from Adam to Jesus, the average generation was 55 years. But no matter how you do the math, we are the generation when Jesus returns.

Folks, when it comes right down to it, don't we all have a witness in our spirits that Jesus is coming soon? The Holy Spirit is not witnessing to us, "Hey, take your time. We've got all the time in the world." No, there's an urgency about what He is speaking to us in this hour.

These signs bless us, push us, encourage us, and buoy our faith in God's flawless accuracy as they come to pass before our eyes, but they don't really surprise us because we see and know. We should have a song in our hearts and a radical joy among us as we watch it all unfold.

#3 REVIVAL OF THE ROMAN EMPIRE IN 1957— DANIEL 2:40 // DANIEL 7:23-24 // REVELATION 13 & 17

This sign is significant because it is the platform for the Antichrist. It is the European Union (EU) that will bring him to the forefront. In other words, the Antichrist will come from revived Rome.

In 1957, the Treaty of Rome, which extended the earlier cooperation within the European Coal and Steel Community and created the European Economic Community, established a customs union. The EU came together in the 1990s as a politico-economic union of 28 member states located primarily in Europe.

#4 HEBREW LANGUAGE RESTORED—ZEPHANIAH 3:9

Never before in your lifetime has there been a language lost and recovered in this way. The complete revival of the Hebrew language took place in Europe and Palestine toward the end of the 19th century and into the 20th century. There is no other example of a language becoming a national language with millions of "first language" speakers.

Eliezer Ben-Yehuda, a Jewish writer, said 115 years ago in Israel, "Hey, we need to speak Hebrew here." Yehuda went on to lead a language revival movement until modern Hebrew was born. He's considered the father of modern Hebrew and came out with new words, edited the first dictionary, and successfully restored the language to public use.

#5 ETHIOPIAN JEWS BROUGHT BACK TO ISRAEL IN 1991—ZEPHANIAH 3:10 // EXODUS 37:2 // ISAIAH 43:6 // EZEKIEL 36:24-28

In Ezekiel 36:24, speaking to the Jewish people, God said, "For I will take you from among the nations, gather you out of all countries, and bring you into your own land." God did exactly what He said. Operation Solomon was a covert Israeli military operation to airlift Ethiopian Jews to Israel in 1991. Non-stop flights of 35 Israeli aircraft transported 14,325 Ethiopian Jews to Israel in 34 hours and 4 minutes.

Lucifer's plan was to separate and annihilate the Jews and prevent Bible prophecy from coming to pass, but he failed big time. Jews from all over the earth said "something" drew them back to Israel. We know that "something" was God.

As Jews were brought home to the Tel Aviv airport, they would fall on their knees and weep. They were not even born again, but God led them back to their homeland where He will ultimately deal with them for the seven-year Tribulation in His great mercy.

#6 FERTILITY OF THE LAND OF ISRAEL— JOEL 2:22-23 // ISAIAH 35:7

Today, Israel produces about 95 percent of the crops needed for domestic consumption. Much of the bounty, as well as agricultural technologies and expertise, is exported to other countries and shared with developed and developing nations. Israel has become the Middle East's breadbasket.[2]

Is this by accident? Of course not. God is making Israel prosperous, which is part of the latter rain we read about in Joel 2:22-23. The latter rain for the Church is the presence of God—salvations, healings, miracles. But the latter rain for Israel is God reestablishing them as a nation and bringing abundance in every area.

This is the vine (the Church) and the fig tree (Israel) yielding strength (Joel 2:22). There's such a parallel of spiritual prosperity in the Church and financial prosperity for Israel during the past 100 years. Check it out!

YEAR	ISRAEL	THE CHURCH
Early 1900s	Chaim Weizmann invented a fermentation process to produce acetone that helped England win WWI.[3] He later became the first president of Israel.	Azusa Street Revival

YEAR	ISRAEL	THE CHURCH
1917	General Edmund Allenby flew over Jerusalem during WWI dropping leaflets that demanded the surrender of the Turks because he did not want bloodshed in the Holy City. The leaflets read, "Surrender immediately, you don't have a prayer, signed Allenby." It turns out, an Arabic interpreter translated the message incorrectly and wrote Allenby's name as "Allah Bey" or "the son of god" [Allah].[4] In other words, the Turks believed a prophet was sent by god, so they hoisted a white flag and surrendered the city without a single shot.	Kenneth Hagin was born. His low-key teaching with zero fanfare pioneered the Word of Faith movement that taught the Church the authority of the believer. Jesus appeared to his mother before he was born, instructing her to name him John because he would have a part in getting the earth ready for the Second Coming. His mother told the Lord she didn't want to and called him Kenneth. Interestingly, Hagin in Hebrew means "one to go before to prepare people for the coming of the Lord." It's identical to the definition of John the Baptist.
1948	Israel made a nation	Healing Revival
1967	Jerusalem won back	Charismatic Renewal

#7 ECONOMIC PROSPERITY OF ISRAEL—AMOS // ISAIAH

Both Amos and Isaiah prophesized that Israel would see prosperity, and without a doubt, the economic prosperity of Israel preaches to everyone. Israel has so many success stories—explosions of creativity producing advances in technology, science, computers, medicine such as such the MRI; the CAT scan; PillCam, a swallowable medical camera; the Flexible Stent; Firewall, the original protection against malware; Sniff-Phone that smells disease; Disk on Key, the world's first USB drive; Watergen that produces drinking water from thin air; Waze navigational system, and more.[5] We could go down the list of things Israel has invented because the hand of God is on that nation.

In addition, Israel enjoys fertility in many categories. The Israel's Golan Heights is said to be an "energy bonanza with the potential of billions of barrels" of oil.[6] In fact, I read an article in *Fast Company* magazine that said there may prove to be more oil in the Golan Heights than in Saudi Arabia.

#8 REBUILDING THE TEMPLE—ISAIAH 27:11-12 // EZEKIEL 43:19 // DANIEL 9:27; 11:31; 12:11 // EXODUS 25:8

This is a significant prophetic signpost because Scriptures make it clear that just before Jesus returns, the Third Temple of God will stand again on the original location. Orthodox Jewish efforts to rebuild the Temple are underway now on many fronts.[7]

The actual rebuild of the Temple will not take place until the Tribulation period. After the Church leaves, the Antichrist will be revealed, and the Temple will then be rebuilt. But the fact that there are efforts underway now is an important sign.

In fact, the Jews are ready to rebuild at any moment. They even have a makeshift portal Temple that can be put up in a day.

#9 Reestablishing the Temple Mount— Isaiah 2:2 // Revelation 11:1 // Ezekiel 43:19 // 2 Thessalonians 2:4

The Temple Mount is the holiest site in Judaism. It is the location or actual mountain where temples have been, and the Temple will be rebuilt. There is no more important piece of real estate on the earth. Why? This will be the Lord's address forever!

All this focus on the Temple Mount and rebuilding the Temple shows that the time of Messiah is at hand. In Israel today, thousands of Jews are working to rebuild the Temple and the altar and have even made preparations to begin sacrifices. In fact, according to a recent poll in Israeli newspaper *Haaretz*, one third of Israel believes a new Temple should be erected on the Temple Mount.

#10 Foxes on the Temple Mount—Lamentations 5:18 // Zechariah 8:22; 14:9 // Ezra 5:1-2

The Jerusalem Post has reported foxes walking near the Western Wall,[8] which preaches loudly the accuracy of Bible prophecy. It is written in Lamentations 5:18 that Mount Zion, where the Temples stood, will be so desolate that "foxes will walk upon it." That never could have happened in the Old Testament when the glory of God filled the Temple.

The prophecy of destruction has been fulfilled, and therefore, we are awaiting the fulfillment of Zechariah's prophecy that the Temple will be rebuilt. The Messiah is coming to restore the desolation. Jesus is coming soon!

#11 TEMPLE MOUNT INSTITUTE PREPARES FOR TEMPLE WORSHIP—EZEKIEL 43:19 // DANIEL 9:27

After the Church is raptured, Israel will rebuild the temple and revert back to Old Testament times for seven years. In other words, God will deal with the Jews like He did under the Old Covenant. This is yet another sign that everything needed to fulfill Bible prophecy is lining up now.

Founded in 1987, the Temple Mount Institute is dedicated to every aspect of the biblical commandment to rebuild. A group of men there whose last names are Cohen researched their lineage and determined they are still from the Bible line of priests. In fact, the word *Cohen* in Hebrew means *priest*. For the past 20 years or so, these priests have been preparing once again to offer animal sacrifices in the temple.

God is getting the instruments ready as well. During a trip to Israel, I saw the Menorah or ancient Hebrew lampstand used in Jewish worship. It was encased in Plexiglas because it's valued at approximately $3 million dollars. All the items and instruments needed to begin sacrifices to purify the Jews are slowing being assembled.

#12 RITUAL BATHS FILLING UP AT THE TEMPLE MOUNT

Ritual baths that have been dry for 2,000 years are filling up. The baths are located south of Jerusalem in the West Bank, and two baths close to the spot are overflowing again with water thanks to abundant winter rains in 2020.[9] These two pools were discovered in separate excavations led by archaeologists in 1990 and 2000.

This is a sign of the times and a fact that preaches to rabbis because, according to Jewish tradition and Levitical law, the baths must be refilled for Temple sacrifices before the Messiah returns. As we've noted, Scriptures tell us that sacrifices and temple worship will be reinstituted during the Tribulation.

#13 Oil of anointing found in 1989—Exodus 30:25; 37:21 // Daniel 9:24 // Psalm 133 // Zephaniah 3:10 // Isaiah 43:6

Israeli archeologists, searching caves near the Dead Sea, discovered what they believe is a 2,000-year-old jug of once-fragrant oil. It is the same variety used to anoint the ancient Israeli kings and will be used to anoint Jesus during a ceremony at the Second Coming.

The substance inside the small juglet was verified to be the Shemen Afarshimon of Psalm 133. Scientists tested it and learned it's the exact ingredients described in the book of Leviticus. This oil was found in the same location where the Dead Sea Scrolls were discovered. How cool is that? It's been preserved and sitting there waiting all along until it's needed for Jesus. Is our God not meticulous?

#14 The world is set up for a one-world government—Daniel 7:24 // Revelation 17:12-13

The phrase one-world government is not in the Bible; however, it does allude to a single-world government existing under the rule of the Antichrist in the last days.

Get this. In 1998, an airline alliance was founded that's called Oneworld. Fourteen airlines are in the alliance reaching around the world.

#15 ONE-WORLD CURRENCY IN THE FUTURE— DANIEL 7:23 // REVELATION 17:12-13

In October 2021, the U.S. Federal Reserve launched a review of the potential benefits and risks of issuing a digital currency, as central banks around the world experiment with the potential new form of money.[10] A cyber yuan in China also stands to give Beijing power to track spending in real time.[11] These initial moves into digital currency open a small door into the once implausible one-currency world.

#16 ONE-WORLD RELIGION—DANIEL 7:24 // REVELATION 17:12-13

The Catholic-Muslim Interfaith Council created by Pope Francis announced a new "Chrislam" Headquarters will open in 2022 in the United Arab Emirates to combine a mosque and a church, according to the signed covenant.[12] There have even been ads in the media promoting "One-World Religion Headquarters to Open in 2022."

#17 PREPARATION FOR THE BATTLE OF ARMAGEDDON—REVELATION 16:12,16

The battle of Armageddon is drawing near. Twice in 2016, ISIS tried to dam up the Euphrates, and they continue doing this to keep water from Bagdad. This is a startling sign because Revelation 16:12 prophesies that the dried-up Euphrates will prepare the way for the "kings of the East" to cross into Israel and attack.

Years ago, I stood on the valley of the of Megiddo. I was at Mt. Carmel where Elijah called down fire from heaven, and I heard this jet spool up. Even way down in the valley, I could hear the jet. All of a sudden, a black F-16 shot up out of the hole in the ground right where the Battle of Armageddon will be. It really startled me to know there's already an underground runway out in the middle of the valley. I thought, *My God, I feel like I'm seeing a preview of the Battle of Armageddon exactly where it will take place.*

So much has been prophesied about what will take place on this little of piece of real estate. Even Napoleon Bonaparte, celebrated and controversial 19th-century French military leader of the French Revolution, said Megiddo is the "perfect battlefield."[13] He also said, "Megiddo will be the greatest site for the greatest battle ever." He didn't even know he was talking about the Battle of Armageddon. *Wow.*

#18 CHINA'S ONE-CHILD POLICY—REVELATION 16:12

In the late 1970s, China instituted a one-child policy that resulted in 30 million more men and "the biggest gender imbalance in the world."[14] This created an entire population of young men from 15 to 30 years old with very few girls to date. No wonder they're ready for war and available for military service. By 2021, China upped the quota to a three-child policy, but the imbalance already exists. This Chinese policy lines right up with Bible prophecy that says China will move down on Israel with a strong and ample army that appears to be ramping up even now.

#19 FISH SHOWING UP IN THE DEAD SEA— GENESIS 13:10 // EZEKIEL 47:8-9

The Dead Sea is coming to life fulfilling end-of-days prophecies from Ezekiel who said the land would flourish and bloom when the Jews return. He said the water would flow east from Jerusalem into the Dead Sea, filling it up with fish.

Scientists are shocked to witness signs of life even now from the Dead Sea, which is more than 400 meters below sea level and the lowest place on earth. Sinkholes appearing around the sea are quickly filling up with fish and other forms of life previously unseen there. One expert said the existence of fish in the Dead Sea is a reality that contradicts the laws of nature, and yet it is witnessed by science and explained by Bible prophecy.[15]

#20 SEA OF GALILEE FULL

The Sea of Galilee, also known as Lake Kinneret, has been experiencing a "rapid rise" in the lake's water levels after almost 20 years of steady decline, according to the *Jerusalem Post*.[16] This is prophetically significant and a sign of the Second Coming because the Talmud, a Jewish religious text of law and rabbinical discussion,[17] says the Sea of Galilee will be full when the Messiah comes.

#21 ISRAEL RULED BY TWO BENJAMINS

Rabbi Yitzhak Kaduri, no longer living but highly regarded as an elder statesman of rabbis in Jewish circles, said Jesus appeared to him and revealed Himself as the Messiah. Kaduri wrote this in a letter that was hidden until one year after he died because he felt the information would be divisive—shocking Israel and causing turmoil. In the letters, he prophesied that before the Messiah returns that Israel will be ruled by "two Benjamins."[18]

Never before in history has anything like that happened until 2020 when a surprising turn of events resulted in Israel being co-ruled by Benjamin Netanyahu and Benjamin Gantz.

#22 WATER SOURCE IN PETRA—REVELATION 12:6 // DANIEL 12:11 // ISAIAH 2:10-11 // ISAIAH 2:19,21

The ancient city of Petra, located in southern Jordan near the western border of Israel, is an empty city in an arid desert valley destined to fulfill Bible prophecy. Midway through the Tribulation when the Antichrist says he will kill the Jews, many Jews will flee to Petra for safety. Even now, God is preparing Petra.

A few years back, I saw a fascinating video on Christian Broadcasting Network (CBN) where Pat Robertson showed live footage of a new water source discovered in the caves of Petra where Israel will hide. This is yet another sign of Jehovah making provision for His people and giving the Church a sign of Jesus' soon return.

The city was once a bustling metropolis and center of an Arab kingdom in Hellenistic and Roman times with impressive architecture. Today, almost a million tourists trek there yearly through almost impassable mountains to see this archaeological site.[19] Amazingly enough, 2,500 years ago the Nabataeans who lived there understood hydraulics and developed a sophisticated water technology that God may just be improving and reviving.[20]

#23 RUSSIA AMASSING TROOPS AND EQUIPMENT IN THE UKRAINE—EZEKIEL 38

In 2021, Russia has amassed more than 120,000 troops and equipment, which is being considered provocation for war.[21] Many believe Russia is ready to invade the Ukraine just as they did Crimea. NATO has said they would come to the Ukraine's defense, challenging Russia.[22] French President Emmanuel Macron also said NATO and France will protect the Ukraine. France has been passive along these lines until now, but this was a bold and different stance.

#24 RUSSIA FILLS UP SYRIAN MILITARY BASES THE U.S. VACATED—EZEKIEL 38

In 2021, everywhere America pulled out, Russia filled in.[23] Why is that a big deal prophetically? There are nine bases[24] in Syria that are on Israel's doorstep. Blatantly, Russia is creating a pathway to Israel. Connect the dots in Ezekiel 38, and it's easy to see that Russia's takeover of Israel is more imminent all the time.

#25 TURKEY SURROUNDING ISRAEL—EZEKIEL 38

There is one news article after the other in *The Jerusalem Post* of late reporting that Turkey is systematically surrounding Israel in various training efforts and skirmishes. Turkey is in Libya training Hamas's operatives. Turkey is in northern Syria attacking the Kurds. Turkey is in western Iraq. Turkey is fighting Greece over islands that belong to Greece but are between the two countries geographically. Every one of these is one step closer to the impending Ezekiel 38 War.

Turkish President Recep Tayyip Erdoğan has said he will call on Islam and take Israel from the Jews. In fact, a newspaper considered his mouthpiece published an "urgent call for action to form an 'Army of Islam' to simultaneously destroy Israel."[25]

#26 TURKEY AND IRAN ACCELERATE THREATS TOWARD ISRAEL—EZEKIEL 38

The acceleration of missiles from Iran and connected with Turkey is showing their very public thoughts and verbiage about annihilating Israel. Threats are increasingly blatant and not at all veiled these days. They've said they want to annihilate Israel—even calling it the "rabid dog of the Middle East."[26]

If we got into everything Iran is doing right now to try to take down Israel, it would boggle your mind. We must watch Turkey as well. They are doing some unusual things to become a platform for the Antichrist.

#27 TURKEY PRONOUNCING OWNERSHIP OF JERUSALEM AND THE TEMPLE MOUNT

Erodğan said in 2021 that Jerusalem and the Temple Mount don't belong to Israel.[27] That's crazy! That would be like saying Washington, D.C. and the Washington Monument don't belong to the United States.

The Palestinians even said last year that Big Ben doesn't belong to England. "It belongs to us," they said.[28] How insane! But the Bible says the Antichrist will try to change dates and times in history (Dan. 7:25), and we see a prelude to that with these nations and their not-so-veiled threats toward Israel and the looming Ezekiel 38 War.

#28 LARGEST GATHERING OF PREDATORY BIRDS ARRIVED IN ISRAEL—EXODUS 39:4 // REVELATION 19:17

The clean-up crew for the Ezekiel 38 War—and even the Battle of Armageddon—is arriving in Israel. What clean-up crew? More than 172 species of predatory birds have arrived in Israel, which is the largest gathering ever.[29] It's pretty radical that heaven has the animal kingdom in Israel already on standby.

Interestingly enough, a zoologist in Connecticut who attended one of my services actually told me that number is now 500 species. For sure, there are 500 million birds that pass through Israel during the bi-annual migration season. It's considered the eighth wonder of the world.[30]

#29 RED HEIFER BORN SPOTLESS IN ISRAEL—NUMBERS 19:2

The Second Coming cannot occur until the third Temple is constructed in Jerusalem and a red heifer is born in Israel. The red heifer is specified by the Bible as required for Jewish purification rituals and temple sacrifice during the Tribulation.

In 2018, the first red heifer in 2,000 years was born in Israel. The Temple Institute in Jerusalem announced the calf's birth on YouTube.[31] Again, in 2019, another red heifer was born in Israel that also appears to meet the qualifications.[32]

For many years, red heifers had been born in other countries, but the Bible specified that the red heifer had to be born in Israel and be without blemish. The requirements are very stringent and even require that the red heifer can have no more than two black hairs on its entire body.

#30 MARK OF THE BEAST TECHNOLOGY AVAILABLE—REVELATION 13:16-18

Few people have not heard of the mark of the beast, an end-times symbol of loyalty to the Antichrist whereby no world citizen without it will be able to buy or sell. But most people don't realize that now—for the first time in history—the technology is available to implant this kind of identification in humans.

Today, via the radio-frequency identification technology (RFID), a microchip can be inserted in a human body with information such as a person's medical history. Readers have one or more antenna that emits radio waves and receives signals back from tags in the vicinity, according to the Federal Food and Drug Administration. The tags can contain information up to several pages of data. This process has been used in dogs for some time, but some sources indicate this biometric system will be implanted in all humans by 2025.[33]

I was preaching in Jacksonville, Florida, and a guy came up after the service and said, "I have a chip in my wrist that pays for my groceries."

"You cannot," I answered in disbelief. "The laser won't read your hand."

We went to Publix grocery store, and he told the clerk, "I will pay with my wrist!"

"It will never work!" the clerk said.

"Watch this!" he said. Boop! He already had his information implanted into his wrist. Folks, there's no question about it. Technology to implant the mark of the beast is available.

#31 GLOBAL COMMUNICATIONS AVAILABLE FOR THE WORLD TO SEE THE TWO WITNESSES—REVELATION 11:9-10; 17:8

The Bible prophecies that certain events will be seen by all peoples during three and a half days. For example, the apostle John says the two witnesses will be seen by the whole world. That was not even remotely possible in John's day when news traveled by horseback or mule. In fact, it was laughable 1,500, 100, or even 50 years ago. Yet today, nearly all of us can pull out a smartphone and see news anywhere along with the rest of the world. Today's technology is ready for the whole world to see the two witnesses live in real time and on repeat from the comfort of personal devices. It's not even a challenge!

#32 DEADLY DISEASES OR PESTILENCES ON THE RISE—MATTHEW 24:7 // REVELATION 6:8

In the past several decades, we've seen AIDS, Ebola, Dengue, West Nile, SARS, Avian Flu, and most definitely COVID-19 with its many variants.

#33 FAMINES—LUKE 21:11 // REVELATION 6:5-8 // MATTHEW 24

Jesus spoke of famines, which are frequently pinpointed in world news. In 2021 as many as 811 million people go hungry. World hunger is on the rise. From 2019 to 2020, the number of undernourished people grew by 161 million.[34]

#34 Signs of the Tribulation period: roaring seas, strange tides, hybrid scorpions—Matthew 24 // Luke 21:25-26 // Revelation 9 // Ezekiel 38 // Revelation 13

The world is poised for World War III or the Ezekiel 38 War, which takes place after the Church is raptured and during the Tribulation. Some military generals are already saying it has begun, which you can read more about in Chapter 7.

With everything going on around the world—especially in the Middle East—biblical prophecy of the end times is fast becoming a reality. We talk of famines, pestilences, earthquakes, and other signs of the Tribulation, but here are still more.

Romans 8:22 says, "All creation has been groaning as in the pains of childbirth right up to the present time" (NLT). *All creation* could not be more accurate. The Bible talks of roaring waves and scorpions as precursors to the Tribulation, and we are now seeing both. Notice what Jesus said:

Luke 21:25-27 (NLT)

There will be strange signs in the sun, moon, and stars. And here on earth the nations will be in turmoil, perplexed by the roaring seas and strange tides. People will be terrified at what they see coming upon the earth, for the powers in the heavens will be shaken. Then everyone will see the Son of Man coming on a cloud with power and great glory.

Record tsunamis[35] and strange tides[36] already made headlines in these last days.[37]

Revelation 9 speaks of hybrid scorpions that torment humans during the Tribulation, and amazingly enough, 500 people were hospitalized in Egypt in November 2021 with scorpion bites.[38] Three people died from the venom. What the Bible has prophesied centuries before, we're now seeing in the news as the earth prepares for Jesus' soon return. Folks, the Bible is flawlessly accurate!

#35 CHAOTIC WEATHER AND NATURAL DISASTERS— MATTHEW 24:8 // LUKE 21:25-26 // ROMANS 8:21-22

Fully 77 percent of evangelic Protestants blame the increase in earthquakes, hurricanes, droughts, and other forms of chaotic weather and natural disaster to the fast-approaching "end of the world." Half of Americans and 77 percent of evangelicals believe natural disasters are a sign of the end times as well—not climate change.[39] Apparently, these folks know how to read their Bibles!

Even the unbeliever should recognize something is up with the weather. It's more chaotic than normal—earthquakes, storms, wildfires, and the list goes on.

#36 CHRISTIANS BLAMED FOR CLIMATE CHANGE

As just another sign of the times, Christians were blamed recently for climate change on late-night television. Late-night hosts and comedians Jimmy Kimmel, Stephen Colbert, and Jimmy Fallon teamed up recently to talk climate change.[40] They said Christians don't care about the earth and are the cause of climate change because they believe in an "escape clause" called the Rapture.

#37 PALESTINIAN-ISRAELI CONFLICT—PSALM 83 PARTIALLY FULFILLED IN WARS OF 1948, 1967, AND 1973

People ask me all the time, "What's the difference between the Psalm 83 War and the Ezekiel 38 War?" There are several differences. First of all, the Psalm 83 War is about annihilation. The Ezekiel 38 War is about ravaging goods or spoil.

There already have been three or four wars about annihilation (or Psalm 83 wars) and, perhaps, more to come. In 1948, the Arabs tried to annihilate Israel. In 1967, they tried to annihilate them again in the Six-Day War. In 1973, the Arabs tried to annihilate them yet again in the Yom Kippur War. In 2006, the Gaza War began with the Palestinians doing the same thing in a localized Israeli-Palestinian conflict. In 2016, the Palestinians began building tunnels to get to Israel, but their tunnels began collapsing. They thought the collapses were accidents, but anyone who knows God knows better. Tunnels don't "just happen" to collapse. But, somewhere between God and Israeli skill, they are collapsing just the same.

The Ezekiel 38 War has not happened yet, although nations are lining up for it now, which is covered in more detail in Chapter 7.

#38 DAMASCUS WIPED OFF THE PLANET— ISAIAH 17:1 // JEREMIAH 49:23-27 // AMOS 1:3-5 // ZECHARIAH 9:1-8

Isaiah 17:1 says, "Look, the city of Damascus will disappear! It will become a heap of ruins" (NLT). The Bible is pretty clear about its destiny; something will happen in Damascus that wipes the city off the planet.

How and why? you might wonder. It's all a platform for the Ezekiel 38 War. Look at the armies around Syria right now. Syria still uses chemical weapons—Sarin gas—weekly on Israel. Israel vowed in 2007 that if Syria harmed them with chemical weapons, they would wipe Syria off the map. Syria is increasingly in the news and extremely anti-Semitic. This past year, Israel has flown in weekly to blow up caches of weapons that came from Iran and worked their way down to Damascus. In fact, in October and November of 2021, even after Russian President Vladimir Putin warned Israel not to do so, Israel defended itself with five airstrikes on the outskirts of Damascus. All the ramped-up activity and skirmishes take us close to the fulfillment of the sign.

#39 MUSLIM COALITION FOR EZEKIEL 38—DEUTERONOMY 28:37 // JEREMIAH 29:18; 44:8 // LUKE 21:20-24 // PSALM 83:4-8 // ZECHARIAH 12:2

Israel is surrounded by enemies—Arab nations sworn to destroy and annihilate it. Many of these nations have been forming an alliance. This fact alone lays groundwork for the Ezekiel 38 War, discussed in greater detail in Chapter 7.

Muslim intentions toward Israel are clear. Check this out! The Sahih Al-Bukhari, a renowned religious text revered by the Muslim world, says, "The Hour (last day) will not be established until you fight with the Jews, and the stone behind which a Jew will be hiding will say 'O Muslim! There is a Jew hiding behind me, so kill him.'"

On the other hand, nations that will not attack Israel during the Ezekiel 38 War are even now making peace with Israel. Saudi Arabia is chief among that group of friend nations.

#40 RUSSIA (MAGOG) RISES AS A MILITARY POWER—EZEKIEL 38

Ezekiel 38 tells us that Russia (Magog) will rise as a military power and lead an attack on Israel in the Ezekiel 38 War. Today, most of the southern states of the former Soviet Union are both military powerhouses and following the lead of Putin in Russia following in step.

#41 TURKEY (GOMER) JOINS THE ATTACK ON ISRAEL—EZEKIEL 38

In 2002, Turkey elected a pro-Islamic party to govern the country. In 2005, Hitler's anti-Semitic manifesto *Mein Kampf* became a bestseller in Turkey. In 2007, Turkey elected an Islamist president. And by 2021, Erodoğan said he would call on Islam to take Jerusalem from the Jews. Can you see it? Players are lining up for the Ezekiel 38 War.

#42 IRAN (PERSIA), SUDAN (CUSH), AND LIBYA (PUT) WILL ALSO PARTAKE IN THE ATTACK ON ISRAEL—EZEKIEL 38

Anti-Semitism in the Islamic world is at an all-time high as nations line up for the Ezekiel 38 War.

#43 A TETRAD OF BLOOD RED MOONS— PSALM 19 // ACTS 2:10 // JOEL 2:31

We don't hear a lot of preaching on it, but it's amazing how Lucifer has tried to hide or pervert blatant signs of Jesus' return so we would not understand them even when they're right in front of us. Notice the psalm below.

PSALM 19:1-5 (NLT)

The heavens proclaim the glory of God. The skies display his craftsmanship. Day after day they continue to speak; night after night they make him known. They speak without a sound or word; their voice is never heard. Yet their message has gone throughout the earth, and their words to all the world.

This psalm talks about the heavens declaring God's glory. Of course, Lucifer perverted everything about the stars and moons and focused it all on astrology instead of God, but the Bible says in Genesis 1:14 that the planets signal us.

"Why is it a big deal?" somebody asks. Passover is when Jesus died for us, and the Feast of Tabernacles, when Jesus will come and tabernacle with men, is when Jesus will return at the Second Coming. So what was the sky saying in 2014? "I died for you. I'm coming back. I died for you. I'm coming back." The same thing happened in 2015: "I died for you. I'm coming back." Right in between them, there was a full solar eclipse, and on the day the sun comes up on the center of the equator splitting the earth. Guess what day this occurred? Nisan 1, the religious new year.

The Bible says, "The sun shall be turned into darkness, and the moon into blood, before the great and notable day of the Lord come" (Acts 2:20, Joel 2:31). The heavens were signaling us, and who controls the heavens? God!

NASA called it a tetrad[41]—four blood red moons in a row. Guess when was the last time you had four blood red moons in a row like that?

- **1492:** The Jews were kicked out of Spain, called the Edict of Expulsion. Remember, it was also the year Columbus sailed to America.
- **1948:** Israel was made a nation.
- **1967:** Jerusalem was won back.

It's pretty radical to have four blood red moons in a row. Can you imagine God giving us a more epic billboard than one in the heavens that lights up the night sky?

In 2014, right before April, I was preparing for a service and praying in tongues in my hotel room. I heard myself pray out in English, "April to see. April to see." I thought to myself, *Man, something big is happening in April.* I had been preaching on the blood red moons as an end-time sign for five years at that point, and here a red blood moon was coming in April.

Come 2014, Colleen and I got out in the backyard there in Tulsa and looked up at the blood red moon for an hour and 45 minutes. I watched the moon turn blood red.

The Lord said, "I told you that you would see in April."

"Lord, this is what You have been telling me?"

He said, "I made the moon blood red for you. What do you need?"

You see, even though I preached the message, I still did not realize that's what He was talking about. We are so accustomed to fanfare that He made the moon turn blood red on Passover and Tabernacles four times in a row, and the Church kind of yawned. What we should be doing is screaming at each other, "Hey! Pay attention! Jesus is about to come back!"

#44 SIGN IN THE HEAVENS: WOMAN CLOTHED WITH THE SUN—REVELATION 12

Revelation 12:1-2 says, "Then a great pageant appeared in heaven, portraying things to come. I saw a woman clothed with the sun, with the moon beneath her feet, and a crown of twelve stars on her head. She was pregnant and screamed in the pain of her labor, awaiting her delivery" (TLB). She had Jupiter in her womb for exactly 42 weeks.

On September 23, 2017, the sun was in the Virgo constellation described above where the woman clothed with the sun had Jupiter in her belly for 42 weeks. This was a rare sign—occurring once in 7,000 years.[42] Many believed the heavens were signaling (Ps. 19). In fact, that's why many people thought Jesus would return in 2017.

This Virgo sign has appeared in the sky before at different times—but never before with such flawless dates correlating to something important. Many Jews believe the main reason for the sign in the heavens in 2017 was actually in conjunction with Israel being told they could not police Jerusalem because it was an international city. But telling Israel that Jerusalem doesn't belong to them is crazy! It would be like telling police officers in Washington, D.C. they are unable to police America's capital.

In December of 2017, Israel was warned they could no longer police Jerusalem. Exactly nine months later—with Jupiter in the womb for 42 weeks—the "baby" was born September 23. The "baby" the constellation warned of was the enactment of the law banning the Jews from policing Jerusalem. Since that time, there was a conflict about the policing issue, and Israel resumed its policing powers of Jerusalem.

#45 CHINA'S PRESENT, EXTREME STANCE WITH TAIWAN

China is determined to retake Taiwan while both America and Japan have said they will protect Taiwan. This is precursor for the Battle of Armageddon. Even though China is a huge land-mass, they are not satisfied and trying to accumulate more.

#46 CHINA FLEXING ITS MUSCLES—REVELATION 16:12

The whole world is affected by China's strength right now. As we discussed earlier, this is significant because Revelation 16:12 prophesies the dried-up Euphrates will prepare the way for the "kings of the East" to cross into Israel and attack. China is one of those eastern kings.

In 2021, China threatened to nuke Japan for the third time. We don't typically read these sorts of headlines in our newspapers, but it's true just the same. A lot of times, I have to get foreign news to find out what's really going on. In November 2021, South Korea had to send out jets to intercept nuclear bombers from China and Russia that were flying in their territory.[43] This is China taunting South Korea, which would not have happened even just a few years ago.

Clearly, China is flexing their strength as prophesied. They have frequently gone into Taiwan's airspace and harassed our ships in the North China Sea. They do provocative acts to get attention. Why is this important? China is mobilizing for the Battle of Armageddon.

In August 2021, China surprised the world by introducing a nuclear-capable hypersonic missile that flies at lower altitudes but travels more than five times the speed of sound or roughly 4,000 miles per hour.[44]

#47 SPREADING OF THE GOSPEL FORETOLD—MATTHEW 24:1-14 // MARK 13:10 // REVELATION 14:6

Jesus sat on the Mount of Olives and the disciples came to Him privately asking, "What will be the sign of Your coming, and of the end of the age?" (Matt. 24:3 NKJV). Jesus told them of many signs. Many would falsely come in His name, "And you will hear of wars and threats of wars, but don't panic. Yes, these things must take place, but the end won't follow immediately" (Matt. 24:6 NLT). In verses 7-8, Jesus said there would be war, nation against nation and kingdom against kingdom. He said there would be famines and earthquakes in many parts of the world. But Jesus Himself said all of these signs were only the first birth pains with more to come.

In verses 9-13, Jesus continues describing signs—Christians will be hated all over the world, persecuted, arrested, and killed. False prophets will appear and deceive many. Sin will be rampant everywhere. But still, there is no mention of His coming.

Then notice verse 14 says, "And the Good News about the Kingdom will be preached throughout the whole world, so that all nations will hear it; and then the end will come" (NLT). When will the end come? When the gospel is preached throughout the whole world, so all nations hear it. This amazing amount of gospel going all over the world in one generation signifies the fullness of the Gentiles, which indicates Jesus is about to come back!

#48 RISE OF FALSE PROPHETS—MATTHEW 24:4,11

Jesus talked about the rise of false prophets being a sign of the end of the age or Jesus' soon return in Matthew 24:4 and 11.

When the disciples asked, "What will be the sign of Your coming and of the end of the age?" Jesus said, "Don't let anyone mislead you, for many will come in my name, claiming, 'I am the Messiah.' They will deceive many" (Matt. 24:4-5 NLT). In verse 11, Jesus said, "And many false prophets will appear and will deceive many people" (NLT).

#49 HUMANS COULD DESTROY ALL LIFE— REVELATION 11; 17:8 // ZECHARIAH 14

Never before in history has mankind lived at a time when basically all human life could be destroyed by humans. Yet today, with nuclear, biological, and chemical weaponry, it's no longer impossible.

Jesus said of the Great Tribulation that no one would make it through that, but it would be shortened for the elect's sake (Matt. 24:21-22). Thank God, we don't have to be here for that! (More about the Tribulation and the Great Tribulation in Chapter 11.)

#50 TRAVEL INCREASE—DANIEL 12:4

Daniel had a vision about the end times where God spoke to him, saying, "But you, Daniel, shut up the words, and seal the book until the time of the end; *many shall run to and fro*, and knowledge shall increase" (Dan. 12:4).

Notice how a few other Bible versions translate "many shall run to and fro." When God spoke to Daniel, express travel of the day was a donkey. Today it's a jet. Think about it!

Here's how two other Bible versions translated Daniel 12:4:

- The Living Bible: "But Daniel, keep this prophecy a secret; seal it up so that it will not be understood until the end times, when travel and education shall be vastly increased!"
- God's Word Translation: "But you, Daniel, keep these words secret, and seal the book until the end times. Many will travel everywhere, and knowledge will grow."

#51 KNOWLEDGE DOUBLES EVERY 12 HOURS—DANIEL 12:4

We read in Daniel 12:4 above how God spoke to Daniel in a vision about the end times also bringing an increase in knowledge. There's no doubt about it. Buckle up to read the progression of statistics below.

In 1982, futurist and inventor R. Buckminster Fuller estimated that up until 1900, human knowledge doubled approximately every century. By 1945 it doubled every 25 years.[45] By 1982, it doubled every 12 to 13 months. Today, scientists say knowledge doubles every 12 hours.[46]

#52 RISE IN DRUG USE—REVELATION 9:21

Revelation 9:21 says, "Neither repented they of their murders, nor of their sorceries, nor of their fornication, nor of their thefts." The Greek word translated *sorceries* is *pharmakeia*, which also refers to drug use. There's no question drug use has risen sharply during our generation. Around 275 million people used drugs worldwide in 2020 to 2021—a time of unprecedented upheaval caused by the COVID-19 pandemic. This number was up by 22 percent from 2010. Overdose of prescription opioids and heroin also remain high and are increasingly contaminated with illicit fentanyl.[47] In addition, the number of drug overdose deaths has quadrupled since 1999.[48]

#53 WORLDWIDE PERSECUTION OF CHRISTIANS—MATTHEW 24:9-13

When Jesus was asked about signs signaling His return, He said, "Then you [Christians] will be arrested, persecuted, and killed. You will be hated all over the world because you are my followers. And many will turn away from me and betray and hate each other. And many false prophets will appear and will deceive many people. Sin will be rampant everywhere, and the love of many will grow cold. But the one who endures to the end will be saved" (Matt. 24:9-13 NLT).

Anti-Christian attitudes are mirrored throughout society, culture, and the media today, and we see all through the Bible that this will be the way it is before the return of Jesus. I heard recently on MSNBC a speaker said, "The problem with America is conservative, white male Christians who are actually terrorists." There was a time when such a statement would be appalling and not tolerated.

The plan of God always goes full circle. The early church was persecuted at the beginning, and it will be the same at the end.

#54 RISE OF BABYLON—GENESIS 10:10 // ZECHARIAH 5:11 // ISAIAH 13

Pay attention in the days ahead to Babylon, just south of Bagdad in modern-day Iraq. In Bible days, this was the location of the Tower of Babel (Gen. 10:10). According to Bible prophecy, this city will reemerge in the end times. In fact, more than one-tenth of the book of Revelation is devoted to prophecies about this city. From Babylon, the Antichrist is introduced to the world as a savior figure who brings solutions to a troubled world as he assumes power. The Jews will think he is the Messiah.

The Antichrist will believe it's advantageous to be nice to the Iraqis and Islamic groups and, therefore, will build up Babylon situated between the two. It will become a center of commerce seemingly overnight, and more money will circulate there as a result. The Antichrist will use Babylon as a platform to connect various groups.

Then, midway through the Tribulation, the Antichrist will move his headquarters to Jerusalem where he walks in the Temple during sacrifices and says, "Sacrifices are no longer needed. I'm here. I'm god."

Interestingly enough, Saddam Hussein spent hundreds of millions of dollars[49] rebuilding portions of Babylon. In 2021, France's President Emmanuel Macron has spoken of pouring money into the restoration of Babylon as well.

#55 MOCKERS OF THE SECOND COMING— 2 TIMOTHY 3:1-3 // 2 PETER 3:3

The Bible prophesied long ago that people would mock the Second Coming.

2 PETER 3:3-4 (TLB)

I want to remind you that in the last days there will come scoffers who will do every wrong they can think of and laugh at the truth. This will be their line of argument: "So Jesus promised to come back, did he? Then where is he? He'll never come! Why, as far back as anyone can remember, everything has remained exactly as it was since the first day of creation."

#56 SEXUAL IMMORALITY RAMPANT— JUDE 18 // REVELATION 9:21

"In the last days there will be people who don't take these things seriously anymore. They'll treat them like a joke, and *make a religion of their own whims and lusts."* These are the ones who split churches, thinking only of themselves. There's nothing to them, no sign of the Spirit!" (Jude 18-19 MSG). "And they did not repent of their murders or their witchcraft or their *sexual immorality* or their thefts" (Rev. 9:21 NLT).

In this last-days cultural climate, we see blatant sexual immorality and the sex industry growing exponentially to keep up.

#57 SEXUAL PERVERSION, HOMOSEXUALITY, SAME-SEX MARRIAGE—LUKE 17:26-30 // GENESIS 19 // JUDE 7

LUKE 17:26-30 (NLT)

When the Son of Man returns, it will be like it was in Noah's day. In those days, the people enjoyed banquets and parties and weddings right up to the time Noah entered his boat and the flood came and destroyed them all. And the world will be as it was in the days of Lot. People went about their daily business—eating and drinking, buying and selling, farming and building—until the morning Lot left Sodom. Then fire and burning sulfur rained down from heaven and destroyed them all. Yes, it will be "business as usual" right up to the day when the Son of Man is revealed.

Many of the marriages during this era were same-sex marriages. Homosexuality was flaunted and legal during the days of Noah and Lot. Genesis 19 speaks to Sodom in particular.

Jesus warned that the last days would be like the days of Noah and Lot, and who would argue that we live at a time when perversions of every kind are pushed at us as if they are normal?

In 2015, the U.S. Supreme Court struck down a ban on same-sex marriages and legalized it in all 50 states. The White House lit up with a rainbow. Interestingly enough, on the same day the Supreme Court passed a law saying if you are born in Jerusalem, you can't have Israeli citizenship on your passport. Jerusalem is Israel's capital, but still, there is pressure to take it away from them because the devil tries stealing territory for his kingdom everywhere he can.

#58 VIOLENCE AS IN THE DAYS OF NOAH—LUKE 17:26 // GENESIS 6:11-13 // MATTHEW 24 // LUKE 21

The violence in Noah's day could not have been worse. "As far as God was concerned, the Earth had become a sewer; there was violence everywhere. God took one look and saw how bad it was, everyone corrupt and corrupting—life itself corrupt to the core. God said to Noah, 'It's all over. It's the end of the human race. The violence is everywhere; I'm making a clean sweep'" (Gen. 6:11-13 MSG).

Today, exponential violence around the world mirrors the days of Noah. As mentioned in Chapter 2, we could not have a more exact replica. Corruption and violence are blatant and aggressive just about everywhere and even spilling in the streets.

In the U.S. alone, there are two million people in the nation's prisons and jails with a 500 percent increase over the past 40 years.[50] Murders in the U.S. jumped by nearly 30 percent in 2020 compared with the previous year to become the largest single-year increase ever recorded in the country, according to the Federal Bureau of Investigation (FBI).[51]

#59 CONSTELLATIONS—EZEKIEL 38 // ZECHARIAH 13

In May 2016, the planet Mercury crossed the sun at sundown at the Temple Mount. The planets and moon formed a sickle, and the constellation Orion changed its tool to a hammer. The hammer and cycle are Russia's symbol, and the sickle is a sign of Israel going through the threshing floor or the Great Tribulation or Jacob's trouble. God is trying to warn Israel!

#60 BETHLEHEM STAR IN YEAR 2016—MATTHEW 2:1

In 2016, I was watching Lester Holt on the NBC Nightly News, and he announced a celestial event happening. He said we have Jupiter, Regulus, and Venus coming together to create the Bethlehem Star.[52] I had friends of mine who lived in San Francisco on the west coast who said it looked like one huge star. All three of those planets came together to form the Bethlehem Star. Guess what the constellation was? Leo. He's the Lion of the Tribe of Judah. The Bethlehem Star hadn't been in here 2,000 years, but Jesus said there would be signs in the heavens. Come on, man.

In terms of signs in the heavenlies, what is the Bethlehem Star? At the birth of Jesus, the magi or the three wise men from the east (Matt. 2:1) were from Daniel's school in Persia. These guys were wise but without the internet, television, newspapers, or the like. They would lie on their buildings and watch the skies. They knew their heavens way better than we do.

Kepler, a scientist, discovered Kepler's Laws of Planetary Motion years ago, and he determined the heavens are all completely mathematical. That's how NASA uses Kepler's Laws of Planetary Motion to this day to engineer their shuttles to go there and land at a certain time. It's all math, and as a result, they can enter a date in the computer for 2,000 or 4,000 years ago and know exactly what the heavens looked like. At the birth of Jesus, three stars came together.

There was an attorney in Nashville, Tennessee whose daughters wanted to have a nativity set, and he decided to do it right. He began studying Kepler's Laws of Planetary Motion and entering information in his computer. He said, "If I'm going to have a star hanging out in my front door, I want to know what it means. I want to know what was really going on." He began to see that at the birth of Jesus, three stars came together: Jupiter, Regulus, and Venus. Here's where it gets interesting. Jupiter is a *king star*. Regulus is a *regal king star*. Venus is a *mother star*, and all three came together. No, I am not telling you men are from Mars and women are from Venus, but I am telling you that the heavenlies are signaling you. They are telling you that Jesus is coming back *soon!*

Regulus and Jupiter did retrograde motion and formed a halo right over Bethlehem. There were two halos right over Bethlehem at the birth of Jesus, and the wise men traveled 700 miles by camel because they knew a king would be born. Guess what the constellation was at the birth of Jesus? Virgo. Why? Because of the virgin birth.

#61 FRENCH PRESIDENT MACRON BROKERS PEACE WITH JORDAN AND EGYPT TO RAMP UP ATTACKS ON ISRAEL—EZEKIEL 38

I'm not at all surprised that French President Macron stands with those against Israel. What's really interesting is that his first name is Emmanuel, which means literally "god with us," and his last name Macron means "the mark." I'm telling you, if Macron is not the Antichrist, he's missed a big opportunity.

Yes, I realize that the apostle Paul said the Antichrist won't be revealed until the Church is Raptured, but in my opinion, Macron is very likely to be the Antichrist. Among many other reasons, he's flexed his muscles with Lebanon and Bagdad, trying to appear as a hero.

If you read through the Tim LaHaye *Left Behind* series, you'll see that Macron is doing everything the Antichrist will do. To top it off, Macron is part Syrian and part Jew. Bible scholars have argued for years about whether or not the Antichrist will be Jewish. Some scholars suggest the Antichrist will have rejected or abandoned a religion such as Islam or Catholicism.

Interestingly enough, Macron is part Jewish and part Syrian (an Islamic nation). Although he was raised in a non-religious family, he was baptized Catholic by his choice at age 12.[53] However you slice and dice it, he qualifies for what we know about the Antichrist.

#62 RISE IN ANTI-SEMITISM—DEUTERONOMY 28:37 // JEREMIAH 29:18; 44:8 // LUKE 21:20-24 // REVELATION 12

History confirms that the Jews have been persecuted like no other group. Hitler tried to exterminate them during the Holocaust, and the Antichrist will try the same thing during the Tribulation. Today, anti-Semitism is a global epidemic.[54] The world largely has turned against Israel in a wave of anti-Semitism only matched by pre-Holocaust attitudes.

A classic example is the absurdity of the world's reaction to Hamas attacking Israel with more than 4,000 rockets in 2021.[55] It's unjust and unbelievable that Israel would be told to calm down while the rocket barrage continued. Reports such as these will only escalate until the Messiah comes in as a hero to save the day and stop war.

#63 NUCLEAR WEAPONS NOW A REALITY—ZECHARIAH 14:12

Many of the things Zechariah prophesied would have been hard to comprehend in his day. Zechariah 14:12 says, "They will become like walking corpses, their flesh rotting away; their eyes will shrivel in their sockets, and their tongues will decay in their mouths" (TLB). Thousands of years later, the radiation hazards that follow nuclear weapons explain a lot.

#64 RISE IN VEGETARIANISM—1 TIMOTHY 4:3-4

Speaking of the last days, 1 Timothy 4:3-4 says, "They will say it is wrong to be married and *wrong to eat meat*, even though God gave these things to well-taught Christians to enjoy and be thankful for. For everything God made is good, and we may eat it gladly if we are thankful for it" (TLB).

By the way, folks, Jesus was *not* a vegetarian. In Genesis 18, Jesus enjoyed a steak dinner.

#65 LAND PARTITIONED—JOEL 3 // DANIEL 11:39

Joel and Daniel both prophesied that Israel's land would be partitioned in our lifetime. It's a controversial issue. In fact, unusually enough, every Israeli prime minister who's been elected got elected opposing land division. Nevertheless, every prime minister has ended up dividing land. This has been going on for the past 20 to 30 years.

What it establishes more than anything is that there's great pressure to divide the land. In fact, I believe it's very likely the Antichrist will offer a solution to the problem on his platform. He'll want to divide the land to appease the Palestinians.

#66 NO KING FOR ISRAEL UNTIL JESUS RETURNS—HOSEA 3:4 // DANIEL 7:22

Hosea prophesied that the returning Jews would have no king until Jesus returns (Hos. 3:4-5). As foretold, Israel has been without a king for over 2,500 years. But Israel is about to have a king—King Jesus, the Messiah! In many ways, the ancient prophets were better attuned to our times than we are.

When Daniel was overwhelmed by what he knew of the Tribulation, do you remember what Gabriel told him? He said, "The Ancient of Days will prevail!" Wow!

#67 EASTERN GATE REMAINS CLOSED UNTIL JESUS RETURNS—EZEKIEL 44:1-3

Today, as prophesied, the Eastern Gate, facing the Mount of Olives, remains sealed until Jesus will enter Jerusalem through it when He returns.[56] Different religions thought they could block the Messiah from returning by making the area a cemetery, but Jesus could just raise the dead!

#68 THE BIBLE PROPHESIES THAT ISRAEL WILL PLANT TREES—ISAIAH 41:18-20

Speaking of Israel, God says:

ISAIAH 41:18-20 (NLT)

I will open up rivers for them on the high plateaus. I will give them fountains of water in the valleys. I will fill the desert with pools of water. Rivers fed by springs will flow across the parched ground. I will plant trees in the barren desert—cedar, acacia, myrtle, olive, cypress, fir, and pine. I am doing this so all who see this miracle will understand what it means—that it is the Lord who has done this, the Holy One of Israel who created it.

Since 1900, roughly 250,000,000 trees have been planted across Israel, and it is the only country in the world that ended the 20th century with more trees than it had in 1900. In 1948, roughly 2 percent of Israel was covered in trees and this has now grown to around 8.5 percent.[57]

#69 JESUS FORETOLD OF TERRORISM—LUKE 21:11

Jesus foretold of fearful sights in Luke 21:11. The Greek word for *fearful* is *phobetron,* which can be translated *terror.* That means some 2,000 years ago Jesus warned us of an uptick in terrorism.

Up until the 1970s, as a society we heard very little about international terrorism and next to nothing about domestic terrorism. From 9-11 forward, terrorist activities are almost daily in the news somewhere. In fact, the Global Terrorism Database documents more than 200,000 international and domestic attacks have occurred worldwide since 1970.[58] Without question, terrorism is steadily on the rise.

#70 RABBIS THINK NOVEMBER 2021 BLOOD MOON A WARNING—GENESIS 1:14

November 18-19, 2021, another blood moon was seen. It was the longest lunar eclipse in 100 years, lasting three hours and 28 minutes. Jewish rabbis frequently interpret blood moons as warnings. They interpreted this one in conjunction with their belief that U.S. President Biden has plans to divide Jerusalem.

#71 WEST BANK SETTLEMENTS PROVOKE EZEKIEL 38 WAR—EZEKIEL 38

All hell is breaking loose in response to an Israeli announcement that they will build settlements in the West Bank. U.S. President Biden is against this as are many nations surrounding Israel.[59] Israel has made it clear they will move ahead despite objections, saying they want to finally build on land that became theirs in the Six-Day War in 1967. Those opposed say Israel only "occupies" the land. How crazy is that?

#72 ACCURACY OF SAINT MALACHY PROPHECY

While in Rome in AD 1139, St. Malachy received a vision showing him 112 Catholic popes in succession from his day to the end of time. The Irish archbishop who was canonized a saint wrote poetic descriptions of each pontiff along with their family names, birthplaces, and coat of arms.[60] According to the St. Malachy's prophecies, Pope Francis is the last pope before judgment day. The History Channel said this is statistically impossible, and yet, the list was written in the 12th century through today.

#73 RUSSIA RESTORING ARCH OF TRIUMPH IN SYRIA'S PALMYRA

In November 2021, it was announced that Russia will restore the Roman Arch of Triumph in Palmyra, Syria, which is pretty striking news.[61] What's the big deal? The arch stood at the entrance to the temple used to worship Ba'al.[62] The Talmud, the primary text of Jewish law, says it's the last sign before the Messiah returns.[63] Palmyra is where the Tower of Babel was located, so it all goes back to rebellion at the origins of humanity. This is where Elijah called down fire from heaven to defeat the priests of Ba'al.

#74 DEAD SEA TURNS RED—GENESIS 19

A pool of water near the Dead Sea mysteriously turned blood red September 15, 2021. The pool is located in modern-day Jordan, but it just happens to be the biblical region of the ancient cities Sodom and Gomorrah. What's really amazing is that the waters turned red on the Jewish Day of Atonement

(September 15-16, 2021). If this isn't God showing off, I don't know what is. This is huge!

Is this a sign? Sure, it is! I believe God was saying even sexual sins—such as those common in the ancient cities of Sodom and Gomorrah—are covered by the blood of Jesus.[64] Jewish leaders were freaked out by what happened, and so far, scientists have no definitive explanation.[65] God is doing everything He can to get our attention in this hour.

#75 BIRDS FALLING FROM THE AIR—HOSEA 4:3

We read earlier in Romans 8 how the whole earth and all creation is yearning and groaning with birth pangs for the coming of the Lord. Another sign along this line is the prophet Hosea speaking of the last days. Hosea 4:3 says, "That is why your land is in mourning, and everyone is wasting away. Even the wild animals, the birds of the sky, and the fish of the sea are disappearing" (NLT).

In northwestern Spain in December of 2021, hundreds of birds mysteriously fell from the sky "like rain" and hit the pavement, people, cars, and more.[66] Government officials still are probing the unusual occurrence.

#76 SUN SIGNS—REVELATION 16:8-9 // 2 PETER 3:10 // PSALM 19:1-5 // ROMANS 8:19-23

Scripture says in the last days, the sun will scorch the inhabitants of the earth (Rev. 16:8-9). Although this prophecy is a divine judgment on unrepentant man, will it result from nuclear war or ecological disaster? Second Peter 3:10 says a day comes when the elements will melt, and NASA agrees.[67]

Solar flares have increased intensity lately, and it has NASA's attention. In December 2021, NASA warned of "swirling sun debris created by a solar storm."[68] In October 2021, a massive solar light was a powerful eruption.[69] Scientists have even been concerned it could disrupt cell service.[70]

I find it interesting that in December 2021, for the first time in history, NASA's Parker Solar Probe actually touched the sun to investigate this 4.5-billion-year-old star at the center of our solar system.[71] Increasingly, Bible prophecies and news headlines are merging.

#77 A SIGN JUST BEFORE THE COMING OF THE LORD

Midway through Donald Trump's presidency three years ago, we experienced a super moon. When Trump was born June 14, 1946, there was also a blood moon—what NASA calls a wolf moon. Then 700 days later, Israel was made a nation on May 14, 1948.[72]

When Trump was elected, Benjamin Netanyahu had been in office seven years, seven months, and seven days. Trump was elected when he 70 years old, seven months, and seven days. Notice the pattern here. Is it more than a coincidence?

Trump's presidency was an important one if for no other reason than after 70 years, he moved the American Embassy from Tel Aviv to Jerusalem.

And, most interesting of all, when you say the name of his ticket—Trump/Pence or *trumpence*—you are speaking of the coming of the Lord because Jesus will return on the Feast of Trumpets. Don't get mad at me, now. I'm just relaying the facts.

#78 STARTLING U.N. VOTE ABOUT THE TEMPLE MOUNT— ISAIAH 14:12-17 // ISAIAH 51:17 // ZECHARIAH 8:22 // PSALM 132:13-14

In December 2021, 129 of the U.N. members voted that the Temple Mount does not belong to the Jews, but rather, it belongs to Islam. Only 11 countries stood with Israel, which is shocking! Let's connect the dots here to see why this is such an important sign. The Battle of Armageddon—the war of all wars—will be fought over Jerusalem. Why? Because Jerusalem is the city where the Temple Mount is located and where Jesus will set up His throne. Psalm 132:13 says, "The Lord has chosen Jerusalem; he has desired it for his home" (NLT). "This is my permanent home where I [God] shall live" (Ps. 132:14 TLB). But Lucifer is saying, "If I cannot ascend to the throne in heaven to be like God, then I'll just take His throne on earth." Everything comes down to that one piece of prime real estate.

That makes it pretty clear that the global pressure to take Jerusalem away from Israel is a satanic plot to establish Jerusalem as the Palestinian capital and center of Islam. And it's happening right before our eyes. This action is also another step closer to the setup for the Tribulation or the "cup of trembling" for all nations (Isa. 51:17) and, ultimately, the Battle of Armageddon.

#79 CHINA AND RUSSIA ARMED AND READY FOR BATTLE OF ARMAGEDDON WITH SUPERWEAPONS—REVELATION 16:12

In the same week in December 2021, China and Russia boasted of new and highly sophisticated weaponry never seen before on the face of the earth.[73]

Sign #46 mentioned that in August 2021, China announced a new hypersonic, nuclear-capable missile. But refusing to be left behind, by December 2021, Russia touted that they lead the world with their new hypersonic missile. It travels more than 20 times the speed of sound[74] in the upper atmosphere, cannot be detected by radar,[75] and is said to have such great maneuverability that it would be impossible to defend against. Putin was quoted as saying by the time other countries catch up, Russia will likely have developed counteractive technology.[76]

Why is this a sign? It means that the two main countries that attack during the Battle of Armageddon are armed and ready. Revelation 16:12 says, "Then the sixth angel poured out his bowl on the great Euphrates River, and it dried up so that the kings from the east [primarily China and Russia] could march their armies toward the west without hindrance" (NLT).

SIGNS AND MORE SIGNS

For more signs, updates, and details continually added and expanded, follow the weekly *End of Days Update*, hosted by Joseph Morris on YouTube.

WHAT'S NEXT?

You've read many signs of Jesus' soon return, and you've seen the precise and flawless Bible accuracy predicting these signs thousands and thousands of years ahead. Now, may we all say: Dear Father, we see the signs, and we respond accordingly.

"Yes, someone might say, "but how do we respond? Now what?" I'll tell you what. Use your God-given authority to pray over your spouse, children, entire family, house, church, job, city, and more. Decree things like never before. Begin to say, "It is written that I am redeemed from the curse of the law. I run my race and finish my course with joy. I fulfill every assignment God has for me. Money comes into my hands so I can under-write the work of the gospel."

Hammer faith-filled statements over yourself and your family as hard as ever. Be more of a confession freak than ever. Do you remember how you used to be in the early days when you first got a hold of God's Word? That's what you need to be doing now—all the way to Jesus' return.

You are blessed, and you have come to the kingdom for such a time as this. Prophetic words have been spoken over this generation. Jesus Himself spoke of the day you are living in right now. That wasn't true in the Dark Ages. That wasn't true 1,000 years ago. That wasn't true 100 years ago, but it's true today. It's true right now.

Friend, I cannot give you the exact day and time Jesus will return, but after reading 75+ signs, you should be well aware that we are in the season. All the signs point to the fact that Jesus' return is very, *very* near.

SOLD OUT

After reading about some 75+ signs of Jesus' soon return, what time is it? It's time to be sold out for Jesus. What's the last thing Jesus instructed you to do? Make sure you are doing it! The minute you commit to do whatever He tells you to do, an influx of new revelation and the equipment to do it comes so you can run farther and faster.

Friend, Jesus is about to come back. What would you say to Him if you were raptured tonight? Could you look Him in the eye and say, "I finished my course! I did what You told me to do! I gave it my all"? This is no time to give only a percentage of what He's deposited in you. It's time to be wildly sold out! When you commit and get busy, the blessing of God comes on your life.

Jesus is coming back for you. Will you be ready to meet Him?

CHAPTER 5

A GREAT TRANSITION OF DISPENSATIONS

WE ARE ENTERING a season of dramatic change. We are blessed to be living right before God comes back to the planet because Adam's lease is about up. We are also living in the dispensation of the Church Age, which is rapidly drawing to a close. Above all, I hear the Holy Ghost saying, "There's a great transition coming!" The dispensation or era of human and church history is about to be dramatically altered, and we have front-row seats.

From Malachi to Matthew, there was 400 years of silence. No one was speaking for God before the first coming; no one was saying a word. It was quiet until God raised up John the Baptist, and the Bible says John prepared the way for Jesus (Matt. 3). Jesus Himself said there had not been a greater prophet since John nor would there ever be, and yet the least in the kingdom of God today has more anointing than John the

Baptist. That means you have more grace on you to be a voice than John did. Let that sink in for a second.

It's no wonder God has provided you with more supernatural power and equipment. It's all about what He has called you to do. You are an awakening voice right before the coming of the Lord, and all around us is a dynamo of Holy Ghost activity preparing for Jesus' return. All kinds of things are happening and will continue happening until the sky breaks open and Jesus appears.

A Big Change Coming

In the late 1980s, Kenneth E. Hagin, a 20th-century prophet who carried a strong message of faith, prophesied that right before the coming of the Lord, people will go to the other side and return. When he spoke that out, I thought he meant people would be translated, and they may well be. But I've also realized how many people have died and come back to write books about their experiences. Some of the accounts are downright weird, so it's critical to base everything on the Word of God.

I read some books and think, *Oh dear Jesus, the author lost his mind.* They go all wonky and new age. Still, many people die and come back to write about legitimate heavenly encounters because the world is getting ready for a transition. In these last days, we will hear more and more preaching on heaven. We will hear more and more about supernatural encounters because God is preparing us for what's ahead!

I also recall a prophecy about the last days by Sister Jeanne Wilkerson, a prophetess who lived in Tulsa, Oklahoma, and one fiery lady. In the 1980s, I listened to her speak when I was

17 and attending RHEMA Bible Training Center. Brother Hagin called her up to the platform, and she began to prophesy that right before the coming of the Lord there would be wildfires all over America. Sister Wilkerson said these fires would signify sin burning in the hearts of men.

A while back, after landing at the Ontario, California airport, I was driving on I-10 and startled to see one of those wildfires coming toward us on the freeway. It jumped the lane and caught the middle median on fire. Then it jumped again and caught the other lane on fire. It was something to see. Wildfires like this have been on the rise in the past 20 years or so, and they are not confined to California.[1] They've occurred in Texas, Colorado, New Jersey, Europe, and many places beyond.

The Holy Ghost also said something to me a while back about the change in dispensations. "Watch! In every dispensation change you'll see such an increase of angelic activity," He said. Without any fanfare, without any weirdness there will be a flurry of angelic activity to lead people to Jesus. We see this very thing in the book of Acts. In Acts 10, an angel appeared to Cornelius and told him to go down to Joppa where he would hear words to be saved. In Acts 8, an angel appeared to Philip about witnessing to the Ethiopian. In Acts 9, Jesus appeared to Ananias, telling him to go lay hands on Paul, which activated revelation gifts of the Spirit such as word of wisdom and word of knowledge. As a result, the New Testament got written. God often uses heavenly activity to accelerate things—getting more done in a shorter period of time.

Listen carefully! The end of the Church Age will finish like it started. What will we see at the crux of the end times? What will it look like right before the coming of the Lord? It will look at Acts 2, 3, 4, 5, and 6. You and I will finish writing the book of Acts.

John G. Lake, an early 20th-century Pentecostal leader, missionary to South Africa, and well known for a healing ministry with over 100,000 document healings, said an angel appeared to him and showed him the book of Acts. The angel said, "This is Pentecost as God gave it. Contend for this. This and this alone will meet the need of the human heart."[2] We must contend for finishing off this Church Age in the book of Acts style. That's why the Holy Ghost was talking to me about angels. The plan of God goes full circle. Right now, we are at the end of this dispensation, and this dispensation will finish exactly like it began.

> We are blessed to stand on the threshold of a season when we will see increasing demonstrations of the glory of God.

We will enjoy outpourings of the Holy Ghost everywhere, including outside the walls of the church with normal people yielding to God. The book of Acts did not feature only great preachers or apostles doing the works of Jesus in temples. No, believers took the gospel, the gifts, and the supernatural to the streets—out where the people are. That's what God desires today! He wants the whole body of Christ doing the works of Jesus everywhere people are, just as we're called to do.

We are blessed to stand on the threshold of a season when we will see increasing demonstrations of the glory of God. The articulation of the glory of God will be made known to this generation so all will see how wonderful Jesus is. May every one of us walk in the full measure of what Jesus left us 2,000 years ago.

A DISPENSATIONAL TIMELINE

To better understand the dispensational change just ahead, let's consider a timeline of dispensations and how they have changed down through the ages. The word *dispensation* means "a system of order, government, or organization existing at a particular time." It is a common system of Bible interpretation that divides the spiritual history of mankind into categories. The term itself is not found in the Bible, but the seven dispensations make it easier to understand the timelines.

The seven dispensations are the Dispensation of Innocence, the Dispensation of Conscience, the Dispensation of Human Government, the Dispensation of Promise, the Dispensation of Law, the Dispensation of Grace, and the Millennial Kingdom of Christ.[3]

On pages 291-294, we have included classic dispensational charts prepared by Rev. Clarence Larkin, a famous Baptist pastor who lived during the late 1800s and early 1900s. His writings and charts on dispensationalism have greatly influenced the Christian world in the area of eschatology.

HOW GOD RESPONDS PER DISPENSATION

Before we delve into each dispensation, I want to make an important overall point that will bring a lot of things into focus for you. It is vital you get this! If you get a hold of this one point, you will comprehend the end-time dealings of God in the earth today. If you don't understand this one thing, a whole lot of things just won't make sense.

The point is this: God treats people differently and responds to events differently depending on the dispensation. Understanding this makes all the difference in understanding how and why God reacts as He does.

For example, on a timeline of the ages, you and I are living at the close of the Church Age or the Dispensation of Grace. In this dispensation, God has given the Church authority. You will see that is not the case in every dispensation.

Remember in Acts 1:6, Peter and John and the other disciples thought Jesus was coming back right away to set up His Millennial Kingdom? Isaiah had prophesied, "For unto us a child is born, unto us a son is given: and the government shall be upon his shoulder" (Isa. 9:6). In one verse, Isaiah went from the birth of Jesus and skipped all the way over to the government resting on His adult shoulders.

During His earthly ministry, Jesus told the disciples, "That thou art Peter, and upon this rock I will build my church; and the gates of hell shall not prevail against it" (Matt. 16:18). The disciples responded, asking, "Church? What's a church?" They wanted a king and a kingdom.

When soldiers came to arrest Jesus in the Garden of Gethsemane, Peter pulled out his knife and cut off the soldier's ear (John 18:10). Peter wasn't going for his ear, by the way. He was going for the guy's head because Peter thought, *Here it is. The moment has come. Jesus is going to be the Messiah*. Peter and the other disciples did not understand that gap called the Church Age for two days or two thousand years.

The Old Testament prophets saw some things about the First Coming of Jesus or His birth, and they definitely saw about the Second Coming. But they thought these events were right together, so the Church Age was a complete mystery. The Rapture was also a complete mystery. That's why if you talk to your unsaved friends about the Rapture, they think you're crazy because it's not for them.

In the beginning, God created the heavens and the earth, and He turned the earth over to Adam (Gen. 1). Unfortunately, Adam and Eve sinned and turned it over to the devil (Gen. 3). While the devil still has a short-term lease on the earth, Jesus died on the cross and restored authority to the Church, making it clear that the devil is under our feet (Eph. 2).

The Church Age is such a distinct time when Jesus said, "I am he that liveth, and was dead; and, behold, I am alive for evermore, Amen; and have the keys of hell and of death" (Rev. 1:18). "I will build my church; and the gates of hell shall not prevail against it" (Matt. 16:18). Then Jesus said, "Here are the keys. You go into all the world and preach the gospel. You lay hands on the sick. You cast out devils. You go in my place for me" (Mark 16:15-18). Right then and there, Jesus authorized the Church; He put the Church in charge down here on earth.

For the past two thousand years, even though people often say God is in control, He is *not* in control. Technically speaking, the Church is in control.

Again, this point is critical. Recognizing that God treats people differently in different dispensations will help you understand what I'm about to say. Right now—during the Church Age—God responds differently than He has in the past or will in the future. For example, Germany prospered after killing six million Jews in the Holocaust during World War II (1939–1941). Why? How? Because we are in a dispensation of grace. It shocks some people and makes others mad. If you listen to some preachers, God is ready to kill everybody, but the truth is, God is not mad at anybody. He laid all that on Jesus.

It's important that we understand this before we delve into the topic of the Rapture. Otherwise, we will misunderstand and misinterpret God's actions. For example, I hear people say frequently, "God is judging America." I heard that a lot in 2005 when Hurricane Katrina devastated New Orleans. Here's my response: "If God judged New Orleans, He didn't do a very good job because people are still alive there." The truth is, God did *not* judge New Orleans in 2005, and He did not judge Germany in 1941 because we are in a dispensation of grace.

Listen, folks, when God sends judgment, there are no people left. Consider Sodom and Gomorrah in the Bible (Gen. 18–19). When God sent judgment, the people were toast. Of course, some nations reap what they sow. But in that case, a tragedy is not the Lord's judgment but the result of people being stupid and making poor choices. If people sow bad seeds, people reap a bad harvest, but that is not the Lord's fault. I'm sure that statement went over well. Stop the presses. Goodbye, everybody. Start the car, Colleen. I'll be right there.

THE SEVEN DISPENSATIONS

In every dispensation, God has given man an opportunity for a future and a hope, but in every dispensation, man has messed it up. The dispensations are in order below:

The Dispensation of Innocence: From the creation of man to the fall of man (Genesis 1:28-30 and 2:15-17).

God created the heavens and the earth and formed man in His own likeness. God gave Adam and Eve authority and dominion over this new world. God gave them an opportunity, but it ended with the fall of man.

The Dispensation of Conscience: From the time Adam and Eve were evicted from the garden to the worldwide flood (Genesis 3:8–8:22).

Man was left to rule himself by his own will and conscience, but it ended in lawlessness, corruption, and violence so God wiped it all out with the flood. We think of the flood as judgment but, in reality, it was protection. The flood was necessary to keep a righteous bloodline in the earth so Jesus ultimately could be born.

The Dispensation of Human Government: Began just after the flood.

God commanded Noah to build an ark and made promises to him as a result. God promised not to curse the earth or flood it again. He also commanded Noah and his sons to repopulate the world. Instead, Noah's descendants worked together to build the tower of Babel (Gen. 11:1-9). Man said, "You know what? We will make our own way to heaven." So, this dispensation also ended in failure. God countered by confusing their languages, creating nations and cultures that spread around the world. This was the beginning of human government.

Interestingly enough, during the past several years, ISIS was destroying all the artifacts where the tower of Babel was built.

This is where the Assyrians were located. Why is that a big deal? Because the Bible says the Antichrist will be an Assyrian—a thought pattern emerging in the forefront even now.

The Dispensation of Promise: From the call of Abraham through Israel's bondage in Egypt.

The call of Abraham, the lives of the patriarchs, and the Jewish people in bondage all fall under this dispensation. This is the time when Abraham's descendants waited for the fulfillment of God's promise to make them a great nation and give them their own land (Gen. 12:1-7). Once they left Egypt, they were officially a nation led by God into the wilderness toward the Promised Land.

The Dispensation of Law: Lasted 1,500 years, beginning with the Exodus and ending with the crucifixion and resurrection of Jesus Christ.

Man receiving the Ten Commandments and the Mosaic Law fall here and outlined what God expected of His people. The point of the Law was to show the people they needed to trust God rather than themselves. In this dispensation, God gave His people laws to point them to Jesus, but they could not fulfill the laws on their own. This dispensation ended at Calvary with Jesus dying to fulfill the Law for us. What a flawless and perfect system God designed that Jesus would take our place and do for us what we could not do for ourselves.

The Dispensation of Grace (the Church Age): From the resurrection of Jesus through the Rapture of the Church.

What's so cool in this dispensation is that God is not judging or critiquing us but looking at us through the corrective lens of Jesus' redemptive work on the cross. He sees you and me as righteous and complete in Jesus.

I mentioned in Chapter 1 how Jesus appeared to me in 1987 with a mandate to preach on the end times. Four years later in 1990, He appeared to me again because I hadn't done my job. As I said earlier, I was overcome and crying uncontrollably because of the goodness coming out of Him. Jesus could have reprimanded me and told me how I had failed Him, but He just looked at me. His goodness led me to repentance (Rom. 2:4).

Here's the point. Jesus was not critiquing me, grading me, or judging me. In this dispensation, He does not grade anybody. He may get frustrated because He wants us to do what we are told and do our best, but He still does not judge us.

> There are different standards and protocols for how God responds in the various dispensations.

Jesus does not say, "You missed it. You're toast." I hear weird and extreme preaching along those lines, but it is not accurate. In this dispensation, God is not angry with you, and He is not judging you. However, there are different standards and protocols for how God responds in the various dispensations. In all other dispensations, God dealt with man on his own merits, but the Dispensation of Grace is different.

Jesus made all the difference in this dispensation as our Advocate and Lawyer. Lucifer accuses us, but Jesus defends us. Jesus stands right up and says, "Not today, devil. I redeemed him. I purchased her. I made him whole. I made her righteous.

He's not only forgiven but justified. My death and resurrection covered it all!"

Jesus had to redeem all mankind to be flawless so God could function with you and you could enjoy His presence. Through Jesus' shed blood, God made you perfect and holy. The law could not make you perfect. All it could do was show you that you were not good enough. God dealt with man differently in the Dispensation of Law.

In this Dispensation of Grace, God told us to judge ourselves. He never sends anybody to hell; people choose hell by default because they do not choose Jesus. "But why must people go to hell when they die?" somebody asks. If sinful people were not incarcerated in hell, they could operate outside of their bodies like a god; they could kill and destroy. God puts people in hell to protect you. Imagine if Hitler could have operated outside of his body. He did horrific evils in his body, but outside of his body like a god, he could have killed everybody.

In the Dispensation of Grace today, Jesus fulfilled the law at Calvary and said, "It is finished." What was finished? The Law. Redemption was not finished because Jesus had not yet gone into the heart of the earth to defeat the devil. But Jesus left the cross and went to hell to pay the penalty for Adam's sin.

In Colossians, Paul was bold enough to say it this way—Jesus "blotting out the handwriting of ordinances that was against us, which was contrary to us, and took it out of the way, nailing it to his cross" (Col. 2:14). Your boldness and confidence to be caught up in the air with Jesus at the Rapture is not based on your works or your perfection but *His*. Once you received Jesus at salvation, you became *in Him*. You are now part of His body.

This is the concept that really freaks people out—our dispensation technically ends in apostasy, which is happening right now. We don't like to talk about it or preach about it, but it's true just the same. The Bible told us that in this hour before Jesus returns, men would behave badly.

Second Timothy 3:1-5 paints an ugly, ungodly picture. See if it sounds familiar:

> *This know also, that in the last days perilous times shall come. For men shall be lovers of their own selves, covetous, boasters, proud, blasphemers, disobedient to parents, unthankful, unholy, without natural affection, trucebreakers, false accusers, incontinent, fierce, despisers of those that are good, traitors, heady, highminded, lovers of pleasures more than lovers of God; having a form of godliness, but denying the power thereof: from such turn away.*

The Message Bible puts it this way:

> *Don't be naive. There are difficult times ahead. As the end approaches, people are going to be self-absorbed, money-hungry, self-promoting, stuck-up, profane, contemptuous of parents, crude, coarse, dog-eat-dog, unbending, slanderers, impulsively wild, savage, cynical, treacherous, ruthless, bloated windbags, addicted to lust, and allergic to God. They'll make a show of religion, but behind the scenes they're animals. Stay clear of these people.*

We don't have time to preach on all the negative aspects of the last days because we need to focus on the positive ones. Yet, we need to recognize that the environment around us is exactly what the Bible said it would be—apostasy. Nevertheless, we will finish off the book of Acts with revival just like it started. The Bible says in James that God is waiting on the precious fruit of the earth, and the Bible talks about Job getting double what he lost. So, we have great things to look forward to as we finish off the Church Age. We will have a grand and glorious revival right in the middle of apostasy.

What happens next? The Rapture! The Church is caught up with Jesus in the air, and the seven-year Tribulation begins on the earth. The Church Age is a specific time when we have been given authority on the earth. At the Rapture, the Church is taken off the earth, which is the purpose of catching away the Church. The Tribulation could not happen while the Church is here operating in its authority.

In fact, 2 Thessalonians 2:1-12 (NKJV) tells us the Antichrist cannot be revealed until the Church leaves:

Now, brethren, concerning the coming of our Lord Jesus Christ and our gathering together to Him, we ask you, not to be soon shaken in mind or troubled, either by spirit or by word or by letter, as if from us, as though the day of Christ had come. Let no one deceive you by any means; for that Day will not come unless the falling away comes first, and the man of sin is revealed, the son of perdition, who opposes and exalts himself above all that is called God or that is worshiped, so that he sits as God in the temple of God, showing himself that he is God.

Do you not remember that when I was still with you I told you these things? And now you know what is

restraining, that he may be revealed in his own time. For the mystery of lawlessness is already at work; only He who now restrains will do so until He is taken out of the way. And then the lawless one will be revealed, whom the Lord will consume with the breath of His mouth and destroy with the brightness of His coming. The coming of the lawless one is according to the work-ing of Satan, with all power, signs, and lying wonders, and with all unrighteous deception among those who perish, because they did not receive the love of the truth, that they might be saved. And for this reason God will send them strong delusion, that they should believe the lie, that they all may be condemned who did not believe the truth but had pleasure in unrighteousness.

At the end of the Church Age, God is preparing like He did in the Old Covenant to deal with man in an outward way where everything is visible. During the Tribulation, there will be seven years of fireworks to get Israel to turn to God. God is so cool, so smart. He's got it all figured out.

The next events are the Tribulation and the Great Tribula-tion, the Second Coming, and the Millennial Reign of Christ, all outlined in upcoming chapters.

A CHANGE IN TONE

Look with me at Ezekiel 38 to see how God's tone changes at the Ezekiel 38 War, discussed more in Chapter 7. This change in tone is the reason I went through the dispensations, so you could understand how God deals differently with people in different dispensations.

EZEKIEL 38:14-16 (MSG)

Therefore, son of man, prophesy! Tell Gog, "A Message from God, the Master: When my people Israel are established securely, will you make your move? Will you come down out of the far north, you and that mob of armies, charging out on your horses like a tidal wave across the land, and invade my people Israel, covering the country like a cloud? When the time's ripe, I'll unleash you against my land in such a way that the nations will recognize me, realize that through you, Gog, in full view of the nations, I am putting my holiness on display."

Remember, in our current dispensation—the Church Age or the Dispensation of Grace—Jesus put the Church in charge. He told us to go preach the gospel, and He would confirm the Word with signs following. But the moment the Church leaves in the Rapture, everything changes. All of a sudden, it's rat-a-tat-tat with a baseball bat.

> The moment the Church leaves in the Rapture, everything changes. All of a sudden, it's rat-a-tat-tat with a baseball bat.

God is so cool. Russia will try to swoop down and overtake Israel, but God will show off for Israel. He is courting her, and He will defend her. God said, "I will do this so the heathen may know I'm God." He's so awesome!

Consider how differently God responds according to the dispensation of time. God did not intervene during the Holocaust when six million Jews were horrifically tortured and killed.

Why? God did not have the authority to intervene because He had given the authority to the Church.

"Brother Joe, you're freaking me out," someone says. "Are you saying it's the Church's fault that so many Jews died?" Yes. That's exactly what I'm saying. Jesus gave the Church authority on earth, and the Church should have used it!

But this time around when the Church is raptured, the dispensation changes. And when Russia invades Israel, God will intervene and say, "Oh, no, you don't. I've got Israel's back."

EZEKIEL 38:23

Thus will I magnify myself, and sanctify myself; and I will be known in the eyes of many nations, and they shall know that I am the Lord.

Right now, it's up to the Church to make Jesus known. But when the Church departs and the seven-year Tribulation begins, God says, "I'm doing this on My own." His plan reminds me of children's church years ago when there were pictures posted everywhere when the Old Testament was taught so kids could understand it all. In the same way, God will do a show-and-tell mentality during the Tribulation until everyone gets it. It's pretty cool! Let's look at Ezekiel 39:

EZEKIEL 39:6-7

And I will send a fire on Magog, and among them that dwell carelessly in the isles: and they shall know that I am the Lord. So will I make my holy name known in the midst of my people Israel; and I will not let them pollute my holy

name any more: and the heathen shall know that I am the
Lord, the Holy One in Israel.

God's tone changes completely right after the salt of the earth—the Church—departs. The change in dispensation changed everything. Notice how many times as the verses continue that God refers to them as "the heathen." He wants them to turn so badly that He will do different things to show off and get their attention. We will look at more details about this in Chapter 11 about the Tribulation. I'm explaining this now to make the point that we are living at the very edge of this dispensation—about to step into the next one.

A CROSSOVER OF DISPENSATIONS

Throughout Bible history, at a point of crossover, some things actually do *cross over.* For example, when the dispensations were changing, John the Baptist began to baptize people for the remission of sins. That had never been done before. How was it even possible? The dispensation was changing, and it was time for Jesus to die on the cross and pay for the remission of sins.

At this hour, we're at a crossover point between the Dispensation of Grace and the Millennial Reign of Christ. I believe we will begin seeing things indicative of the next dispensation like people being translated. During the Millennial Reign, people will be translated frequently and move around at will. It won't be weird or strange—just life everlasting in demonstration.

The glory of God will come on older people who seemingly will be as though young again. It will be a work of the Holy Ghost to show you how close you are to bumping into the next dispensation. The dead will be raised. Limbs will grow. There will be supernatural outbreaks of the power of God left and right with no weirdness, no fanfare. It will be the supernatural unfolding naturally. It will just be heaven functioning in the Church, getting the earth ready for the Millennial Reign of Christ.

During the Tribulation, God will show off to get Israel and the heathen to turn to Him, but right now before we leave, we will see previews of the next 1,000 years. People will look at the Church and get a glimpse of the liberty and glory of the visible King for 1,000 years. The whole earth is being set up for God to deal with Israel right before the Church departs. That's why we need the Church to wake up and get busy! We've got a lot of activity to cram into a little sliver of time.

I'm a real *Star Wars* freak, but we used to joke about *Star Wars* when it came out in 1977. We laughed at the ad like, "What? That's it? Whatever." But it ended up being the biggest-grossing movie in history. The previews enticed me, and then when I actually saw the movie, it was way cooler than I even imagined. Right now, we are seeing previews of the Millennium, and you are in the trailer. You and I will be walking, talking previews for the resurrection and the next dispensation.

The timeline is capped off with the Second Coming of the King of Kings and Lord of Lords. Boom. The Bible says the Mount of Olives splits in half (Zech. 14:4), and its area goes up in the air about 150 feet. The waters will come by His throne, and as the waters get near Jesus, it will quicken and heal all the water for the entire earth because there's so much life in Him (Ezek. 47:8). Just getting near Jesus fixes everything. But He's not just *near* you and I; He's *in* us.

The Messianic Dispensation or the Millennial Kingdom of Christ: From the defeat of Satan (Rev. 20:1-3) and ushering in 1,000 years of peace when Jesus will reign on earth (Rev. 20:4).

This will fulfill many prophecies, declaring Jesus as King of Kings. Other names for the dispensation are the Millennial Age or the Dispensation of the King. During this time, animal sacrifices will be reinstituted, but they will point back to Calvary, not forward to Calvary as they did in the Old Testament. "Why will sacrifices be needed?" someone might ask. There will be men and women with Adam's stain on them who defile the temple, and animal sacrifices or the shedding of blood will be needed to purify the surroundings where God will dwell.

> The timeline is capped off with the Second Coming of the King of Kings and Lord of Lords. Boom.

There are more verses about the Millennial Temple—God's House—than almost anything in the Bible. God is very particular about His location. You can read Ezekiel 40–46 to understand the flawlessness and the detail about God's property. But think about this. Right now, you are a mobile throne, and God likes mobile homes. If you get a hold of that revelation, it will buoy your faith, and you will never allow sickness in your body again.

At the end of the Millennium or Messianic Dispensation, Satan will be released to gather all the rebels who revolted at the end of the Millennial Reign of Christ.

The Perfect Age

After the seven dispensations of fallen man, the earth will be renovated by fire. We then will enter what's called The Perfect Age. God will bring the New Jerusalem down to the earth. It will be heaven on earth—literally—because God loves the earth that much.

CHAPTER 6

THE RAPTURE

TAKE A GOOD look at your body and remember what it looks like because it won't be long before your mortal body will put on immortality. Death will be swallowed up in life and, at last, you will lose the stain of Adam. You will have a brand-new glorified body that never dies, never gets sick, never ages, walks through walls, and instantly translates from heaven to earth. Your earth suit with its sin nature of Adam will become only a distant memory. It's going to be wonderful!

For the most part, the Rapture is not talked about in the Gospels, but we do find one shadow of reference to the Rapture in John 14. It's pretty powerful!

WILL YOU MARRY ME?

Actually, this split-second reference to the Rapture in the Gospel of John is an extreme statement. Basically, Jesus asked His disciples to marry Him.

John 14:1-3

Let not your heart be troubled: ye believe in God, believe also in me. In my Father's house are many mansions: if it were not so, I would have told you. I go to prepare a place for you. And if I go and prepare a place for you, I will come again, and receive you unto myself; that where I am, there ye may be also.

This was a Jewish wedding proposal. I can just imagine Jesus' staff—Peter, James, and John—saying, "Whoa, whoa, whoa! *What?*" They were just normal guys, but there was nothing normal about this proposal. Jesus freaked them out! It would have freaked me out, but as you know, Jesus often said interesting things just like that to get people's attention and prepare them for what was to come.

> Jesus walked up to His staff and said, "Oh, by the way, will you guys marry Me?"

Think about it. Jesus walked up to His staff and said, "Oh, by the way, will you guys marry Me?" They were like, "Uh, hold on. Guys don't ask guys to marry them. Jesus has been out in the sun too long. Something is up here. Jesus says some interesting stuff, but this is, 'Will you marry me?'"

In the Jewish wedding tradition, a man would ask a woman to marry him and then pay the purchase price for her. In other words, there would be a redemption, and she would be set apart for the marriage. In the same way, Jesus paid the price of redemption for the Church with His own life and blood.

And now we—the Church—have been set apart waiting for the Rapture.

According to tradition, the groom would go to his father's house and ask to marry the daughter. Upon his agreement, the father would then set about building a honeymoon suite for the couple, but the son would not know when the suite would be finished. Jewish tradition tells us the average wait time was about a year for the father to complete the wedding chamber or house.

Then, one day, the father would say to his son, "Okay, your room is ready! Go get your bride." During the time the room was built, the bride was to be continually preparing for her groom to come for her. She was to be ready and waiting!

People think, *Well, you can't know when the bridegroom is coming back.* Not so! That's just plain wrong teaching. Brides knew almost to the day when the bridegroom was returning, and they were anxiously waiting!

How many of you who are married knew when your wedding would take place? Did it catch you by surprise? No. Many people even send out "save the date" announcements. When our daughter, Lauren, got married, she had nine bridesmaids fly to California, and I've never worked so hard in all my life. Lauren said, "Hey, you will be able to do this, Dad. It's no big deal." I tell you what, nothing about her wedding caught me by surprise. I worked 24/7 just trying to get all the stuff done for the ceremony.

Yet when it comes to the Rapture, most people think it will be a surprise. Sure, it will be a surprise for the world, but it should not be a surprise for the bride—the Church. The bride of Christ should be expectant, ready, and anxiously waiting!

The apostle Paul said, "But you aren't in the dark about these things, dear brothers and sisters, and you won't be surprised when the day of the Lord comes like a thief" (1 Thess. 5:4 NLT).

Jewish tradition specified that after the purchase price was paid, the bride would be set apart or sanctified. She would prepare herself as she got closer to the wedding date. Meanwhile, I've interviewed families in Israel who explained that how soon the groom returned for the bride was all based on money. If the family had a little bit of money, it would be like a tenth of a honeymoon chamber and take a while to build. If they had a lot of money, an elaborate room would be built quickly. The father would decide, *This is how much money I will spend on your room.* But it would almost always be about a year regardless of the money involved. Clearly, no one was clueless. The groom was preparing, and the bride was preparing.

Unfortunately, the Church has taught that no one can tell when Jesus is coming back. But the truth is, you *can* tell! Once you get into the Scriptures, it really becomes quite clear.

A Jewish father would tell his son, "I've got your room ready. Go get your bride!" The groom would run down with a shout and get his bride who had been getting herself ready. She would be preparing day by day with her ears perked up so she could run to meet him. Church, we, too, should have our ears perked up and be ready to run to meet our Groom. At the Rapture of the Church, Jesus will come down for us with a shout, and we will meet Him in the air, so shall we ever be with the Lord. Come on, folks!

Like we said earlier, our mortality will put on immortality. Hallelujah! For us that means we are never to get tired again, never to get sick again, never to gain weight again. (By the way, my weight is flawless. I just need to be 6 feet 3 inches. I'm the perfect weight for that height.) Praise God, everything will get corrected when we are quickened by His Spirit. Our cells will be quickened, and we will get a brand-new body. Aren't you looking forward to that day?

WHAT PAUL SAYS ABOUT THE RAPTURE

In 1 Thessalonians, the first letter written by Paul, the theme of his writing is the coming of the Lord. In fact, Paul wrote the letter because the Thessalonians thought they were in the Tribulation. They were under so much persecution that Paul had to speak up, saying, "Hey, whoa, folks. Let me address some issues here!"

The Thessalonians had been taught the immediacy of the return of the Lord to the point that they were saying, "Something is wrong here! People are dying and going home to be with the Lord. What's up? I thought Jesus was going to come back before that?" Paul wrote them a letter saying, "Don't worry. Everything is cool."

As you read what Paul wrote about the Rapture, notice his tone and keep it in mind. Paul wants you hopeful and happy with no sorrow because that's the way Jesus wants you.

1 Thessalonians 4:13-18

But I would not have you to be ignorant, brethren, concerning them which are asleep, that ye sorrow not, even as others which have no hope. For if we believe that Jesus died and rose again, even so them also which sleep in Jesus will God bring with him. For this we say unto you by the word of the Lord, that we which are alive and remain unto the coming of the Lord shall not prevent them which are asleep. For the Lord himself shall descend from heaven with a shout, with the voice of the archangel, and with the trump of God: and the dead in Christ shall rise first: then we which are alive and remain shall be caught up together with them in the clouds, to meet the Lord in the air: and so shall we ever be with the Lord. Wherefore comfort one another with these words.

Let's read the same passage from the New Living Translation in more modern language:

And now, dear brothers and sisters, we want you to know what will happen to the believers who have died so you will not grieve like people who have no hope. For since we believe that Jesus died and was raised to life again, we also believe that when Jesus returns, God will bring back with him the believers who have died. We tell you this directly from the Lord: We who are still living when the Lord returns will not meet him ahead of those who have died. For the Lord himself will come down from heaven with a commanding shout, with the voice of the archangel, and with the trumpet call of God. First, the believers who have died will rise from their graves. Then, together with them, we who are still alive and remain on the earth will be caught up in the clouds to meet the Lord in the air. Then we will be with the Lord forever. So encourage each other with these words.

Does the last verse say we should scare one another with these words? No. The teaching of the Rapture is to bring comfort, so encourage each other. This is good news! As we've said before, there is bad news ahead—but not for the Christian. In fact, the King James Version says "comfort one another with these words." The New Living Translation says "encourage each other with these words," and in the margin of most Bibles, it says *exhort* one another with these words. This is our glorious hope! There should be a joy in the Church that we are about to be caught up. We are about to see Jesus face to face.

"Can you really be that bold about Jesus' return?" You can if you can read.

What generation will be here when the Rapture happens? Your generation, this generation. When you go through all the signs and do the math, however you want to do it, it's still you. "Hey, Joe," somebody asks, "Can you really be that bold about Jesus' return?" You can if you can read.

People confront me daily saying, "You cannot tell when the Lord is coming back." Yet Jesus had a whole tribe in the Old Testament called the Tribe of Issachar. First Chronicles 12:32 says they were "men that had understanding of the times, to know what Israel ought to do." The scripture indicates if you know what time it is, you know what to do. On the other hand, if you don't recognize the time, you won't know what you're supposed to do or recognize there is a change coming.

I've heard people say, "The Rapture is simply a doctrine of the Church that surfaced in the late 1800s." No. It came from right here in the Bible. It started with Jesus giving His disciples a wedding proposal. It came when Paul said to the Thessalonians, "Don't worry. Jesus will come back with a shout, and the dead in Christ will rise first."

The Message translation quotes 1 Thessalonians 4:13-18 this way:

> *We can tell you with complete confidence—we have the Master's word on it—that when the Master comes again to get us, those of us who are still alive will not get a jump on the dead and leave them behind. In actual fact, they'll be ahead of us. The Master himself will give the command. Archangel thunder! God's trumpet blast! He'll come down from heaven and the dead in Christ will rise—they'll go first. Then the rest of us who are still alive at the time will be caught up with them into the clouds to meet the Master. Oh, we'll be walking on air! And then there will be one huge family reunion with the Master. So reassure one another with these words.*

Isn't this something? Every loved one who has gone on to be with the Lord will instantaneously be reunited with their flesh. Their molecules will recollect; their spirits will rejoin their bodies, and you will meet them in the air. What a reunion!

Jesus will say, "Come up hither!" and every one of those bodies will be completely remade at the same exact second your body is remade. Hallelujah! People ask, "Can the Lord heal me?" He already healed you 2,000 years ago, but He will change your whole molecular structure with the shout of the archangel, the trumpet of God. Woohoo! Together, we will rocket right out of the earth to meet Jesus in the air.

Do you remember seeing pictures in old movies where the graves burst open at the Rapture? Not so—the graves will not burst open. Men and women will come right through their caskets just like you will go right through the ceiling. Nothing will contain you! When Jesus says, "Come up hither!" every born-again person on the planet will go north. Wow! Hallelujah! Talk about an evacuation!

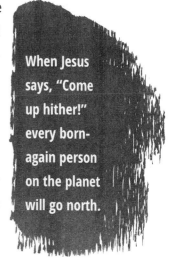

When Jesus says, "Come up hither!" every born-again person on the planet will go north.

No matter the country, when an army prepares to go into battle, the ambassadors are always evacuated first. God is also coming back for His ambassadors—and that's *you.*

RAPTURE QUALIFICATIONS

In 1 Thessalonians 4:14, Paul listed the qualifications for going up in the Rapture.

> *For if we believe that Jesus died and rose again, even so them also which sleep in Jesus will God bring with him.*

As I travel and speak on end times, I hear a lot of frustrated people comment on this verse. I hear people say, "If you're perfect, you will go up in the Rapture. If you're not perfect, you will not go up in the Rapture." The truth is, if you are born again, you will go up. Friend, it's not about you—it's about Jesus coming for His body.

I want to be clear about this: You are either born again or you're not. There is no in between. It's true that you cannot be a great, mature, and powerful Christian if you are carnal and living like the world, but you are still a Christian. You may not be doing what you should do, but that does not mean you lose your reborn nature; it does mean you are yielding to your carnal, fleshly nature.

There's a whole teaching right now that says if people don't believe in the Rapture or don't have faith for the Rapture, they won't go up in the Rapture. That's not biblical. Too many Christians have made it about "me." They ask, "Am I cool enough, good enough, godly enough, holy enough to go in the Rapture?" Yes, you are holy enough because Jesus made you holy (1 Cor. 1:30). Jesus made you the righteousness of God in Him (2 Cor. 5:21).

I've heard people ask, "What if the Rapture occurs, and I'm not doing everything I should be doing and doing some stuff I shouldn't be doing?" Listen, folks, I'm not giving you a license to sin; people will sin without a license. But I am telling you that Jesus purchased you and that qualifies you for the Rapture.

I travel ministering in churches all the time, and I'm asked all kinds of questions about this: "I drank the wrong cup of coffee, will I still go in the Rapture? I had some thoughts I shouldn't have, what will happen to me? I did some things I'm not proud of, am I qualified?" Listen—there is no bad strain of Jesus' blood.

If you accepted Jesus as your Lord and Savior, then His blood washed you clean.

While I was preaching in Galveston, Texas, an angry lady walked up to me and said, "How dare you say if you're born again, you're going up in the Rapture." I thoroughly explained salvation to her—that it's not by works but by faith and grace. The Holy Ghost loves to magnify Jesus, and this is what He said to me about that lady: "Ask her whose works she would rather trust in—Mine or hers." Hebrews 1:3-4 says, "when he had by himself purged our sins, sat down on the right hand of the Majesty on high: being made so much better than the angels, as he hath by inheritance obtained a more excellent name than they." All by Himself, Jesus redeemed you, and Hebrews makes the point over and over again.

I'm stressing this point because I want you to have joy about the Rapture. I hear people all the time confess their biggest fear is whether or not they will go up in the Rapture. So, let me ask: are you saved? If you answer yes, then you're going up. If answer no, let's fix that now. Turn to pages 295-296 and pray to receive Jesus as your Savior.

If you are born again, it's crazy to doubt you will go up in the Rapture. If I had only one leg and hopped everywhere I went, I would really look forward to receiving my other leg. It would be so wonderful to reunite with my leg. I'm sure you agree that sounds ridiculous. Likewise, Jesus is looking forward to rejoining His entire body—both legs and all the rest. Again, we've made salvation about us—am I cool enough, am I sharp enough. It does not matter—you are born again.

It's important to look at the Greek translation of these words. At the Rapture, there's an examination that's made, and the same word *examination* is used in reference to the Second Coming. At the Rapture of the Church, the righteous go up to meet Him in the air. At the Second Coming, the wicked are plucked off the earth, but both scriptures say "he makes an examination." You're either lit or not lit. There's no in-between. I know it makes religious people mad, but that's too bad. God's Word is the final authority.

If you are a Christian, Jesus has redeemed you. Period. The Rapture should produce zero fear for you. You don't need to earn your way to heaven or make your way there—Jesus already made the way. Come on! Jesus purchased you with His own blood. How dare anyone say His blood was not perfect enough to wash away sin.

Hebrews 1:3 says by Himself Jesus purged our sins, so how dare we question if the blood is powerful enough to cleanse. "With his own blood—not the blood of goats and calves—he [Jesus] entered the Most Holy Place once for all time and secured our redemption forever" (Heb. 9:12 NLT). The Contemporary English Version says, "Then Christ went once for all into the most holy place and freed us from sin forever. He did this by offering his own blood instead of the blood of goats and bulls."

When the trumpet sounds at the Rapture and, all of a sudden, Jesus says, "Come up hither! Come up to the throne of God!" every born-again Christian will rock a brand-new body to heaven. Talk about a bright future! Your social calendar is already full. You have the Reward Seat of Christ to attend and the Marriage Supper of the Lamb. You have appointments with God, and you are living right before it all takes place.

Friend, live holy, and don't be stupid! It's no time to be acting like the devil. That would be idiotic. Why would you want to be wearing a spotted garment when you're about to meet Jesus in the air?

What would you think if I wore a sports jacket, took it off to dip it in the mud, and then put it on again? Wouldn't that be ridiculous? Who wants to wear a dirty garment? Or let's say you have two dresses in your closet, but one was ruined in the mud. Would you ever be torn about which one to wear? No. At the Rapture of the Church, Jesus will "subdue all things unto himself" (Phil. 3:21). The entire verse reads, "He will take our weak mortal bodies and change them into glorious bodies like his own, using the same power with which he will bring everything under his control" (NLT).

> Friend, live holy, and don't be stupid! It's no time to be acting like the devil.

A Body Retrofitted for Glory

In Luke 24, Jesus gives you some insight about the new body you will receive when you meet Him in the sky. Very early on Sunday morning the women who went to Jesus' tomb with spices found the stone had been rolled away from the entrance. Two angels told the women that Jesus had been raised from the dead. Later that same day, Jesus appeared to two men on the road to Emmaus as they were talking about all that had happened.

LUKE 24:15-24 (NLT)

As they talked and discussed these things, Jesus himself suddenly came and began walking with them. But God kept them from recognizing him.

He asked them, "What are you discussing so intently as you walk along?"

They stopped short, sadness written across their faces. Then one of them, Cleopas, replied, "You must be the only person in Jerusalem who hasn't heard about all the things that have happened there the last few days."

"What things?" Jesus asked.

"The things that happened to Jesus, the man from Nazareth," they said. "He was a prophet who did powerful miracles, and he was a mighty teacher in the eyes of God and all the people. But our leading priests and other religious leaders handed him over to be condemned to death, and they crucified him. We had hoped he was the Messiah who had come to rescue Israel. This all happened three days ago.

"Then some women from our group of his followers were at his tomb early this morning, and they came back with an amazing report. They said his body was missing, and they had seen angels who told them Jesus is alive! Some of our men ran out to see, and sure enough, his body was gone, just as the women had said."

Jesus had some pretty straight words for the two men:

LUKE 24:25-27 (NLT)

Then Jesus said to them, "You foolish people! You find it so hard to believe all that the prophets wrote in the Scriptures. Wasn't it clearly predicted that the Messiah would have to suffer all these things before entering his glory?" Then Jesus took them through the writings of Moses and all the prophets, explaining from all the Scriptures the things concerning himself.

As the men were nearing Emmaus and the end of their journey, Jesus acted as if He was going on. But they begged Him to stay because it was late:

LUKE 24:32-35 (NLT)

They said to each other, "Didn't our hearts burn within us as he talked with us on the road and explained the Scriptures to us?" And within the hour they were on their way back to Jerusalem. There they found the eleven disciples and the others who had gathered with them, who said, "The Lord has really risen! He appeared to Peter." Then the two from Emmaus told their story of how Jesus had appeared to them as they were walking along the road, and how they had recognized him as he was breaking the bread.

As the two men excitedly told the disciples how Jesus had appeared to them, Jesus suddenly appeared again:

LUKE 24:36-53 (NLT)

And just as they were telling about it, Jesus himself was suddenly standing there among them. "Peace be with you," he said. But the whole group was startled and frightened, thinking they were seeing a ghost! "Why are you frightened?" he asked. "Why are your hearts filled with doubt? Look at my hands. Look at my feet. You can see that it's really me. Touch me and make sure that I am not a ghost, because ghosts don't have bodies, as you see that I do." As he spoke, he showed them his hands and his feet.

Still they stood there in disbelief, filled with joy and wonder. Then he asked them, "Do you have anything here to eat?" They gave him a piece of broiled fish, and he ate it as they watched.

Then he said, "When I was with you before, I told you that everything written about me in the law of Moses and the prophets and in the Psalms must be fulfilled." Then he opened their minds to understand the Scriptures. And he said, "Yes, it was written long ago that the Messiah would suffer and die and rise from the dead on the third day. It was also written that this message would be proclaimed in the authority of his name to all the nations, beginning in Jerusalem: 'There is forgiveness of sins for all who repent.' You are witnesses of all these things.

"And now I will send the Holy Spirit, just as my Father promised. But stay here in the city until the Holy Spirit comes and fills you with power from heaven."

Then Jesus led them to Bethany, and lifting his hands to heaven, he blessed them. While he was blessing them, he left them and was taken up to heaven. So they worshiped him and then returned to Jerusalem filled with great joy. And they spent all of their time in the Temple, praising God.

Jesus walked and talked with people and many completely recognized Him. He ate food. And boom. He walked right through a wall. Don't you love it? Jesus walked *right through a wall.* There's nothing normal about that! The disciples freaked out. After the shock of seeing Him go through a wall, they thought Jesus was a spirit. To prove otherwise, Jesus said, "Feel me. A spirit doesn't have flesh and bone." Where was His blood? He left it at the mercy seat for you and me.

"How do you know Jesus walked through a wall?" somebody asks. Verse 36 says as the two followers of Jesus were telling the disciples what happened on the road to Emmaus, Jesus was "suddenly standing there among them" and greeted them. He sure didn't knock on the door! He didn't need to.

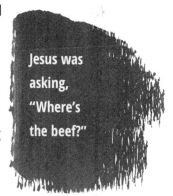

Jesus was asking, "Where's the beef?"

Did you also notice the first thing on Jesus' mind? After explaining He wasn't a ghost, His first question was, "Got anything to eat?" He ww anted to know where the meat was. He didn't ask about kale or salad. No, Jesus was asking, "Where's the beef?"

Sometimes Christians have this tendency to think that when we are raptured, we will all go to heaven and become like robots, losing all personality. No. Some people think we will lounge around on fluffy clouds playing harps all cherub-like. No. Religious tradition has given us some crazy, totally unscriptural ideas. (Wait until you read Chapter 14 and discover how supernaturally natural the Millennium will be.)

Listen to me now. Jesus was showing the disciples—and you—just how supernaturally natural the glorified body is.

Jesus was showing you His glorified body as a picture of your future. He was showing you that you won't be a ghost. You will still have an appetite. You will walk right through walls. You will still have muscle and bone and will still be recognized. How cool is that?

As I travel teaching on end times, there's one question I get more than any other. A sweet little lady will almost always raise her hand and ask, "Will I know my husband in heaven?"

I usually answer, "Do you want to know your husband in heaven?"

The real answer is of course you will. You will carry everything from here to there. You will get a new body, but you won't forget everything you know. You will not turn into a freak. Listen, if you like sports, you will play sports. If you like music, you can learn all the instruments. If you like art, you will paint masterpieces. Life with Jesus will be more glorious than you can possibly imagine.

I tell you right now that for the first six months of the Millennium, I'm going to play at St. Andrews Golf Club. I will be translated to Augusta, Georgia, to the National Golf Club there, then I'll be going on to Hawaii, and translated back to St. Andrews. I can play all these courses back to back because it won't get dark. I can golf 24 hours a day.

"Will you really want to do that?" somebody asks. Yes! You see, when it comes to heaven and the Millennium, some people's thinking is so weird and distorted. Many people do not understand that God wants you enjoy yourself. Just as it thrills me to see my daughter happy, it thrills God to see His children happy, joyful, smiling, laughing, and enjoying life.

When you understand that about Him, it's easier to understand how awesome the Millennium will be. Man, you will experience some fulfillment. A while back I played the guitar, and although I wasn't very good, I really had fun playing old rock songs from the '70s. I had some different guitars over the years, but at one point, I had a Fender Strat until the Lord said, "Give it away." He said, "Give it to that guy right there." As it turned out, the young man had just asked his mom for a guitar that day, and his mom said, "Well, believe God for it!"

Over the years, I would buy a guitar, give away a guitar, and buy a cooler one. As I walked into the music store one day thinking I would buy another guitar, the Lord said to me, "Why don't you learn to play every instrument? You're going to live forever." I was like, *Whoa.* It kind of messed with me. Think about that. God is giving you a glorified body to get your flesh ready for forever.

Remember the cherubim and the seraphim around the throne of God that I mentioned earlier? The seraphim covered the mercy seat—two wings that cover the face, two wings that cover the feet, and two wings that fly. They cry, "Holy, Holy, Holy." How would you like to have a job like that 24/7? Right now, your flesh, the rods and cones in your eyes, and so much more cannot handle the brightness or the magnificent presence of God. So how wonderful that God will make you a brand-new body retrofitted to handle the glory of God.

Throughout the Scriptures, we read that when people encountered God, they hit the floor or the ground. Daniel had to be picked up a couple of times. Ezekiel had to be picked up—once by his hair. Their human bodies could not handle the glory of God, so God will retrofit our bodies to handle His presence. A retrofitted body is a matter of functionality to go before the throne of God.

Imagine this. The Bible says there is no need for the sun in heaven because of the glory that's in His face (Rev. 21:23). Wow. I believe in heaven we will think, *The sun is coming up! No, no. It's Jesus walking toward us.* In Him it pleased the Father that all the fullness of the Godhead would dwell bodily (Col. 1:19). Whoooo! Hallelujah!

> God will make you a brand-new body retrofitted to handle the glory of God.

Travel will be a whole different experience as well. Like angels, we will be able to instantly be somewhere else. Remember angels do always behold the face of their Father for the children they protect (Matt. 18:10). So, obviously, angels travel back and forth from heaven to earth pretty quickly, and we will too.

The Word of God doesn't give us every detail about our futures, but we already read where Jesus' glorified body walks through walls, eats, and behaves normally. In John 21:5, Jesus yelled from the shore, asking, "Have you caught any fish?" He didn't make weird, eerie noises like we would expect in some scary Hollywood movie: "Ooooooh, woooo" all muffled and ghost-like. No. Peter recognized Him instantly and yelled, "It's Jesus!" as he jumped out of the boat and swam over to Him (John 21:7).

Peter did not yell, "Aaaah, it's a freak!" Too often we let our minds take the freaky route rather than the normal route.

Anything God plans for us will be very, very cool. God loves to put a little stamp right on our beautiful hope that we will be with Him forever.

FEAST CALENDAR POINTS TO RAPTURE TIMING

To bless and strengthen our hope for Jesus' return, let's consider the calendar of feasts, which shows us something important about the timing of the Rapture. Why are the feasts indicative of Rapture timing? First, Jesus has flawlessly fulfilled every single feast. Second, feasts are dress rehearsals. Most weddings and plays have dress rehearsals, so everyone knows their positions, cues, and lines. God also gives us rehearsals for what's ahead.

The first Bible feast is the Passover, a major event even today on the Jewish calendar. It was instituted by God to commemorate the deliverance of the Israelites from Egyptian bondage and saving of the firstborn from the destroyer (Exod. 12, 13, 23, 34). A lamb without blemish was killed—both as a sacrifice and a symbol of Jesus the Lamb of God at Calvary on Passover. As the blood was applied to Israeli doorposts, the death angel literally *passed over* those homes. Jesus is the Lamb of God who took away the sin of the world and was sacrificed for us on Passover.

The next feast was the Feast of Unleavened Bread. The Israelites took three pieces of bread and folded the middle piece, pierced it, and broke it. This is symbolic of Jesus the Bread of Life born in Bethlehem. *Bethlehem* means home of the bread. Isn't it cool? The Feast of the First Fruits followed to celebrate the first fruits of harvest.

Normally, a crucifixion takes longer than when Jesus was on the cross. Criminals were hung on the cross and a slow death was part of the spectacle—a sort of crime deterrent. But Jesus had a feast to keep! Jesus hung on the cross, taking our sin, poverty, and sickness upon Himself and then died quickly on Passover. He was buried at the Feast of Unleavened Bread, and He rose again on the Feast of First Fruits.

Jesus met the timing of each feast flawlessly, which had been prophesied. When you talk to a Jewish person about this, it freaks them out because it proves Jesus is the Messiah.

The next feast is Pentecost where the Holy Ghost was poured out. Is there another feast that has not yet been fulfilled? Yes, the Feast of Trumpets or Rosh Hashanah or Feast of Gatherings. The word Rosh Hashanah in Hebrew literally means "head of the year." The biblical name is Yom Teruah or literally "day of shouting or blasting." I believe the Rapture of the Church will take place on the Feast of Trumpets.

Somebody might say, "If you know that, then you would know when the Rapture will be." Yes, that is exactly right. I know exactly when the Feast of Trumpets starts in Israel and when it's finished, and the whole time each year I'm on high alert. I've said to the Lord, "Hmm, this is a perfect time for You to come." There are several things about Feast of Trumpets that make sense for the Rapture to occur during that time.

Of course, I don't know the specific year the Lord is coming back. I would never preach that! That's crazy! But I can tell you with great confidence that whatever year Jesus chooses, it will probably be during the Feast of Trumpets. If I am wrong, you can correct me as we are on our way up in the air. We can sit down and talk it over in heaven.

Let me explain why I think this way. Number one, the Feast of Trumpets represents the beginning of a coronation of a king. In any coronation, there is always a private ceremony for the family and a public ceremony for everyone else. When we are raptured, we will attend a private ceremony where Jesus will be crowned as King of Kings and Lord of Lords. At the Second Coming, Jesus will be presented to the whole earth in a public ceremony as the King of Kings and the Lord of Lords.

> There are several things about Feast of Trumpets that make sense for the Rapture to occur during that time.

The next event is the start of Seven Days of Awe before the Day of Atonement. That's a picture of the seven years of Tribulation. In other words, the Church is raptured, and there are seven days of awe for the rest of the world. That's a perfect correlation to seven years of Tribulation.

The Feast of Trumpets always falls 29.5 days after the last new moon, but they never knew exactly which day it would be. They didn't know whether it would fall on the 29th or the 30th of the month because it was so many days from the previous one. The Sanhedrin, a tribunal assembly in every ancient city of Israel with religious, civil, and criminal jurisdiction, would go out with two witnesses to determine when the new moon was and announce it. That's why Jesus said no one knows the day nor the hour. He was talking about the Feast of Trumpets.

The Sanhedrin would go outside, look up in the sky together, and then complain, "Not yet! It's not today!" Then one day, they would look in the sky and say, "This is it! It's today!" So when Jesus said, "No one knows the day or hour when these things will happen, not even the angels in heaven or the Son himself" (Matt. 24:36 NLT), they all knew that Jesus was referring to the Feast of Trumpets. Jesus was trying to give the Church a clue that you will be raptured on the Feast of Trumpets.

Once again someone might say, "Well, if you know that, then you know when the Lord is coming back." Yes, that's right! Just like you knew when your wedding was, you know when the Groom is coming for His Bride, the Church, and you know when you will be raptured. I know that freaks people out, but it's true just the same.

Recently, I made that statement and a lady blinked at me like a frog in a west Texas hailstorm, as Brother Hagin used to say. People are so shocked on all these topics because the Church either has not been taught or has been taught incorrectly about Jesus' return and the timing of it all.

The next feast is the Feast of Tabernacles, which in Jewish history recognized God's salvation, shelter, provision, and faithfulness. I believe the Second Coming will happen during the timing of the Feast of Tabernacles when Jesus returns and bodily tabernacles with men.

But listen to me! The Rapture is signless, but for the Second Coming, there is sign after sign after sign. It is so wonderful that we have all these things coming to pass in our lifetime. Think about it. You never have to die.

BIBLE PRECEDENT OF RAPTURES

The Christian world has come up with so many weird doctrines about the Rapture because it is unusual. Then again, just because it's unusual does not mean it is unscriptural. Enoch was raptured. Elijah was raptured. And the Church will be raptured. In fact, let's look at some Bible examples of rapture.

Elisha and the sons of the prophets knew the very day Elijah would be raptured. Second Kings 2:1 says, "When the Lord was about to take Elijah up to heaven in a whirl-wind, Elijah and Elisha were traveling from Gilgal" (NLT).

> The Rapture is signless, but for the Second Coming, there is sign after sign after sign.

Notice this conversation between Elijah and Elisha in 2 Kings 2:9-12 (NLT):

When they came to the other side, Elijah said to Elisha, "Tell me what I can do for you before I am taken away." And Elisha replied, "Please let me inherit a double share of your spirit and become your successor." "You have asked a difficult thing," Elijah replied. "If you see me when I am taken from you, then you will get your request. But if not, then you won't." As they were walking along and talking, suddenly a chariot of fire appeared, drawn by horses of fire. It drove between the two men, separating them, and Elijah was carried by a whirlwind into heaven. Elisha saw it and cried out, "My father! My father! I see the chariots and charioteers of Israel!" And as they disappeared from sight, Elisha tore his clothes in distress.

The Bible says Enoch walked by faith and was a spokesman for God, making him a perfect type or symbol of the Church. He also had a son named Methuselah, but Enoch departed right before the flood came. Genesis 5:24 says, "And Enoch walked with God: and *he was not;* for God took him." Notice what Hebrews says below.

HEBREWS 11:5 (NLT)

It was by faith that Enoch was taken up to heaven without dying—"he disappeared, because God took him." For before he was taken up, he was known as a person who pleased God.

How would you like to have job prophesying about the Second Coming of the Lord before Jesus even came the first time? Talk about awkward! Imagine telling people that Jesus will come back with 10,000 saints while people are asking, "Who's coming back? What saints? We don't know any saints." Enoch had to preach like that, and then he was taken to heaven without dying, caught up because the wickedness of the day was so bad that God took him off the earth.

GENESIS 5:22-24 (NLT)

After the birth of Methuselah, Enoch lived in close fellowship with God for another 300 years, and he had other sons and daughters. Enoch lived 365 years, walking in close fellowship with God. Then one day he disappeared, because God took him.

Enoch was taken off the earth. Elijah was taken off the earth. These two aren't the only raptures in the Bible. The New

Testament tells how Jesus and His disciples sang together, "When they had sung a hymn, they went out to the Mount of Olives" (Matt. 26:30 NKJV), where Jesus left for heaven. Jesus Himself was raptured.

ACTS 1:1-3 (NLT)

In my first book I told you, Theophilus, about everything Jesus began to do and teach until the day he was taken up to heaven after giving his chosen apostles further instructions through the Holy Spirit. During the forty days after he suffered and died, he appeared to the apostles from time to time, and he proved to them in many ways that he was actually alive. And he talked to them about the Kingdom of God.

Then Acts 1:8-11 (NLT) says:

"But you will receive power when the Holy Spirit comes upon you. And you will be my witnesses, telling people about me everywhere—in Jerusalem, throughout Judea, in Samaria, and to the ends of the earth." After saying this, he was taken up into a cloud while they were watching, and they could no longer see him. As they strained to see him rising into heaven, two white-robed men suddenly stood among them. "Men of Galilee," they said, "why are you standing here staring into heaven? Jesus has been taken from you into heaven, but someday he will return from heaven in the same way you saw him go!"

Jesus compared the Second Coming to the days of Lot and the days of Noah. Notice what the angel told Lot.

GENESIS 19:15-24 (NLT)

At dawn the next morning the angels became insistent. "Hurry," they said to Lot. "Take your wife and your two daughters who are here. Get out right now, or you will be swept away in the destruction of the city!"

When Lot still hesitated, the angels seized his hand and the hands of his wife and two daughters and rushed them to safety outside the city, for the Lord was merciful. When they were safely out of the city, one of the angels ordered, "Run for your lives! And don't look back or stop anywhere in the valley! Escape to the mountains, or you will be swept away!"

"Oh no, my lord!" Lot begged. "You have been so gracious to me and saved my life, and you have shown such great kindness. But I cannot go to the mountains. Disaster would catch up to me there, and I would soon die. See, there is a small village nearby. Please let me go there instead; don't you see how small it is? Then my life will be saved."

"All right," the angel said, "I will grant your request. I will not destroy the little village. But hurry! Escape to it, for I can do nothing until you arrive there." (This explains why that village was known as Zoar, which means "little place.")

Lot reached the village just as the sun was rising over the horizon. Then the Lord rained down fire and burning sulfur from the sky on Sodom and Gomorrah.

The angel told Lot that he *could not* do anything until the righteous departed, and Noah rode the flood of sin, corruption, and torrential rains like the righteous who endure. Both are perfect pictures of the Church leaving and Israel riding through the Tribulation period for seven years. God is so cool to give us clues!

The Bible talks about more raptures during the Tribulation. The two witnesses will be caught up to heaven (Rev. 11), so there is ample biblical precedent that people on earth, all of a sudden, leave earth and depart to heaven.

The Greek word for *rapture* is actually *harpazo,*[1] which means "snatched up or caught up." Interestingly enough, however, the word *rapture* is not in the literal Greek. But in the Latin, the word *rapture* is *rapturo*, which means "snatch or take away." This just shows you that the word *rapture* is in the New Testament. Think about it—walking with God and then shooo! Think of all the *Invasion of the Body Snatchers*-type movies. I'm sure folks will come up with a bunch of New Age explanations for why people have disappeared after the Rapture. But no matter what you call it, how wonderful that God will evacuate you because of what's getting ready to happen on the earth.

1 THESSALONIANS 5:9-11

For God hath not appointed us to wrath, but to obtain salvation by our Lord Jesus Christ, who died for us, that, whether we wake or sleep, we should live together with him. Wherefore comfort yourselves together, and edify one another, even as also ye do.

Verse 11 drives home the point once again that we are to comfort and edify fellow Christians with this news. The teaching of the Rapture was always to bring comfort—never fear. Yet today, there is a religious mentality that has crept into the

Church where so many people are afraid of the coming of the Lord. People often come up to me in meetings and say, "I was afraid to come. I thought it was going to be bad news." But, again, there is no bad news for the Christian!

WALLS OF HUMANITY CHANGE

I think the Rapture scene will look something like when the devil disputed with the angel for the body of Moses (Jude 9). After the devil argued over Moses' body, the archangel said, "The Lord rebuke you." I believe Lucifer will say, "Hey, these Christians are here on the earth, and I have charge over this earth." But the archangel will say, "The Lord rebuke you!" I believe that's what was meant in 1 Thessalonians 4:16 when it said "with the voice of an archangel." All of a sudden, the walls of humanity will change.

There's a picture of this in the Old Covenant when Israel walked around the walls of Jericho shouting until the walls came down. In the same way, we will step into an eternal-type body—never to be troubled with the scar of the fall again. Talk about shouting! We should shout right now! In a moment of time, all the horribleness of this dispensation will disappear from us. No more death. No more sickness. No more separation. Our veins will no longer be filled with blood—the glory of God will course through them. Life will no longer be in the blood but in God's glory! How glorious is that?

THE CHURCH IS A RESTRAINING FORCE

Paul shares more detailed information and revelation with us in 2 Thessalonians 2:1-3:

Now we beseech you, brethren, by the coming of our Lord [the Second Coming] *Jesus Christ, and by our gathering together unto him* [the Rapture of the Church because we will be gathered together unto Him], *that ye be not soon shaken in mind, or be troubled, neither by spirit, nor by word, nor by letter as from us, as that the day of Christ is at hand. Let no man deceive you by any means: for that day shall not come, except there come a falling away first, and that man of sin be revealed, the son of perdition.*

Notice again that this passage tells us of two events: "the coming of the Lord" refers to the Second Coming and "our gathering unto Him" refers to the Rapture. Let me also call your attention to the phrase "a falling away" in verse 3. The Greek word there is *apostasia* or "the apostasy." Is there a difference between *apostasy* and *the apostasy* or *apostasia*? Yes! *Apostasy* is a departing from the faith. *Apostasia* is the exact word used when Enoch departed before the flood, and it means departing, period—as in an exit—goodbye.

This verse did not refer to departing from the flood. If a departing from the faith could have brought the Antichrist, he would have come during the Dark Ages. The apostle Paul is saying here that the Antichrist cannot even be revealed until the Church departs. The moment the Church does depart, Satan is in power and has full access to everything. The Church is a restraining force in the earth, and the devil for this time is being held in check by the Church.

Christian friend, you have so much authority that God must pull you off the earth before the seven-year Tribulation or you would be dictating what happens on the earth. You would be redirecting asteroids.

"Where in the world do you come up with that?" somebody asks. In James 5, Elijah prayed that it would not rain for three and a half years, and it didn't rain for three and a half years. That's a picture of the Church. If Elijah can dictate natural rain, we can dictate spiritual rain. That whole chapter is about the dominion we have as the body of Christ on the earth.

God must take the Church off the earth so the Antichrist can come on the scene because He gives the devil the last part—or three and a half years—of the Tribulation. Jesus had three and a half years, and the Antichrist will have three and a half years. The Antichrist will function the three and a half years on his own or with demonic influence, but then Lucifer will go bodily into the Antichrist and incarnate him. Just like Jesus took on flesh, Lucifer will take on flesh. Again, that cannot happen while the Church is on earth because we have so much power.

Let's read a little further in 2 Thessalonians 2:7-8 (NLT):

For this lawlessness is already at work secretly, and it will remain secret until the one who is holding it back steps out of the way. Then the man of lawlessness will be revealed, but the Lord Jesus will slay him with the breath of his mouth and destroy him by the splendor of his coming.

Man, I love what is ahead for Lucifer. His future is pretty bleak, and he deserves every bit of it. He was defeated 2,000 years ago, but he's going to get the absolute tar beat out of him at the Second Coming. He will be thrown in that pit, and I, for one, will be throwing garbage down in the pit. I'm going to become a garbage man in the Millennium. "What do you do, Brother Joe?" "I grab up all the garbage I can find to throw at Lucifer."

The thought pattern in God's Word is straightforward about the Rapture: The Church has an appointment. We are expected at the Reward Seat of Jesus Christ. I've heard people say, "Yes, but the Church must be here for the Tribulation period because it is to purify us." No true! The Tribulation period is to motivate the Jews to accept the Messiah. As a Christian, I've already accepted Jesus as my Messiah; I don't need to go through the pressure. Clearly, the purpose of the seven-year Tribulation is pressure because some people are so hardheaded, they won't change unless they are relentlessly clobbered or pelted.

During World War II, this type thinking was called a foxhole mentality. Soldiers might wonder if there is a God or choose not to serve Him until the gun battles ramped up. When soldiers were crouched in a foxhole with missiles flying straight at them, most soldiers changed their minds and thought, *Well, this is a good time to get saved—like NOW!*

Yeah right, it's a good time to get saved because you think you're about to die. During the Tribulation, there will be seven years of that kind of pressure and a whole lot more. But you see, you and I don't need to be here for that because we've already accepted Jesus as Lord and Savior.

RAPTURED IN THE FALL

I honestly believe that come fall of whatever year, there will be such a joy and an unction in the Church that Jesus is about to come. There will be such an anticipation in the Church, and we will be sensing, *Wow! This is it! We are about to meet Him face to face!* For those of us who are married, we can think about how we acted right before our wedding. It will be the same for all of us as the Bride of Christ.

Before a wedding, the bride and groom usually go through a couple of days of reflection before they say "I do." I believe it will be the same for the Christian who says, "Wow. Big change is coming!" All of a sudden, we will be caught up in the air to attend the Reward Seat of Christ, and Jesus will be crowned King of Kings right before us.

We will stand in front of Jesus face to face. We will see the scars on His hands and the crown on His head, and we'll think, *How could it be that He chose to die for me?* We will worship Him like we've never worshiped before, and there will be honor and dominion and power unto the Son of God who was and is and is to come. The fulfillment of our redemption will take place right then and there.

> I honestly believe that come fall of whatever year, there will be such a joy and an unction in the Church that Jesus is about to come.

Listen to me now! The Rapture will be a beginning—not an ending. You are not done when you are raptured, which is why you have so much in your heart yet to do. Somebody says, "I don't want the Rapture to happen yet. I have so many things I still want to do for Jesus." You feel that way because you are not done. (We'll get into that more in the chapter on the Millennium.) Friend, you are just tasting the powers of the world to come.

What happens when you get just one bite of your favorite big, juicy cheeseburger or favorite sandwich? You want more! You get just a taste, and you get irritable doing without. "I want the whole cheeseburger," you say. That's where you are right now in time. You've had a bite of what's to come spiritually, and you want more. Right now, you are in the process of learning the ways of God because you've got such a great big change coming.

You, Christian friend, you are about to be raptured.

CHAPTER 7

NATIONS LINING UP FOR THE EZEKIEL 38 WAR

HAVE YOU EVER noticed that before a big football game the players get out on the field to toss the ball around, practicing field goals and passes? Then, all of a sudden, when the players begin lining up to kick off, you know it won't be long before the game is on. That's what we're seeing right now. For the first time in thousands of years of history, nations that will come against Israel right after the Church is raptured are literally lining up and getting into position for the Ezekiel 38 War.

This lineup makes it pretty clear that the Church leaves soon. Moreover, the nations of the world are aligning against Israel exactly as the Bible said they would. It's not similar—it's *precise.* And it's flawless to watch.

Jesus came to earth at a specific time, and He will return at a specific time. Meanwhile, we live in this pressure vacuum while the earth prepares for Jesus' return—whether it be opposing nations and their armies, Gentiles and Jews, or even the Church. Everyone is under this umbrella of pressure squeezing right down to the end because Jesus of Nazareth is about to be revealed as King of Kings and Lord of Lords.

Joel saw it and said, "Wake everybody up!" (Joel 3:9). Isaiah saw it. Hosea saw it. Every prophet saw it and was in awe of God coming back to the planet. The first coming was quiet, but the Second Coming will be the universal grand finale event of all events. Even now in preparation, there are rumblings and birth pangs from every corner of the earth and even in the heavens. A lot of what happens as we count down to the return of Jesus involves that one little piece of real estate called Israel. That's definitely true when it comes to the Ezekiel 38 War.

> A lot of what happens as we count down to the return of Jesus involves that one little piece of real estate called Israel.

Revelation 19:15 says of His return, "From his mouth came a sharp sword to strike down the nations. He will rule them with an iron rod. He will release the fierce wrath of God, the Almighty, like juice flowing from a winepress" (NLT). Malachi 3:2 asks, "But who will be able to endure it when he comes? Who will be able to stand and face him when he appears? For he will be like a blazing fire that refines metal, or like a strong soap that bleaches clothes" (NLT).

There's a showdown coming all right! Ezekiel says when Russia comes down on Israel, it's the only time you see God intervene for Israel so the heathen will know He is God. God takes 82 percent of Russia out in one fell swoop, or five sixths of Russia, according to Ezekiel 38:20.

NATIONS BOLDLY LINE UP

The nations that don't attack Israel in the Ezekiel 38 War are making peace with Israel now while those nations that move against Israel are boldly lining up. Let's compare how the nations divide up in Ezekiel 38 with what's currently happening in world news, and you'll see clearly how close we are to the Rapture of the Church.

EZEKIEL 38:1-3 (NKJV)

Now the word of the Lord came to me, saying, "Son of man, set your face against Gog, of the land of Magog, the prince of Rosh, Meshech, and Tubal, and prophesy against him, and say, 'Thus says the Lord God: "Behold, I am against you, O Gog, the prince of Rosh, Meshech, and Tubal."'"

It's interesting that these nations God calls out are today Russia and Turkey, which just happen to sit above Israel geographically.

EZEKIEL 38:4-12 (NKJV)

I will turn you around, put hooks into your jaws, and lead you out, with all your army, horses, and horsemen, all splendidly clothed, a great company with bucklers and shields, all of them handling swords. Persia [Iran], *Ethiopia* [Cush and Sudan], *and Libya are with them, all of them with shield and helmet; Gomer* [Turkey] *and all its troops; the house of Togarmah from the far north and all its troops—many people are with you.*

Prepare yourself and be ready, you and all your companies that are gathered about you; and be a guard for them. After many days you will be visited. In the latter years you will come into the land of those brought back from the sword and gathered from many people on the mountains of Israel, which had long been desolate; they were brought out of the nations, and now all of them dwell safely. You will ascend, coming like a storm, covering the land like a cloud, you and all your troops and many peoples with you.

Thus says the Lord God: "On that day it shall come to pass that thoughts will arise in your mind, and you will make an evil plan: You will say, 'I will go up against a land of unwalled villages; I will go to a peaceful people, who dwell safely, all of them dwelling without walls, and having neither bars nor gates'—to take plunder and to take booty, to stretch out your hand against the waste places that are again inhabited, and against a people gathered from the nations [Israel], *who have acquired livestock and goods, who dwell in the midst of the land."*

In this next verse, you will see that America, Australia, and European nations are mentioned.

Ezekiel 38:13 (NKJV)

Sheba, Dedan [Saudi Arabia], *the merchants of Tarshish* [Spain and other European nations], *and all their young lions* [England, America, and part of Australia] *will say to you, "Have you come to take plunder? Have you gathered your army to take booty, to carry away silver and gold, to take away livestock and goods, to take great plunder?"*

All the other nations mentioned in Ezekiel 38 have old historical ties with Turkey or are portions of Turkey and Russia. The main players are Russia, Turkey, Iran (Persia). Ethiopia and Libya are involved as well. Ezekiel 38 says Israel will be attacked from the *far north*, so let me say this to help you visualize the area. In your mind, run a straight line north of Israel, and you'll see it heads directly into Russia, Turkey, and connects with eastern Asia. The borders were different in Bible days versus now, but it's still all connected and points to the exact same region. The Bible clumps Turkey with western Russia and doesn't really define the two.

All of these nations are systematically helping the Palestinians surround Israel even now. These nations are blatantly and aggressively verbalizing their end-game goal to annihilate Israel.

Turkey's President Recep Tayyip Erodğan said last year that Jerusalem and the Temple Mount don't belong to Israel.[1] That's crazy! That would be like saying Washington, D.C. and the Washington Monument don't belong to the United States.

The Palestinians even said this past year that Big Ben doesn't belong to England. "It belongs to us," they said.[2] How insane. But the Bible says the Antichrist will try to change dates and times in history (Dan. 7:25), and we see a prelude to that with these nations and their not-so-veiled threats toward Israel. Even now, they are demonstrating the spirit of the Antichrist.

Erodğan has said he would call on Islam, and they will ascend to the Temple Mount and take Jerusalem. Does that not sound familiar? Does it not remind you of Lucifer who said, "I will ascend to the sides of the North and be like the Most High" (Isa. 14:12-14)? It's that same spirit, that same mentality.

Turkey's actions are so bold that they are almost unbelievable. Turkey is training Hamas in Libya. Turkey is working its way into Greece. Turkey is already in northern Syria. Turkey is in the edge of Iraq. Technically, Turkey has Israel surrounded.

Russia also has nine airbases in Syria. Every single week, Israel must bomb the outskirts of Damascus to preemptively strike munitions plants there. Russia has said they won't allow Israel to do it anymore, but Israel does it anyway. On top of it all, Iran is close to getting a nuclear weapon.

The Bible says in Isaiah 17:1 that Damascus will no longer be a city. I don't know whether that happens before or after the Rapture, but a lot of end-time scholars believe it's the action that instigates the beginning of the Ezekiel 38 War. Certainly, Damascus being wiped off the map would be a perfect precursor to bring Russia and Turkey down on Israel. I believe we'll also see radioactivity during the Ezekiel 38 War. The Bible talks about troops returning to deal with it when they are more suited to handle the hazards (Ezek. 39).

AFGHANISTAN IN THE NEWS

A lot of people are wondering if the turmoil in Afghanistan in 2021 has anything to do with the Ezekiel 38 War. Of course it does. It is a precursor to how quickly nations can be altered, and it is also a pathway for how Russia will come down on Israel. The group that took over Afghanistan is among those who want to annihilate Israel. Afghanistan is a doorway to a corridor that makes way for Russia to invade Israel.

The Bible says the Euphrates River runs dry right before the Second Coming, and ISIS has been damming up the Euphrates over and over again. All these groups are doing things to facilitate what happens at the Second Coming. So, when you see nations altering themselves in a day, you're seeing a setup for what happens just before we leave.

WORLD WAR III

We read in Ezekiel 4 that God puts a hook in Russia's jaw, and they come down to Israel for food or money. Turkey is the instigator, but Russia is the invader. The Ezekiel 38 War is all about Russia coming down on Israel for spoil. Even now, these guys are showing their true colors, and you have a front-row seat.

Ezekiel 38 is showing us that right after the Rapture of the Church, World War III will break out on the face of the earth. Russia has for some time now attempted to provoke war. They fly their airplanes in the Baltic Sea and over Alaska without their transponders on, which you can only do when you're at war. (Transponders send out beacons alerting other nations where your planes are.) They buzz our Israeli and American jets and spy planes. A Russian submarine came up right off the coast of Los Angeles a while back, and the captain came out and literally thumbed his nose at America. Their actions are to provoke confrontation, which didn't happen 30 years ago. It didn't happen 20 years ago, but it happens frequently today.

After Russia invaded the Ukraine and Crimea in 2014, Putin seemed to develop a new thought pattern: We can do whatever we want to do. Russia demonstrates this attitude in many ways, and it's especially disconcerting that the U.S. Secret Service theorizes that Russian President Vladimir Putin has Asperger's Disease, which is a type of autism.[3] Think about the fact that the head of a nation that has more nuclear weapons than almost anybody in the world all lined up for war may have mental issues. Like I said, right before your eyes, Russia is setting up for World War III.

FINANCIALLY STRAPPED RUSSIA

After the Rapture, something happens to Russia. They will say, "Hey, we're taking Israel because we need her oil." Keep in mind that by the time the Church is raptured, Russia will likely be completely bankrupt. For years, I've heard on-and-off-again reports of Russia facing near bankruptcy.

Several years ago, I was preaching right around Kennebunkport, Maine, where President George W. Bush was staying. Putin came to meet with him there, and his security team bought liquor with counterfeit $100 bills. Even then, they were printing their own money because they have no money.

As a result of the continuing war in Syria, do you know what the attrition is on all the Russian airports? A whopping 82 percent of their airplanes cannot fly because they don't have the money to maintain them. I believe it will be easy for God to take out Russia because nothing works. I've preached there many times, and even in the middle of the day, the electricity and water go out. They say they are fixing wires and pipes, but I believe it all comes down to no money. The real reason it's such a dilapidated country is because of godlessness. A country that reverences Jesus and honors God has blessings upon it.

EPIC CHAOS

Right after the Church leaves, there will be chaos all over the earth. Obviously, the media will come up with some pretty wild ideas about why so many people have disappeared. It will have catastrophic effects. Think of unsaved parents whose young children are raptured. Entire churches will be emptied out. What about airplane pilots who disappear mid-flight? Let me just tell you that it will not go unnoticed, and the massive chaos will set the stage for the greatest harvest in the Bible that takes place right after we're raptured.

In the midst of Russia taking over Israel and Christians around the world vanished, the world will face a great wake-up call. Many people will be saying, "The churches of those crazy Christians are all empty. Maybe they knew something that we don't." Russia will be saying, "We need cash, and Israel is ripe for taking." All combined, the scene is set for epic chaos.

Russia already just happens to have a S300 missile defense system set up in Syria. It's got the most technologically advanced cyber warfare set up on the mountains of Syria to the point that Israel recognizes Syria eavesdrops on everything they do.

The whole world is set up for war. Twenty years ago, America and many other nations would have said, "We stand with Israel. If you fight Israel, you will fight us as well." That isn't necessarily the attitude right now. Beginning in 2014, America took a different position. In fact, not only did they take the position not to support Israel, but they also tried to basically prop up Iran to destroy Israel. There was a time that was unimaginable, but today it's the making of news headlines.

Do you understand the significance of this? Right before our eyes, the nations have lined up setting the stage for the Ezekiel 38 War. I wish I had a bazooka I could fire or a trumpet I could blow to get everyone's attention. Listen to me!

Right now, in Syria it's the craziest coalition ever. Russia is fighting the Syrian rebels, who are trying to fight ISIS. Russia put up an air defense system that is unbelievably the most sophisticated in the world, and ISIS doesn't have any airplanes. Okay, they put up the most elaborate air defense in the world all over the nation of Syria to fight ISIS, but again, ISIS has no airplanes. Think about it.

> Right before our eyes, the nations have lined up setting the stage for the Ezekiel 38 War.

A SHOWDOWN WITH GOD

"Hey Joe, what do you mean that everything is in position for the Ezekiel 38 War?" The incidents are ready to fall like dominoes. The Rapture happens, the Church or the restraining force against evil is gone. Russia needs money; its mighty weapons are in place. Russia looks at prosperous and bountiful Israel and says, "Let's just help ourselves!"

Let's read Ezekiel 38:14-16 as we did in Chapter 5 but this time from the New Living Translation:

Therefore, son of man, prophesy against Gog. Give him this message from the Sovereign Lord: When my people are living in peace in their land, then you will rouse yourself. You will come from your homeland in the distant north with your vast cavalry and your mighty army, and you will attack my people Israel, covering their land like a cloud. At that time in the distant future, I will bring you against my land as everyone watches, and my holiness will be displayed by what happens to you, Gog. Then all the nations will know that I am the Lord.

Russia will try to swoop down and overtake Israel, but God will show off for Israel. He will defend her. God said, "Then all the nations will know that I am Lord (or God)." He's so awesome!

Let's look at Ezekiel 38:23:

Thus will I magnify myself, and sanctify myself;
and I will be known in the eyes of many
nations, and they shall know that I am the Lord.

Continue reading in the next chapter in Ezekiel 39:6:

And I will send a fire on Magog, and among
them that dwell carelessly in the isles:
and they shall know that I am the Lord.

Pay attention to the word *carelessly*, which means confidently. Let me give you Joe's conjecture on this. My personal take is that right after the Rapture, the earth will see nuclear war. I believe that is the fire that comes on those isles. *Isles* is the word for coastal cities like Los Angeles, New York, Miami, etc. And again, this is Joe talking, but I believe these port cities will probably be nuked from Russia. Notice what the Bible specifically says in Ezekiel 39:

EZEKIEL 39:7

So will I make my holy name known in the midst of my
people Israel; and I will not let them pollute my holy name
any more: and the heathen shall know that I am the Lord,
the Holy One in Israel.

As we discussed in Chapter 5, God's tone changes after the Church leaves. God boldly deals with the heathen.

After the Ezekiel 38 War, munitions burn for seven years. In fact, there's so much radioactivity that they mark things and come back after they are better equipped to deal with it. "What happens after the seven years?" someone might ask. The Second Coming. Jesus returns to the Mount of Olives with the brightness of His coming and stops war.

While you're alive in 2022, you are watching Russia amp up. Man, I wish I had a printout of everything they've done recently. Russia is positioning more and more armaments in Syria, and they have let Hezbollah thwart Israel at every opportunity. Hezbollah is an Islamist political party and militant group in northern Israel that openly declares they want to annihilate Israel. They have 100,000 rockets and keep getting more from Russia.

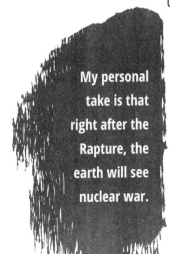

My personal take is that right after the Rapture, the earth will see nuclear war.

Former Israeli Prime Minister Benjamin Netanyahu said to Russia a while back, "You do one more shipment down to Hezbollah, and we will fire on you." So, there's all these little things that happen right before a world war, and you're watching the mechanics of it. The nations are gearing up for it because we are about to depart. This should send all of us a clear, loud message. It should tell us: "Lift up your head!" Why? The war that we have just talked about happens after we are gone. Friend, live in the mentality that you're about to be caught up in the air to meet Jesus because you are!

CHAPTER 8

PROOF CHRISTIANS WON'T BE HERE FOR THE TRIBULATION

YOU DON'T NEED to be fearful about anything happening around you or anything yet to come in the last days. God has given every Christian dominion to walk protected on the earth, so don't allow yourself to think of the Rapture as some escape theology based in fear. You are about to be raptured because you have appointments with God—the Reward Seat of Christ and the Marriage Supper of the Lamb. You will leave the planet while God deals with the Jews for seven years. You are not supposed to be here for the Tribulation, and as we look at Daniel's 70th week, I'll prove it to you.

You do not need to be afraid of anything ever because Satan has nothing on you. That should be the believers' stance—*always*. You should have zero fear because He who sent you is with you (John 8:29). Like we have said over and over, there is plenty of bad news ahead—but there is absolutely no bad news for the Christian.

TOLERATE ZERO FEAR

While preaching in Pittsburgh years ago, I said, "I dare the devil to try to kill me in a car wreck. I dare him to give me cancer. I dare him to make me blind." Silence filled the room and several people gasped. Mind you, I didn't say the devil could; I just dared him to try. Why would I say that? Because God has already promised that surely goodness and mercy will follow me all the days of my life (Ps. 23:6). God has already said, "Greater is he that is in me than he that is in the world" (1 John 4:4). Angels have charge over me (Ps. 91). We should not have more faith in the devil's ability than God's.

> Like we have said over and over, there is plenty of bad news ahead—but there is absolutely no bad news for the Christian.

"Where did you learn to talk like that?" somebody might ask. I learned it from Brother Hagin. He was preaching in southern California when the Asian flu came through that area in the 1950s. So many football players had the flu that they had to cancel games. When preachers in the area told Brother Hagin about it, he said, "I'll tell you right now that I'll never have the Asian flu."

The other preachers said, "I wouldn't say that for all the money in the world."

"Why not?" Brother Hagin asked.

"Because the devil might hear you."

"That's the very dude I want to hear me!" Brother Hagin answered.

When I talked like that in Pittsburgh, I freaked out the whole group. You could see on their faces that they thought I was crazy or dangerous. But the truth is, I talked like that in Pittsburgh for the same reason I mention it here. Too often Christians back away from boldness, and yet boldness is the atmosphere for the manifestation of Jesus. We need some last-day boldness in the Church.

Everybody in Pittsburgh got even quieter when I said, "I dare the devil to kill my family. I dare him to kill me. I dare him to kill me in a car wreck." After the service, a woman walked up to me shaking and making weird demonic noises and said, "I will kill you and your family."

Thinking one of my crazy minister buddies hired this woman to prank me, I said, "Go ahead so you can get your money's worth." I did begin to wonder how my buddy convinced her to speak with such passion. *Wow!* I thought, *this is a great performance*. Then all of a sudden, she started talking really filthy and cursing. I suddenly realized, *This is not my buddy pranking me. This woman is really possessed*. I cast the devil out of her, and she fell down like a catfish out of water.

Here's my point. This woman filled with Lucifer was bold enough to walk right up and tell me what the devil would do to me. How dare someone filled with Lucifer be bolder than someone filled with God? How dare we be afraid of the devil? How dare we tolerate fear at all?

You notice that I had a confrontation the minute I said, "I dare the devil to try to do that." We think of that as bold. But that is not bold—that's normal Christianity. Too many Christians have gotten way too accustomed to a diluted gospel, so when we see normal Christianity, we think it's too bold. Come on now!

I find as I travel around the world teaching on the end times, the Tribulation, and so forth that I must go to extremes to get Christians confident in their salvation, confident that nothing can separate us from Jesus. He said in the world you will have tribulation but be of good cheer, Jesus has overcome the world, and we are in Him (John 16:33). That's why Jesus said, "Greater is he that is in you, than he that is in the world" (1 John 4:4).

There is dominion in us. There is dominion in you. As Christians, we need to be confident and own the peace that belongs to us.

End-time preaching should strengthen your faith overall, buoy your faith in the Rapture, and fill you with the hope that purifies you to the point that you're skipping around your house all giddy because you are about to see Jesus face to face. The Bible says to exhort one another with this news. That means call people nearer to God. Yes, you are to say, "Hey! The Lord is coming back soon, and we're about to meet Him in the air!" The devil hates it, but too bad, so sad. He's a *loser*.

DANIEL'S 70TH WEEK

As we delve into the scriptures about Daniel's 70th week, let me say from the get-go that the info is really detailed but understanding it will make everything fit in place on the end-time topic. When you see how orderly the scriptures are, you cannot help but think, *How cool is our God!* Let's begin reading in Daniel 9:1-3 (NLT):

> *It was the first year of the reign of Darius the Mede, the*
> *son of Ahasuerus, who became king of the Babylonians.*
> *During the first year of his reign, I, Daniel, learned*
> *from reading the word of the Lord, as revealed to*
> *Jeremiah the prophet, that Jerusalem must lie deso-*
> *late for seventy years. So I turned to the Lord God*
> *and pleaded with him in prayer and fasting. I also*
> *wore rough burlap and sprinkled myself with ashes.*

Israel was in captivity for 70 years, and eventually Daniel was smart enough to say, "Hey, I'm going to find out why they're in jail." He put on sackcloth and ashes and determined to find out why in prayer. God showed him why and showed him all the nations on the earth all the way up to the coming of the Lord. Isn't it cool that God always gives you exceedingly abundantly above all you can ask or think?

Daniel went back to the books and found out Israel was supposed to let the land rest every seven years. The Israelites would be so blessed throughout the sixth year, but on the seventh year, the land was to rest with no planting. Unfortunately, Israel fudged on one seventh year and kept fudging another year, another year, another year. Guess how long they missed God and broke the law? It totaled 490 years, which means they owed back 70 years.

See how precise God is in Old Covenant time? God told them to let the land rest, and they disobeyed Him for 490 years. So God decided, "Okay, I'll put you in jail and make you pay the land back for 70 years." Think about that for a minute. That's a huge deal!

Do you remember in Matthew 18 when Peter asked Jesus how many times he was to forgive somebody? Jesus answered 70 times 7, or 490 times. I guess that was the length of forgiveness in the Old Covenant. So how long did Israel mess up? It was 490 years. Keep that number in your mind, and we'll come back to it.

Now skip down a few verses where Gabriel gives Daniel information.

DANIEL 9:23-25

At the beginning of thy supplications the commandment came forth, and I am come to shew thee; for thou art greatly beloved: therefore understand the matter, and consider the vision. Seventy weeks are determined upon thy people and upon thy holy city, to finish the transgression, and to make an end of sins, and to make reconciliation for iniquity, and to bring in everlasting righteousness, and to seal up the vision and prophecy, and to anoint the most Holy. Know therefore and understand, that from the going forth of the commandment to restore and to build Jerusalem unto the Messiah the Prince shall be seven weeks, and threescore and two weeks: the street shall be built again, and the wall, even in troublous times.

Notice verse 24 again, "Seventy segments of seven are determined upon thy people and upon thy holy city." In other words, God said Israel blew it for 490 years, and God gave them another chance of 490 years. All seventy segments of seven are 490 years. That's just a different way of saying it.

Gabriel tells him that God is giving them another opportunity. How sweet of Him. But who is it determined upon? The Jews and the Holy City. Who? The Jews and the Holy City. It has nothing to do with the Church. God is so precise in the Old Covenant. Israel broke the law for 490 years; He put them in jail for 70 years to pay it back. Gabriel goes, "Guess what? The Lord is giving you guys another 490 years. How cool is that?"

Gabriel tells them why in verses 24 and 25. This was God saying, "You can keep time with Me! From the going forth of the commandment to rebuild Jerusalem until Jesus comes is a certain number of years." The fact that there is a certain number of weeks or years is a pretty big statement here.

Now watch. King Artaxerxes saw Nehemiah who was bummed out, depressed, and crying because of Jerusalem. King Artaxerxes said to him, "You know what? Why don't we rebuild Jerusalem?" So he made a proclamation and commanded the rebuilding of Jerusalem (Ezra 7:11-28).

Gabriel said, "From the going forth from the commandment to restore and build Jerusalem until Jesus comes will be a certain number of years." If you add it up, it's 483 years. Remember when Jesus was on the earth, people asked, "Are You the Messiah?" He said, "Go tell them what you see and what you hear." The deaf heard, the lame walked, but Jesus wouldn't really come right out and say, "I am the Messiah." Yet there came a time when it was prophesied the Messiah would come riding into Jerusalem on a donkey (Zech. 9:9). As He rode in, people would lay down palm branches, crying, "Hosanna! Hosanna! Blessed is He that comes in the name of the Lord."

They said, "Oh, that means You're the Messiah." Others said, "Oh, don't say that. You're admitting You're the Messiah." He said if they wouldn't do it, the rocks would cry out. Because it was exactly 483 years from when that commandment came forth.

The Bible says when the commandment came forth, He's going to come after 483 years. Why did He promise that? 490. He owes them seven years of Old Covenant time. That's Daniel's 70th week. That's the book of Revelation. In other words, the Church must leave so God can pay them back those seven years that He owes them. Again, it has nothing to do with the Church.

> This is why I can confidently say that you will not and cannot be here because it's not for you.

We as the Church do our part and depart. God will raise up 144,000 Jewish evangelists, 12,000 from each tribe who will go out and preach. They will go to all the vacant churches and tell people to turn and repent. When the first seal is opened up, those guys will be preaching like a house on fire, and they will reap a wonderful harvest.

Again, God promised them 490. He came after 483. He owes them seven years. Who does He owe? The Jews and Jerusalem. Not you and me—not the Church. The seven years are for the Jews—just for them. This is why I can confidently say that you will not and cannot be here because it's not for you.

We in the Church want to be so significant, but we are not everything. We will do our part, and God will hand off the baton exactly like Elijah handed it off to Elisha. There are types and shadows of this throughout the Scriptures.

It should take some pressure off the body of Christ to realize that we are to do the best we can to finish the Church Age. We go into all the world and preach the gospel as hard as we can with all our hearts, all our soul, all our might, but there are actually some things we don't do and won't do because we depart. We in the Church have a tendency to think it's all about us, but it is not.

Why was Israel broken off and why did God raise up you and me? Because of Israel's unbelief and murmuring. A whole nation missed their destiny, and God had to raise you up because of irritability. Usually in my meetings, at this point I say, "Goodnight, everybody. Drive safely. Start the car, Colleen, I'll be right there." I realize this isn't popular, but it's the truth.

JUDE 14-16 (NLT)

"Listen! The Lord is coming with countless thousands of his holy ones to execute judgment on the people of the world. He will convict every person of all the ungodly things they have done and for all the insults that ungodly sinners have spoken against him." These people are grumblers and complainers, living only to satisfy their desires. They brag loudly about themselves, and they flatter others to get what they want.

We read here that irritability would be the climate right before the coming of the Lord. This is God saying, "You can keep time with Me! From the going forth of the commandment to rebuild Jerusalem until Jesus comes is a certain number of years." Think about it. If a whole nation missed their destiny because of irritability, what does that tell us now? It sends a clear message: Don't be irritable. Don't murmur. Don't complain.

First Timothy 6:14 says, "Keep this commandment without spot, unrebukable, until the appearing of our Lord Jesus Christ."

Do you understand how much boldness that gives you that you will not be here for the Rapture? "Well," someone says, "I believe the Church will depart mid-Tribulation because the wrath of God is the latter part of the Tribulation." No, that's not correct. Jesus cannot open the seals while the Church is on the earth, and the first seal is the Antichrist. So that shoots down that theory.

Why are we going through this detail? Because scriptural accuracy produces joy and hope. Now, if you want to go through the Tribulation, you can tribulate all you want. You can also lie down in the road and get run over by a car, but if you think that's a good idea, you're nuts. The mentality in America is scary. We try to attribute a lot of crazy ideas to God like God will beat you up or make you sick to teach you something or make you stronger. That's insane. If going through hell made a person a better Christian, I'd be glowing in the dark by now.

Seriously, would a good parent break his child's arms to show him or her how bad it is to have a broken arm? Never. If a parent did, the parent would go to jail. But our Father God—bless His heart—gets blamed for injuring us to teach us or break our wills.

Let's look at Daniel 9:26:

And after threescore and two weeks shall Messiah be cut off, but not for himself: and the people of the prince that shall come [talking about the Antichrist and the revival of the Roman empire] *shall destroy the city and the sanctuary; and the end thereof shall be with a flood, and unto the end of the war desolations are determined.*

Notice the math here adds up to 483 years. It's amazing how so much is compacted in this one verse. It talks about who will crucify Jesus and who will handle the platform for the Antichrist. It talks about who will destroy the city like the Romans did in A.D. 70. Daniel is prophesying and Gabriel's giving him a couple of points. I'm sure even Daniel is blown away at what Gabriel is giving him, "and the end thereof shall be with a flood, and unto the end of the war desolations are determined."

Then look at Daniel 9:27:

And he [the Antichrist] *shall confirm the covenant with many for one week: and in the midst of the week* [midway through the seven years] *he shall cause the sacrifice and the oblation to cease, and for the overspreading of abominations he shall make it desolate, even until the consummation, and that determined shall be poured upon the desolate.*

There's a lot said there so let's unpack it a bit. The Antichrist is here on earth and in power before midway through the seven years, and the devil uses or manipulates him. But midway through the seven-year Tribulation, Lucifer enters into the Antichrist and actually possesses him or takes control of him. That means Lucifer has 42 months to operate through a man. I explained earlier that equals the three and a half years just as Jesus had during His ministry on earth. (We will discuss this in more detail in Chapter 11 on the Tribulation.)

Most of the time from beginning to the end of this book, we are taking a hardcore look at the black-and-white facts of the Scriptures. But here what I'm about to say is conjecture. In other words, I'm going to guess on this certain point. The Bible says the Church must depart before the Antichrist can be revealed, but the Bible does not specify the timing of when that will happen. The Bible does say the Tribulation begins when the Antichrist signs an agreement with Israel for seven years, but no scripture defines the timeline for this event. It may be two months, seven months, one year, or four years before they sign an agreement.

So even though the Church is raptured, the Bible does not say the Tribulation begins immediately afterward. Still, I'm guessing it will be within a year or two of the Rapture just because of the compression of everything that occurs. There are a couple of other variables we will look at in Chapter 11.

Consider the very direct and blatant opposites between the "ministries" of Jesus and the Antichrist during the three-and-a-half-year period. Jesus went about doing good and healing all who were oppressed of the devil for God was with him (Acts 10:38). The Antichrist goes about stealing, killing, and destroying for Lucifer will be with him.

Also, think about the fact that midway through the Tribulation is 42 months. Elijah prayed that it wouldn't rain for how long? It was 42 months. As Elijah went up to heaven, some kids started mocking Elisha and yelling, "Get out of here, baldy! Go up! Go up, bald head!" Suddenly two female bears came out of the woods and mauled 42 of them to death (2 Kings 2:23-24). We see that 42 is a number of judgment.

Think about the Iran-Iraq War from 1980 to 1988. It was mainly the Iraq War at the Tigris and Euphrates valley. I remember images of Colin Powel, the American general at the time, sitting with a giant map behind him of the Tigris and Euphrates. Countries were going back into Iraq back then as forerunners for all the countries that are right there right now. Even then, we saw the setup for that seven-year Tribulation period in motion. Russia has a base in Baghdad along with England, France, Germany, and the United States.

I'm thinking you have all these nations come together for that 42-month period, the Great Tribulation. It's a seven-year tribulation, but half of it is 42 months. You have all of them doing that right now. My friend, this is a very, very sobering time to live, but it is also time for the greatest rejoicing known to man. All the promises God has spoken, He will very precisely bring to pass.

NO SUCH THING AS PALESTINIAN PEOPLE

Do you realize there is no such thing as Palestinian people even though the area is now occupied? The European Union (EU) gives the people $400 million a year, and America gives the Palestinians $800 million to a billion dollars a year. The moment Israel gave Gaza to the Palestinians, they started firing rockets from Gaza. Every time I call one of my Israel buddies he tells me, "We're on our way to the bomb shelter again." The people in Gaza keep firing rockets into Israel; it's just insanity there.

In Dubai in the United Arab Emirates (UAE), they built the highest, tallest building in the world, and it even has a Formula One racetrack and a golf course. Israel gives Gaza to the Palestinians on beachfront property. In response, they fire rockets at Israel, and no one says a word in the world.

Even David weighed in on this issue when he called Goliath an uncircumcised Philistine. David was so bold! David was saying he would defeat Goliath because he had no covenant. The word *Palestine* comes from the word *Philistine*—which in Hebrew means *no covenant.* Satan named the land *no covenant* because God said, "I swear by no greater oath than Me, Myself—the land is yours" (Gen. 22:16; Heb. 6:13).

In 2016, the EU said the land was occupied by Palestinians who wanted to force Israel out of their land. But it was not occupied by another because God promised it to Israel. Even through the law of battle, Israel won Jerusalem. In the 1948 War of Independence, Israel won the land back. Yet the whole world is getting ready for Daniel chapter 9. It's uncanny how everything around us is setting up for the culmination and fulfillment of the Scriptures. Right now, in your lifetime, you are watching Lucifer flex his muscles.

The Bible says the devil finds out he has a short time when he enters into the Antichrist (Rev. 12:12), but Lucifer doesn't know until then. He doesn't get what time it is right now. In fact, people misquote that scripture all the time. Lucifer doesn't know what time it is until he's cast out of heaven midway through the Tribulation, comes to earth, and goes into the temple to present himself to God. Then he finds out he has three and a half years left. The Bible is telling us that the devil is so stupid he cannot tell time. People give him way too much credit.

Listen, folks! We're talking here about the war of the ages. Every movie where you see the hero come in at the end and save the day in some way replicates how the earth is getting ready for the hero of the ages: Jesus Christ of Nazareth. King Jesus will lead the charge, and there will be so much glory coming out of His face that it will light the sky. Absolute radiance will emanate from our King of Kings and Lord of Lords, and we will be right next to Him on white horses.

I've flown on plenty of planes and ridden plenty of motorcycles, but I don't know much about horses, especially flying ones, but we're all going to find out. At the Second Coming, the Church will fly back with Jesus, and Lucifer will finally be stopped.

At the Rapture, when the King of Kings is about halfway down out of heaven, we will rise to meet Him in the air. We will go up for the Reward Seat of Christ and the Marriage Supper of the Lamb. Talk about a party. Oh, come on!

Think about a meal with a billion people. How awesome is that? We'll stand before Him at the throne, the sea of glass, clear as crystal. It's the only element that cannot hide a flaw. You'll be flawless before the throne. It says the water is smooth. No more storms. Oh, come on! You ought to shout over that. Woohoo!

Thank God we have the ability to speak to storms now; we use our authority and rejoice in it. But it will be awesome to never ever be subject to storms again, and so shall we ever be with the Lord. We exhort one another with these things—with all the things happening in Daniel's 70th week or the book of Revelation.

There are more verses about that period of seven years than anything in the Scriptures. So why is that a big deal? People are afraid of it. People say, "I'm afraid to read the book of Revelation." Don't be. I'm telling you, there's no bad news for the Christian! We'll look at what happens during the Tribulation point by point in Chapter 11, going through the book of Revelation. The Bible says you will be blessed if you read it! God promises to tell you what will happen before it happens, and He's faithful to do it. Lift up your head, friend, your redemption draws nigh.

CHAPTER 9

WHAT'S NEXT FOR THE CHURCH AFTER THE RAPTURE

HOW WELL WOULD it work for someone to walk into a job interview and say, "I know absolutely nothing about your company, but I just wanted to ask if I could come work for you"? We all know the person wouldn't get far. If you are going to apply for a job, you learn about the company and find out the niche it fills. You find out who the CEO is and determine how he or she thinks so you don't walk blindly into a new place. Likewise, the Church should not be raptured blind but well versed in its future.

Every member in the body of Christ should be thinking, *The end times are all about my future. I will be caught up in the air to meet Jesus. I will attend the Reward Seat of Christ and the Marriage Supper of the Lamb. God has only good things ahead for me!*

Lucifer tries to scare the Church at every turn. He wants you afraid you won't make the Rapture. He wants you afraid about the judgment seat of Christ after the Rapture. He whispers, "Just wait—you will be in big trouble at the judgment seat!" But the devil is a liar! Forget what the devil says and keep reading. The apostle Paul says Jesus cannot wait to see you face to face, and God cannot wait to reward you.

THE REWARD SEAT OF CHRIST

Let's say a huge, muscle-bulging weightlifter on the U.S. team does a dead lift, putting up 500 pounds, and wins the gold medal. Do you think he's afraid to go to the podium and collect his reward? No! It's the very reason he worked and trained so hard.

When the International Olympic Committee officials call him to the podium to hang a medal around his neck, does he say, "Oh, gosh, no. Please don't. I don't deserve this"? No way. He proudly and boldly takes his place on the riser like the winner he is, claiming his prize. As he walks to the platform, they unveil the flag from his nation and play his country's national anthem. He stands there decorated for the world to see.

My friend, right after we're raptured—even before the Marriage Supper of the Lamb—your next appointment with the Lord is the Reward Seat of Christ. You will stand before Jesus and His light will read your life. The Reward Seat of Christ is called *bema* in the Greek. The word is quoted as the "judgment seat" three times in the Epistles, but it's not really a judgment seat. That is a mistranslation. The Greek word *bema* means *reward seat.*

Greek, like English, uses the word *judge* in two senses. One sense is condemnation, while the other is giving out rewards. Unbelievers will be judged and condemned. Believers will be judged in the sense of rewards.

Whatever you did for the wrong motive will be toast right there—wood, hay, and stubble. Whatever you did for the good and proper motive, you'll be rewarded gold, silver, and precious stones. Let's see how the apostle Paul explains this in 1 Corinthians 3:6-9:

> *I have planted, Apollos watered; but God gave the increase. So then neither is he that planteth any thing, neither he that watereth; but God that giveth the increase. Now he that planteth and he that watereth are one: and every man shall receive his own reward according to his own labour. For we are labourers together with God: ye are God's husbandry, ye are God's building.*

It's amazing how we think, *If I could plant or if I could water, I'd be happy*. In other words, if we could just do the *other* job, we would be satisfied. No, it doesn't matter what job you do, God gives the increase. Sometimes we want the job that seems zippy or flashy, but Paul points out the particular job doesn't matter. It's God who gives the increase.

It's the word *labor* in verse 8 that lets the air out of some people's sails. As a baby Christian, I didn't like that word and

> Whatever you did for the wrong motive will be toast right there—wood, hay, and stubble. Whatever you did for the good and proper motive, you'll be rewarded gold, silver, and precious stones.

wondered why it was even in the Bible. Some Christians would like it to read, "Every man will receive according to his own *fun.*" Seriously, that word *labor* may not be a cool word, but your rewards will be indicative or equal to your labor.

Let's go a little further in 1 Corinthians 3:10-15:

According to the grace of God which is given unto me, as a wise masterbuilder, I have laid the foundation, and another buildeth thereon. But let every man take heed how he buildeth thereupon. For other foundation can no man lay than that is laid, which is Jesus Christ. Now if any man build upon this foundation gold, silver, precious stones, wood, hay, stubble; every man's work shall be made manifest: for the day shall declare it, because it shall be revealed by fire; and the fire shall try every man's work of what sort it is. If any man's work abide which he hath built thereupon, he shall receive a reward. If any man's work shall be burned, he shall suffer loss: but he himself shall be saved; yet so as by fire.

Verse 12 makes reference to the Reward Seat of Christ. Does a man build with gold, silver, precious stones, wood, hay, or stubble? In verses 13-15, circle the word *work* all four times it used. Now notice that the scripture goes on to say that a man's work will be revealed by fire; and the fire shall try every man's work of what sort it is or how valuable it is.

Notice verse 15 again, which says, "If any man's work shall be burned, he shall suffer loss: but he himself shall be saved; yet so as by fire." In other words, this judgment or examination is not a bad examination. It's called the reward seat, and you will be rewarded for the good motives of your heart.

Everything you did for the wrong motive will be wood, hay, and stubble, but everything you did for the proper motive will be gold, silver, and precious stones. Remember wood, hay, and stubble is all above the ground or symbolic of what people see you do. Those actions will not be rewarded. Gold, silver, and precious stones are hidden in the earth—or heart, in this case—symbolic of what people don't see.

Gold represents your devotional life, for example. How often do you tell the Lord, "I love You"? Let's hope none of us are like Jimmy of "my name is Jimmy, and I'll take all you can gimme." Silver represents the tongue. Proverbs 10:20 says, "The tongue of the just is of choice silver." Your words encourage or discourage. What are the stones? The priest would go into the presence of God, not for himself but to pray for the people. Hidden things like that are why you will be rewarded.

For sure, you don't want to cause a bond fire at the Reward Seat of Christ. *Gawoosh!* You don't want the angels to all back up saying, "Whoa. We've never seen flames like those before. Did you see that fire? What was that all about?" No, you don't want a lot of wood, hay, and stubble. You want to live with proper motives so when the fire hits, there's nothing to burn. The things you did for the proper motive will adorn you with gold and silver and precious stones. The robes you wear and how you are adorned will preach.

Almost weekly, I fly out to preach, and it's interesting to watch military guys board the plane. I may see a private, sergeant, or captain looking crisp in their shiny uniforms. Then, all of a sudden, a general will board the plane with all his badges of valor and stars. He doesn't have to tell you he's faithful; you know it. You can see it. He doesn't announce, "I'm a general who has served with valor. I saved lives and did what my Commander told me to do." No. His uniform preaches for him.

Likewise, the Word of God says you will adorn yourself in your faithfulness. Daniel 12:3 says, "Those who are wise will shine as bright as the sky, and those who lead many to righteousness will shine like the stars forever" (NLT). So be smart as you plan your future!

Again, 1 Corinthians 3:13 says, "Every man's work shall be made manifest; for the day shall declare it." You talk about excitement! You will adorn yourself with your faithfulness. You will have gold, silver, and precious stones all over you. You will be clothed in the next dispensation indicative to what you did in this dispensation. You will be dressed to reflect your motives.

You won't want to be wearing a Speedo bathing suit during the Millennial reign of Christ. People will look at you and say, "Wow, did you not do anything for God during the Church Age?" No, you will want some robes on. I think of my dad who got saved on his deathbed. He will be wearing a skimpy little suit during the Millennium. We'll be throwing robes at him, saying, "Put some clothes on, Dad." But we'll look at men like the apostle Paul and say, "Wow—look! He did the will of God. Look at those shiny medals." Right now, we are preparing for the reward seat. Everything you do for God counts. Even though we're stepping into eternity, it all counts.

You are living right before the Rapture, right before the Tribulation, right before the Second Coming—right before all three major events. So, friends, let's accelerate our pace. Let's put the flesh aside and live for God. Serve like you've never served before. Push. Run. Finish strong.

How We're Rewarded

Paul already pointed out the cool thing about rewards in 1 Corinthians 3:6-8 (NLT):

> *I planted the seed in your hearts, and Apollos*
> *watered it, but it was God who made it grow. It's*
> *not important who does the planting, or who does*
> *the watering. What's important is that God makes*
> *the seed grow. The one who plants and the one*
> *who waters work together with the same purpose.*
> *And both will be rewarded for their own hard work.*

Verse 8 says both the planter and the one who waters will be rewarded for their work. Bottom line, you are rewarded for doing what God has called you to do. If God has called you to be a real estate agent, you get the same reward as your pastor. If God has called you to be a plumber—and you are doing everything God has told you to do—you are a success.

Years ago, while I attended RHEMA Bible Training Center, I was also working a job in downtown Tulsa. I remember driving up to the really cool office building flanked with expensive Jaguar cars parked all around. I thought, *That's success right there!* But the Lord spoke to me and said, "That's not success. Doing what I tell you to do is success!" So, if God tells you to paint houses and you're faithful, you get the exact same reward as Billy Graham.

At the same time I worked downtown as a RHEMA student, I also worked for a ministry running tapes on a two-tape duplicator. With a small machine like that, I often ran tapes all night long to keep the minister in tapes. I may have been groggy from time to time, but it sure pleased God. Listen! If God tells you to cut hair, do it wholeheartedly and with the right attitude; you'll get the same reward as John Wesley.

God will ask, "What did you do during the Church Age?"

You will answer, "I was a barber." All of a sudden, you show up at the Reward Seat of Christ and you're glowing. People are saying, "Check this out! That guy must have been Reinhard Bonnke with all the gold and precious stones." "No," others answer, "He cut hair for a living, but the guy sure obeyed God."

> Get this: John 13 makes John 14 possible. The servant's heart qualifies you for the greater works.

Our standards are all messed up sometimes. We need to get our minds off ourselves and give of ourselves sacrificially. So many people in the body are familiar with John 14 that talks about doing the greater works of Jesus; many Christians can quote the whole chapter. But there are not nearly as many Christians as familiar with John 13, which talks about Jesus washing the disciples' feet and demonstrating a servant's mentality. Friend, get this: John 13 makes John 14 possible. The servant's heart qualifies you for the greater works.

Many years ago, I worked for Ed Dufresne, who was a legitimate New Testament prophet, with a really strong tangible anointing. He's since stepped over to heaven, but the signs and wonders in his ministry were unbelievable. My job was to travel with him in every way he needed help. One of my duties was unloading luggage and boxes from the truck he needed on the road. Young guys in the ministry would say to me all the time, "Man, I want to be around that anointing. I sure wish I could get up close with him."

"Come help me unload the truck," I would say. Guess how many came? Zero.

Here's the point. God is not looking for great preachers. God is looking for availability and a servant's heart. God wants us to be happy and joyful—never murmuring, complaining, or irritable. We need to let God's Word change us. We need to lift up our hearts in thanksgiving and adoration that the King of Kings and Lord of Lords is soon to arrive on the planet.

FEED ME, FEED ME!

How we measure and equate success is so messed up sometimes. Success is doing whatever Jesus told you to do with mercy, kindness, goodness, and grace.

EPHESIANS 4:7

But unto every one of us is given grace according to the measure of the gift of Christ.

Does the verse above say gifts were given to only a few special people? No. They were given to all of us. Paul is telling us to get busy doing these good things and have a glorious time at the Reward Seat of Christ. Paul is telling us that as Christians we have an engine inside of us, encouraging us to do the will of God. It's witnessing, "Let's help people. Let's tell people about Jesus. Let's serve. Let's do the will of God."

Too often we are so conscious of the flesh that we don't recognize that motor is running. But if we slow down and pray in tongues, that motor starts generating information: Lay hands on the sick. Help in the church. Be sure to listen for it because the motor is running all the time in every born-again Christian.

Learn more about these gifts further down in Ephesians 4:11-12:

And he gave some, apostles; and some, prophets;
and some, evangelists; and some, pastors and teach-
ers; for the perfecting of the saints, for the work of
the ministry, for the edifying of the body of Christ.

What was God's purpose in giving these gifts? They are "for the perfecting of the saints for the *work.*" What's going to be analyzed right after you're raptured? Your work. So God called gift ministries into the body of Christ to do what? Why do we hear preaching from different ministry offices? To perfect or mature us for the *work* of the ministry so that we're not naked in the next dispensation. It's to help us put on some clothes!

My personality is to avoid getting in someone's face. Confrontation is not my thing. But as I teach this message, the Holy Ghost comes on me to ask, "How many messages do you have to hear before you'll get off your rear end and do something for God?" Come on!

Too often Christians are like someone who's eaten 575 cheeseburgers saying, "I ought to eat one more burger before I get up and get busy."

"Just how many cheeseburgers have you eaten?"

"Around a thousand today."

"Today?"

"Yeah! Feed me! Feed me!"

Wouldn't that be ridiculous? Yet, the body of Christ has been fed a gazillion pounds of heavenly food, but too many Christians just want more. We don't need more food—we need to mobilize and do the works of Jesus like we're called to do. Time is short, man!

Look at the next verse in Ephesians 4:13:

Till we all come in the unity of the faith, and of the knowledge of the Son of God, unto a perfect man, unto the measure of the stature of the fulness of Christ.

What is the purpose of all these ministry gifts? To edify the body of Christ until we all come in the unity of the faith and the knowledge of the Son of God unto—unto what? Get this now: "a perfect man." That particular word *perfect* is not *mature*; it's the word *wholehearted.* In other words, don't be halfhearted.

The Lord told Abraham, "Walk before me, and be thou perfect" (Gen. 17:1).

Abraham responds, "What are You taking about?"

God answers, "If I say you will be the father of many nations, you will be. If I say you are going to have a son, you will." God answered this way because Abraham was blowing Him off.

Every time you hear from heaven, you can either be, "Yeah, whatever!" or you can respond, "Yes Sir, I am wholehearted about this." God is looking for wholehearted people. Early on, Paul was supernaturally wholehearted in the wrong direction—spouting off things like, "Talk about Jesus, and I'll kill you." But on the road to Damascus, Jesus appeared to Paul brighter than the noonday sun. What was the first thing Paul said to Jesus after that? "Lord, what would You have me to do?" (Acts 9:6).

Paul's first words were not, "Feed me!" They were, "Lord, what would You have me to *do?*" This is good news for all of us. We have a little bit of time left right before the Rapture to accelerate our pace. We can do works for Jesus that will last forever.

My friend, when you get your house in heaven, there will be badges decorating your walls just like you see in children's church. You will walk in and say, "*Wow!* Look at that! I served in my church. I was an usher. I taught Sunday school. I witnessed to people."

The key is to mix wholeheartedness with whatever God tells you to do. Let us mix the Word, the Spirit, and wholeheartedness in our lives right now before we are raptured and get busy with whatever God is calling us to do!

After you are raptured, your first appointment with God will be the Reward Seat of Christ. Everything you've done with the proper motive you will be reminded of in the next life. Every time you open the door for somebody, every time you do something kind for someone, God takes note. He takes note of what you do right—not what you do wrong. It cannot get any cooler than that!

CHAPTER 10

HUSTLE, CHURCH, *HUSTLE!*

BEFORE LONG, THERE'S coming a day when you will hear a trumpet blast to end all blasts and, in the time it takes to blink your eyes, you will be changed to meet Jesus in the air. Death will be swallowed in triumphant life! The plan of God will consummate in the Rapture to finish off the Church Age. What a day to live! We ought to be able to follow you around and write down the signs and wonders the Lord is doing in your life as you write your own chapter in the book of Acts and fill out your resume for the Millennium.

The apostle Paul had something to say about this day in 1 Corinthians 15:51-54, 58 (TLB):

I am telling you this strange and wonderful secret: we shall not all die, but we shall all be given new bodies! It will all happen in a moment, in the twinkling of an eye, when the last trumpet is blown. For there will be a trumpet blast from the sky, and all the Christians who have died will suddenly become alive, with new bodies that will never, never die; and then we who are still alive shall suddenly have new bodies too. For our earthly bodies, the ones we have now that can die, must be transformed into heavenly bodies that cannot perish but will live forever. When this happens, then at last this Scripture will come true—"Death is swallowed up in victory." ...So, my dear brothers, since future victory is sure, be strong and steady, always abounding in the Lord's work, for you know that nothing you do for the Lord is ever wasted as it would be if there were no resurrection.

Let's take as many people to heaven as we can.

The Message puts verse 58 this way, "With all this going for us, my dear, dear friends, *stand your ground. And don't hold back. Throw yourselves into the work of the Master.*"

That's the whole point right there. Don't hold back! It's time to throw yourself into the work of the Master. It's time to hustle, Church, *hustle!*

FINISH OFF THE CHURCH AGE

We have just a little time left and a great destiny to finish off the Church Age in book of Acts style. When I say a little bit of time, I mean there "ain't much." So, let's have an explosion of salvations, healings, and miracles before we exit the planet. Let's take as many people to heaven as we can. Let's let the world know that Jesus is King of Kings, and He's coming soon.

This is such good news for the Christian, but it's a downright scary time for the world. I would not want to be living without

God anytime but especially in the days to come. With everything happening now and everything yet ahead, I would be like, "Dear Jesus! I'm going to dig a hole and climb in."

Don't misunderstand me. The world is not coming to an end; Jesus is coming back to save the world. He will stop war at the Second Coming. Planet Earth will be renovated—not demolished but improved and enhanced. This earth will be here forever. You have God's word on it! Speaking of the rainbow in Genesis 9:12, God said, "This is the sign of the covenant which I make between Me and you, and every living creature that is with you, *for perpetual generations"* (NKJV).

But the Church Age is coming to an end, and you must know all about it. In fact, there are two things God tells us not to be misinformed about: the gifts of the Spirit and the coming of the Lord. On both topics, the Lord wants you spiritually accurate and acute so you can be used by Him.

EPHESIANS 6:10 (MSG)

And that about wraps it up. God is strong, and he wants
you strong. So take everything the Master has set out
for you, well-made weapons of the best materials. And
put them to use so you will be able to stand up to every-
thing the Devil throws your way. This is no weekend war
that we'll walk away from and forget about in a couple of
hours. This is for keeps, a life-or-death fight to the finish
against the Devil and all his angels.

Listen, God told you to be strong in *His mighty power* (Eph. 6:10 TLB)! That means as we hustle to finish off the age, we can expect the absolute wildest, most unexpected victories before

Jesus comes. You and I will see out-of-the-box, unusual, radical, supernatural, biblical, scriptural signs, wonders, and miracles.

HOW TO HUSTLE

The apostle Paul knew all about hustling, and here's what he told Titus on the topic. Titus 2:12-14 (VOICE) says:

> Run away from anything that leads us away from God; abandon the lusts and passions of this world; live life now in this age with awareness and self-control, doing the right thing and keeping yourselves holy. Watch for His return; expect the blessed hope we all will share when our great God and Savior, Jesus the Anointed, appears again. He gave His body for our sakes and will not only break us free from the chains of wickedness, but He will also prepare a community uncorrupted by the world that He would call His own— people who are passionate about doing the right thing.

The King James Version says, in verse 14, that Jesus redeemed a "peculiar people, zealous of good works." Right now is the season for zealous good works. That's why the Lord expects us to hustle for Him. You and I are the last runners of the race, so Jesus expects more push out of us. We're blessed and privileged, and we ought to act like it.

JESUS FIRST

Jesus is well aware that we are so near to stepping into eternity that we cannot afford to put anything ahead of what He's telling us to do. Jesus wants you to enjoy life, sports, and hobbies, but if they are all you think about then something is not right.

Jesus doesn't want you to put anything before your call or your assignment or whatever He may tell you to do.

For example, I love golf. I even ask the Lord to help me with my golf swing, and He does. I'll get up to make a shot and say, "Okay, Lord, You'll have to fix this."

He'll say, "Tuck your right elbow." He helps me every time I play golf. But if I got up to preach and was thinking about my golf swing, something would be terribly out of order. Like I said, I love golf, but I love Jesus way more. He is way more important than golf.

Why am I going through all this in a book on end times? Because we don't have much time before the Head of the Church leans over the banister of heaven on His way down and yells, "Come up hither! Come up to the throne of God!" I want to make sure that with the time we have left, we are not focused on the wrong things or whatever your hobby is. Keep your priorities straight. Too many people don't have time to go to church because they are so busy with activities. How close do we have to get to the Rapture before we make some changes in our lives?

The payoff is just over the top in the Millennial Reign of Christ. Then, you can have all the hobbies you want—learn to play instruments, ski, golf, whatever. A billion years from now, you'll have all the toys you want. But get this—eternity is coming. Play then. Hustle for Jesus now.

Jesus is trying to warn you: "Time is short!" It's not a bad warning. It's a wonderful warning because He wants to adorn you with medals at the Reward Seat of Christ. Wouldn't it be cool afterward to say to those around you, "Check this out!" with your medals glowing.

People will look at you and say to each other, "Wow, did you see all that gold and silver? That person was wholehearted. That person gave Jesus his all. Jesus adorned her faithfulness, and she will wear it forever." We will thump each other during the Millennium and point out different ones. "Wow! That's awesome. That person really made his or her life count!" Make your life count so you have an abundant entrance into heaven. Recognize the importance of the hour and ask Jesus how you can run your race faster. Ask Him where and how He wants you to serve Him. And, above all, put Jesus first!

MAKE YOUR ELECTION SURE

The apostle Peter also talked to us on this subject. Most of us recognize the first several verses in 2 Peter 1 as talking about the elements of faith, but Peter is also telling us how to be productive for the Lord.

2 PETER 1:5-8

And beside this, giving all diligence, add to your faith virtue; and to virtue knowledge; and to knowledge temperance; and to temperance patience; and to patience godliness; and to godliness brotherly kindness; and to brotherly kindness charity. For if these things be in you, and abound, they make you that ye shall neither be barren nor unfruitful in the knowledge of our Lord Jesus Christ.

The word *barren* in verse 8 means unproductive. So right here we see how to be a producer. You add the elements listed to your faith, and you will automatically be a producer. It's important right at the end of the Church Age that we are all productive for the Lord because we're on our way to the Reward Seat of Christ.

Notice the next few verses in 2 Peter 1:9-10:

But he that lacketh these things is blind, and cannot see afar off, and hath forgotten that he was purged from his old sins. Wherefore the rather, brethren, give diligence to make your calling and election sure: for if ye do these things, ye shall never fall.

In modern-day lingo, Peter is saying, "Get ready! Jesus is coming! If you do these things, you won't fail! Your calling and election will be sure."

2 Peter 1:11-14

For so an entrance shall be ministered unto you abundantly into the everlasting kingdom of our Lord and Saviour Jesus Christ. Wherefore I will not be negligent to put you always in remembrance of these things, though ye know them, and be established in the present truth. Yea, I think it meet, as long as I am in this tabernacle, to stir you up by putting you in remembrance; knowing that shortly I must put off this my tabernacle, even as our Lord Jesus Christ hath shewed me.

Peter wrote that shortly he would put off his tabernacle or body and move to heaven, and he went on to explain what is necessary to have an abundant entrance into heaven. Jesus is our entrance to heaven. Jesus is the ticket—the way, the truth, and the life. He's the only way in, yet there are still some things we can do to have a triumphant entrance.

TRIUMPHANT ENTRANCE

I don't want to slide in the gates of heaven and say, "Holy cow, I just made it! Wheeew, that was close!" I want to enter heaven saying, "I'm here! What a ride! I've done the will of God." I don't want to be timid or scared. I want to enter boldly with great joy, knowing I am home. I want to know that during the very last days of the Church Age, I ran hard and fast. I want to be able to say along with Peter that I gave diligence to make my calling and my election was sure and productive. I want an abundant entrance into the everlasting kingdom.

> I want to enter heaven saying, "I'm here! What a ride! I've done the will of God."

I mentioned my dad earlier, who was a rank sinner all his life. He mocked and cursed God until he got saved on his deathbed. Right after he suffered a stroke and was hospitalized, I walked into intensive care and said, "Dad, it's time for you to get saved." I'm so grateful he went home to be with the Lord even though he knew nothing about God's Word and barely slid in.

My dad's first words in heaven were probably, "My crazy wife was actually right." My mother prayed long and hard over my dad and us kiddos. My dad took me to bars, and my mom took me to church meetings. But in spite of my dad's lifestyle, he entered heaven because of the blood of Jesus. Thank God for the blood. Thank God that my dad could live like the devil his whole life, but at the last moment call on the name of the Lord. It's God's great mercy.

Listen to me! You and your loved ones don't have to slide into heaven or barely make it. Peter tells us how we can be assured that when we leave this planet we are raptured and have an abundant entrance into heaven.

"WITHOUT SPOT, UNREBUKABLE"

Christians don't need to be concerned about sliding into heaven, but they should be concerned about whether or not they are obedient to God's will. We don't hear this command-ment preached often, but Paul told Timothy we are to be "with-out spot, unrebukable." Why? So you don't fail to do what you are supposed to do on this earth. This is a pretty big deal! You're not just on this earth killing time.

1 TIMOTHY 6:11-14

But thou, O man of God, flee these things; and follow
after righteousness, godliness, faith, love, patience, meek-
ness. Fight the good fight of faith, lay hold on eternal life,
whereunto thou art also called, and hast professed a good
profession before many witnesses. I give thee charge in the
sight of God, who quickeneth all things, and before Christ
Jesus, who before Pontius Pilate witnessed a good confes-
sion; that thou keep this commandment without spot,
unrebukable, until the appearing of our Lord Jesus Christ.

Paul says in the next few verses that there is something you can do in this life to lay hold of eternal life. He tells you to be "rich in good works."

1 Timothy 6:17-19

Charge them that are rich in this world, that they be not highminded, nor trust in uncertain riches, but in the living God, who giveth us richly all things to enjoy; that they do good, that they be rich in good works, ready to distribute, willing to communicate; laying up in store for themselves a good foundation against the time to come, that they may lay hold on eternal life.

The blood of Jesus gets us saved and in the gates of heaven, but after that too many Christians say, "Feed me, feed me, feed me!" They don't ask to do anything for Jesus, for the kingdom of God, or for other people. They don't ask to do anything period.

> In these last days, the Church needs to think like an athletic team with a two-minute warning.

Jesus wants you to work for eternity. We just read what Peter said, "If you don't do these things, you're blind. You can't see afar off" (2 Pet. 1:9). Well, I am determined to see afar off. I'm going to live with Jesus forever, so I will make this little vapor we call life count for eternity (James 4:14) by being "rich in good works" (1 Tim. 6:18).

Think about the life of John Wesley. What did he leave his wife went he went on to be with the Lord? He left her a cool preaching robe, a few pound notes of money, and something else: the Methodist Church. I've preached in the middle of nowhere in Russia and come across this hill to see a concrete bunker. I thought, *Man, there's a bomb shelter right there. What in the world is that?* I was told it was a Methodist church. All because John

Wesley said, "Give me ten men that hate sin and love God, and I will change the world." I guarantee when you get to heaven, you will know who John Wesley is. I guarantee you that he had a triumphant entrance. He made his life count for Jesus.

Peter told you how to have an abundant entrance and be productive. Paul told you to be rich in good works. These men of God said to watch for Jesus' return and be productive. What does all this tell you? You cannot afford to just live for right now; you must live for eternity. Come on! Sure, you are to be happy and fulfilled in this life, but you are also just passing through. You ain't home.

You might have heard about the old missionary returning from South Africa years ago. He was a great minister and faithfully served God. He had been away from his family for a very long time, laboring in the work of the Lord. At one point, he boarded a ship back to America, and as he entered the Miami harbor, a big jazz band was welcoming and celebrating an actor who had been on a safari.

Feeling sorry for himself, the missionary prayed, "Lord, I've been across the ocean away from my family working and working, and there's nobody here to meet me. This guy has only been on a safari, and he's got a whole jazz band with a ticker tape parade greeting him. How come there's nobody here to meet me?"

"Don't worry!" the Lord said. "You are not home yet!" Come on now! We're blessed in the here and now, but we haven't seen anything yet because we aren't home yet. We're just passing through. We are citizens and ambassadors from another land on our way to eternity. That's why Paul told us to lay hold of eternal life.

CHAPTER 11

THE TRIBULATION AND THE GREAT TRIBULATION

ALL ALONG I'VE said there is no bad news for the Christian, but frankly, there is plenty of bad news for everyone else. Once you understand what happens on earth after the Church is raptured, you will want to share the good news of Jesus' return all the more. You will find yourself telling people, "Get right with God because you don't want to be here during the seven-year Tribulation." Horrific and heinous demonstrations will be unleashed on planet Earth as God applies pressure on those who won't choose to serve Jesus until they have no other choice.

We see the setup for the Tribulation all over the earth even now. It's amazing that it's not more obvious to the world because it's clear that we're on a trajectory toward one-world government, one-world authority, one-world monetary control, and one-man rulership. It's a bleak picture. The Bible says that Israel will sign a contract with the Antichrist that is a covenant with death and hell. Thank God, our covenant with Jesus is called the New Testament, and it is filled with blessings and benefits that Jesus ratified with His own blood.

Yet we are grateful for the insight and revelation the New Testament gives us about what will happen on the earth right after the Church leaves. This glimpse will make us more whole-hearted to do the will of God in this hour.

Even now we are bumping up against the end of the Church Age or dispensation, which ends in the Tribulation. The wrath of God will be poured out on the earth. As we discussed in Chapter 5, God put all the frustration on Jesus, so He wasn't frustrated with us. But the world has mocked Jesus, spat upon Him, and blamed Him for horrible things, and a season is coming when God will say, "I've been agitated for a while, and now you will know just how agitated I was." The earth will experience seven years of graphic changes—so graphic no human will be able to say, "I didn't know anything was going on." I think it will get pretty clear when people are fishing and the water turns to blood or people are picnicking and the sun goes black. There won't be one person who can say, "What Tribulation? I didn't know about any Tribulation?" No one living on the face of the earth will fail to recognize something going on.

Someone might ask, "But God is love. How can He do this stuff?" You are exactly right. God *is* love, and that is exactly why

> We see the setup for the Tribulation all over the earth even now.

there will be a Tribulation for the unsaved. Every facet of the seven-year Tribulation is a massive rescue mission underway. It's the mercy of God in demonstration—desperately trying to reach hardheaded people so they do not spend eternity in hell.

You need to look at these events from God's point of view. Even though it is a period of trouble, it's called a time of Jacob's trouble. In reality, it's the mercy of God in action. Just as the mercy of God dealt with Pharaoh to change his heart, He will deal with the whole world. The miracles are almost identical, and it's all a perfect setup. It's almost like poetry to get Israel, God's family, to finally repent and turn to Him. He will reveal Himself to His brethren at the very end, and what an amazing revelation it will be. The Jews will say, "My God, my God. We rejected Jesus. We pierced Him. We beat Him. We mocked Him. But now we bow to Him and receive Jesus as the King of Kings and Lord of Lords."

> Every facet of the seven-year period is a massive rescue mission underway.

After the Church is raptured, 144,000 Jewish evangelists will be raised up, and the spirit of supplication will be poured upon Israel. The glory of God will come upon them. Right now, we see Jewish people forming associations with Holy Ghost Pentecostal preachers. It's amazing.

As I try to get most of the Jewish guys I know born again, I try to make a point to them, saying, "Hey, if Jesus is not your Savior, you better start killing some animals once again."

"We don't do that anymore," they answer back.

"Then what's covering your sin?" I ask.

There's blindness on them right now, but they love miracles. They love boldness. They love the God of the Old Testament, and God has a plan for them. It's almost remarkable how God is connecting them not just with denominational people but wild, Holy Ghost people. When you know that God is your God, it makes you bold. It's not arrogance; it's knowing that if God be for you, who or what can be against you (Rom. 8:31)?

God is not only a loving heavenly Father but also El Shaddai, literally "the God who is more than enough." When God talked to Israel in the Old Covenant, He displayed Himself as the Almighty God. God made it perfectly clear to Abraham that he was dealing with Someone who was more than enough—the I am that I am. When Jewish guys today see that kind of reflection in the Church, they say, "I know that Spirit." They know the God of the Old Testament, and right now, they recognize some mingling of the two.

I've done everything I could to talk to my buddies who are Jewish into getting saved. I have gone through the feasts with them, asking, "How do you explain this or that?" They look at me puzzled and say, "Ahhhh." They don't know what to do with the fulfillment of prophecies and feasts that prove Jesus is the Messiah. But I know this. God is in the business of divine setups in their lives. We should rejoice that the Holy Spirit is positioning people for right after the Church departs. We know from God's Word that the Jews will rebuild the temple, and there will also be spiritual revival among the people.

Think about it. Twelve thousand evangelists from each tribe—144,000 Jewish evangelists—will spread the gospel loud and clear. They will instantly rise up with platforms to preach from. Jewish people will think, *My God! That wild and crazy Church disappeared, but God who is so marvelous and wonderful has us ready for this hour right before Jesus is manifested on the earth.*

TWO WITNESSES

During the first half of the Tribulation, two men will prophesy for 42 months or three and a half years, so in the midst of everything going on, there will be preaching and prophesying. Midway through the Tribulation, there will be two witnesses who come to earth to prophesy as God's mouthpieces.

In my opinion, I believe it will be Moses and Elijah. They will have power to do whatever they choose to do for a while—until they are killed by the Antichrist. The Bible says people celebrate and give each other presents because the two witnesses will be dead. Then on the third day, the Spirit of Resurrection comes in them, and they are raised from the dead and translated.

People will see this and know, "There is a God that's greater than all this!" In the midst of it all, God will still have a couple of witnesses preach. Nothing stops God continuing to get out His message of repentance so no one has to go to hell. A person would be spiritually dense, hardheaded, haughty, or rebellious to refuse His willingness to save.

UNPACKING MATTHEW 24

Sitting on the Mount of Olives, Jesus spoke plainly with His disciples about signs of His return. The Tribulation is one of those signs—a prelude to Jesus' Second Coming. Look with me at what Jesus explained to them.

MATTHEW 24:3-15

As he [Jesus] *sat upon the mount of Olives, the disciples come unto him privately, saying, Tell us, when shall these things be? and what shall be the sign of thy coming, and of the end of the world? And Jesus answered and said unto them, Take heed that no man deceive you. For many shall come in my name, saying, I am Christ; and shall deceive many. And ye shall hear of wars and rumours of wars: see that ye be not troubled: for all these things must come to pass, but the end is not yet. For nation shall rise against nation, and kingdom against kingdom: and there shall be famines, and pestilences, and earthquakes, in divers places. All these are the beginning of sorrows. Then shall they deliver you up to be afflicted, and shall kill you: and ye shall be hated of all nations for my name's sake. And then shall many be offended, and shall betray one another, and shall hate one another. And many false prophets shall rise, and shall deceive many. And because iniquity shall abound, the love of many shall wax cold. But he that shall endure unto the end, the same shall be saved. And this gospel of the kingdom shall be preached in all the world for a witness unto all nations; and then shall the end come. When ye therefore shall see the abomination of desolation, spoken of by Daniel the prophet, stand in the holy place, (whoso readeth, let him understand).*

Look closely at verse 7 where the passage talks about nation rising again nation and famines, pestilences, and earthquakes in diverse places. In verse 8, it talks about the beginning of sorrows or birth pains. The Amplified Bible, Classic Edition says,

"All this is but the beginning [the early pains] of the birth pangs [of the intolerable anguish]." Mark this verse 8 in your Bible. This is where the Tribulation begins.

Verse 9 goes on to say, "Then shall they deliver you up to be afflicted, and shall kill you: and ye shall be hated of all nations for my name's sake."

Then notice what happens in verse 13: "But he that shall endure unto the end, the same shall be saved." Talking about the Tribulation period, verse 14 says, "And this gospel of the kingdom shall be preached in all the world for a witness unto all nations; and then shall the end come."

For years, Christians have used this verse to send missionaries into all the world, but actually, this is a mid-Tribulation verse. People get mad when I say that and argue, "Jesus can't come back until the gospel goes into all the world." Nevertheless, this passage refers to mid-Tribulation. "How do you know that?" someone might ask. Read the next verse. "When ye therefore shall see the abomination of desolation, spoken of by Daniel the prophet, stand in the holy place, (whoso readeth, let him understand)" (verse 15). Clearly, that is mid-Tribulation.

Jesus was explaining that the gospel of the kingdom will be preached in all the world even *after* the Rapture of the Church. There's a time midway through the Tribulation that angels go out and preach the everlasting gospel to places that have never heard it. The Church does our part for sure, but I hear people trying to say that Jesus cannot come back until the gospel gets preached to every nation. That is just not correct!

Of course, the Church should endeavor to reach the uttermost preaching the gospel. The Lord wants the Church busy and working hard in our time slot. We must do the best we can to share the good news of Jesus Christ, and there should be pressure on the Church to do that. If we don't have pressure on us to do that, we're not being taught correctly. Nevertheless, a lot will happen after the Church is raptured.

In the climate of our day, ministers feel pressure because people are so easily offended. But even though society acts fragile, the Lord wants us get the message out just the same. You will find out as we begin discussing the Tribulation in detail that the Lord is not worried about people being offended. He is trying to prevent them from going to hell.

As Jesus starts opening the seals of judgment, people don't even recognize it. When we look at Revelation, you will realize Jesus referred to opening the seals in Matthew 24. Listen to me. The tone throughout the Gospels is all about Jewish issues, all about the Tribulation period. Jesus doesn't even talk about the Rapture because it was a mystery at that point. This is important to know because when we get all this information straight, the whole plan of God makes way more sense to us.

Get this clear in your mind. God is not mad at you or the Church, but He is agitated at His own nation of Israel for turning their backs against Him. How would you feel? Notice what Jesus says talking to the Jews in the passage below.

MATTHEW 23:37-39 (NLT)

O Jerusalem, Jerusalem, the city that kills the prophets and stones God's messengers! How often I have wanted to gather your children together as a hen protects her chicks beneath her wings, but you wouldn't let me. And now, look, your house is abandoned and desolate. For I tell you this, you will never see me again until you say, "Blessings on the one who comes in the name of the Lord!"

Jesus cursed the fig tree that produced no fruit in Mark 11 while also symbolically rebuking Israel. Why? Because there was no fruit from the nation of Israel. Jesus was born in 2 B.C. and went to the cross in A.D. 30. Within one generation of the cross, Jerusalem was overthrown in A.D. 70. That's 40 years and prophecy flawlessly fulfilled.

Already, you can feel God's frustration in these scriptures, and as we delve into it in more detail, you will think, *Yikes! Holy cow! The Lord seems a little irritated*. And He is. As we go deeper, you will feel 6,000 years of irritation come out. You could say, "Wow! Dad's a little frustrated with His creation." Really that frustration amounts to this: "My Son's body was broken, and His blood was shed for you. You need to repent so you don't have to live forever in hell." Again, He loves them so much.

A COVENANT WITH THE ANTICHRIST

After the Church is raptured, as we said earlier, Israel makes another huge misstep and enters into a covenant with the Antichrist. It sets the stage for everything that follows. We don't know how long the gap is between the Rapture and when Israel signs the covenant. It could be months or years. In my opinion, I don't believe it will be a long time because of the catastrophic events after the Rapture. However, the agreement is signed, the Tribulation period begins and will last exactly seven years.

At the end of the Tribulation, there's a short interval of about 75 days, which is another topic we will consider in Chapter 12.

> Can you imagine how the news media will react after the Rapture? Think about the global economic chaos when a billion people disappear.

Can you imagine how the news media will react after the Rapture? Think about the global economic chaos when a billion people disappear. Think about unsaved parents whose children disappear because they are alive unto God. They will be freaking out and screaming, "My children are gone!" Think about jets in flight with Christian pilots who disappear. Think about believers who vanish while driving on the highway. It will be absolute chaos. We kind of gloss over all that, but it's going to be a big change. Jesus is coming back for His Church, and if you are alive unto God, you're leaving.

REVELATION REVEALED

Look with me at Revelation 4 to read about the beginning of the Tribulation. First of all, isn't it interesting that the devil has taught people for years that they cannot understand Revelation? In services when I quote from Revelation, I can see it on people's faces, "No, no, not that book! I can't understand it!" Yes, you can! Let's just expose that lie and trick of the devil right now.

Before we focus in on Revelation 4, let me give you an overview of the book. Chapters 1 to 3 are about the Church, which is mentioned 17 times. The Rapture takes place in Revelation 4, and from then on, the Church is not mentioned again because we are no longer on earth.

REVELATION 4:1-8 (NLT)

Then as I looked, I saw a door standing open in heaven, and the same voice I had heard before spoke to me like a trumpet blast. The voice said, "Come up here, and I will show you what must happen after this." And instantly I was in the Spirit, and I saw a throne in heaven and someone sitting on it. The one sitting on the throne was as brilliant as gemstones—like jasper and carnelian. And the glow of an emerald circled his throne like a rainbow. Twenty-four thrones surrounded him, and twenty-four elders sat on them. They were all clothed in white and had gold crowns on their heads. From the throne came flashes of light-ning and the rumble of thunder. And in front of the throne were seven torches with burning flames. This is the seven-fold Spirit of God. In front of the throne was a shiny sea of glass, sparkling like crystal.

In the center and around the throne were four living beings, each covered with eyes, front and back. The first of these living beings was like a lion; the second was like an ox; the third had a human face; and the fourth was like an eagle in flight. Each of these living beings had six wings, and their wings were covered all over with eyes, inside and out. Day after day and night after night they keep on saying, "Holy, holy, holy is the Lord God, the Almighty—the one who always was, who is, and who is still to come."

In the next chapter the Scriptures give us a window into how the scroll is given and the seals are broken.

Revelation 5:1-14 (NLT)

Then I saw a scroll in the right hand of the one who was sitting on the throne. There was writing on the inside and the outside of the scroll, and it was sealed with seven seals. And I saw a strong angel, who shouted with a loud voice: "Who is worthy to break the seals on this scroll and open it?" But no one in heaven or on earth or under the earth was able to open the scroll and read it.

Then I began to weep bitterly because no one was found worthy to open the scroll and read it. But one of the twenty-four elders said to me, "Stop weeping! Look, the Lion of the tribe of Judah, the heir to David's throne, has won the victory. He is worthy to open the scroll and its seven seals."

Then I saw a Lamb that looked as if it had been slaughtered, but it was now standing between the throne and the four living beings and among the twenty-four elders. He had seven horns and seven eyes, which represent the sevenfold Spirit of God that is sent out into every part of the earth. He stepped forward and took the scroll from the right hand of the one sitting on the throne. And when he took the scroll, the four living beings and the twenty-four elders fell down before the Lamb. Each one had a harp, and they held gold bowls filled with incense, which are the prayers of God's people. And they sang a new song with these words:

"You are worthy to take the scroll and break its seals and open it. For you were slaughtered, and your blood has ransomed people for God from every tribe and language and people and nation. And you have caused them to

become a Kingdom of priests for our God. And they will reign on the earth."

Then I looked again, and I heard the voices of thousands and millions of angels around the throne and of the living beings and the elders. And they sang in a mighty chorus: "Worthy is the Lamb who was slaughtered—to receive power and riches and wisdom and strength and honor and glory and blessing."

And then I heard every creature in heaven and on earth and under the earth and in the sea. They sang: "Blessing and honor and glory and power belong to the one sitting on the throne and to the Lamb forever and ever." And the four living beings said, "Amen!" And the twenty-four elders fell down and worshiped the Lamb.

Jesus is so worthy, the only One worthy! Again, at this point, the Church has been raptured, and we are in heaven attending the Reward Seat of Christ and the Marriage Supper of the Lamb. But it's a whole different story on earth. The Bible says there is silence in heaven for about 30 minutes. Perhaps we're able to view some things or not. But in my opinion there is silence in heaven for one of the seals because there's so much bad stuff happening it's sobering. It's almost as if even heaven pauses because of what happens on earth.

JESUS OPENS THE SEALS

In the first few verses, you will read where Jesus opens the first of seven seals. He is the rider on a white horse who wears a crown on His head. He carries a bow with no arrows. In other words, His platform is one of peace, and He conquers with peace.

REVELATION 6:1-2 (NLT)

As I watched, the Lamb broke the first of the seven seals on the scroll. Then I heard one of the four living beings say with a voice like thunder, "Come!" I looked up and saw a white horse standing there. Its rider carried a bow, and a crown was placed on his head. He rode out to win many battles and gain the victory.

As the first seal is opened up, the Antichrist is given the power to rule. It's amazing that already today we can feel the world getting ready for this. Someone has to come on the scene with answers for the Palestinian and Israeli issue and the Middle East because there's plenty of conflict and animosity raging there now. At the opening of the first seal, the Antichrist comes into power with all his great ideas to bring prosperity to everyone.

I've heard the left say it's understandable that the Palestinians object to Israel occupying their land. Seriously? Israel has been living there for 3,500 years. This is not to mention that Arabs in Israel are more blessed than Arabs in all the rest of the world. Israel is the only democracy in that whole area where Arabs and everyone else have rights. The truth is, there is no such thing as a "Palestinian people." In 1976, Hafex al Assad, former Syrian president, told Yasser Arafat, former president of the State of Palestine, "There is no such thing as a Palestinian people, there is no Palestinian entity, there is only Syria...we...are the true representatives of the Palestinian people."[1]

Listen to what happened recently. Israelis had to give a moment of silence for Palestinians who were killed for killing Israelis. That's how insane it is right now. That would be like one of our policemen killed someone to save your life, but you were sad for the guy who got killed trying to kill you. It's nuts! That mentality spreads into all the earth when that first seal is opened up.

The Antichrist will come to rule on a platform of peace, and he will bring what seems to be an answer for the whole situation. The monetary collapse in many countries and others bogged down in economic trouble will cause whole nations to be grateful and eager as the Antichrist suggests one-world currency. He will say to these nearly bankrupt nations, "Don't worry about it! We will forgive your debt and start over with one currency." Everyone falls in line because it will seem like a great idea. In reality, however, it will be Lucifer's way of gaining control of the entire earth. He wants everyone to worship him, but you and I know that just won't happen.

The veracity of Bible prophecies should preach to us as we watch events in the news line up right before Jesus comes back to planet Earth.

The Antichrist always comes to deceive people just like Lucifer because he is Lucifer's representative on the earth. These scriptures fall mid-Tribulation when Lucifer actually enters into the Antichrist incarnate. Up until then, the Antichrist is a human motivated by the devil.

REVELATION 6:3-4 (NLT)

When the Lamb broke the second seal, I heard the second living being say, "Come!" Then another horse appeared, a

red one. Its rider was given a mighty sword and the author-
ity to take peace from the earth. And there was war and
slaughter everywhere.

The opening of the second seal brings World War III. This war will be different from World War I and World War II, fought with M-1 carbines, grenades, and bombs. This war will be fought with intercontinental ballistic missiles. Israel has already developed some pretty impressive weaponry like the Arrow 3 Protector, the Iron Dome protector, and David's Slingshot. David's Slingshot is an intercontinental ballistic missile (ICBM) defense system; when a missile is fired at Israel, it will shoot up a thermonuclear warhead and eliminate it in the upper atmosphere. God knows what He's doing, and He's already directing them whether they know it or not.

I've even read that diplomats have said, "There's a setup underway for the entire world to go to war." Thank God, you and I will not be here.

Can you imagine John seeing all this in a vision when God imparted the book of Revelation to him? I'm sure John wondered how God would protect Israel. But today, we can see the technology already in place. In 2016, Israel developed a new unmanned ship that goes into the Mediterranean and can fire missiles at other ships and take out submarines. So cool!

I've read of 10 to 15 Israeli generals who have said, "We're already prepared now for World War III." Israel already has spoken out about World War III. I've even read that diplomats have said, "There's a setup underway for the entire world to go to war." Thank God, you and I will not be here. The world, on the other hand, is about to go through more catastrophic events than ever before. Even worse, this is still only the first half of the Tribulation we are discussing.

REVELATION 6:5-6 (NLT)

When the Lamb broke the third seal, I heard the third living being say, "Come!" I looked up and saw a black horse, and its rider was holding a pair of scales in his hand. And I heard a voice from among the four living beings say, "A loaf of wheat bread or three loaves of barley will cost a day's pay. And don't waste the olive oil and wine."

After World War III, there will be famine. It's probably hard for us to imagine the terror of all this, but to some extent, Hollywood movies provide a general idea of what it will be like. Movies like the *Terminator* help us visualize the horror of anti-ballistic missiles targeting major cities like Los Angeles, Sydney, and New York. After that many nuclear hits around the world, all of a sudden, there will just be no more food.

Some of the seals talk about no grass left and one third of the trees destroyed. People will go through absolute hell on earth. Once again, the whole reason for the Tribulation is to persuade people to repent. Think of how hardheaded a person would be to go through these horrific events and still not repent.

Later, we will talk more about the Second Coming, where still only 50 percent of the people have repented. Referring to the Second Coming, Matthew 24:40-42 says, "Then shall two be in the field; the one shall be taken, and the other left. Two women shall be grinding at the mill; the one shall be taken, and the other left. Watch therefore: for ye know not what hour your

Lord doth come." It's like at Calvary where one thief got saved; the other thief did not.

Again, these are some hardheaded, stiff-necked people, because it's hard to imagine more fireworks than nuclear weapons exploding all over the earth and the food supply vanishing. You would think people everywhere would be saying, "Hmmm, we're not eating, and we've got missiles coming at us just like the Bible prophesied. I need to change my heart." But because of the hardness of heart, God will send even more fireworks to get people's attention.

The whole purpose of all these seals is that every human being will need to decide whether he or she is for Jesus or against Him. There's no in-between. Right now, people say, "I know there's a God, but I'm not sure I want to serve Him." But we're reading about a point where each person will have to decide. That's why the Bible calls it the valley of decision, because all through this seven-year period people will be boldly confronted with the choice.

REVELATION 6:7-8 (NLT)

When the Lamb broke the fourth seal, I heard the fourth living being say, "Come!" I looked up and saw a horse whose color was pale green. Its rider was named Death, and his companion was the Grave. These two were given authority over one-fourth of the earth, to kill with the sword and famine and disease and wild animals.

When this fourth seal opens, the Antichrist is empowered to kill over a quarter of the earth's population, and he gains sections of power over all the earth. At one point, a third of all the earth is killed, which is some two billion people.

What I'm about to say here is conjecture, and as I said earlier, whenever I give you my opinion, I label it. Some of these seals occur in stages. So, all of a sudden, someone in the middle of the Congo may look up in the sky and think, *Hmmm, all the major cities of the world are being vaporized.* But eventually, the Antichrist controls a quarter of the earth. I imagine it will be Turkey, Syria, Iraq, and Saudi Arabia where he will control annihilating everyone. I realize this is sobering, but I want you to see how blessed you are that you don't have to be here.

REVELATION 6:9-13 (NLT)

When the Lamb broke the fifth seal, I saw under the altar the souls of all who had been martyred for the word of God and for being faithful in their testimony. They shouted to the Lord and said, "O Sovereign Lord, holy and true, how long before you judge the people who belong to this world and avenge our blood for what they have done to us?" Then a white robe was given to each of them. And they were told to rest a little longer until the full number of their brothers and sisters—their fellow servants of Jesus who were to be martyred—had joined them. I watched as the Lamb broke the sixth seal, and there was a great earthquake. The sun became as dark as black cloth, and the moon became as red as blood. Then the stars of the sky fell to the earth like green figs falling from a tree shaken by a strong wind.

Isn't it something in verse 10 that the people are crying out to the Father, "Sovereign Lord, avenge our blood!" Then in verse 13, the sixth seal opens, which is different from the others. It is more supernatural than natural. With the first five seals, we saw intercontinental ballistic missiles, famine, and so on. But at the sixth seal, the hand of God alters the heavens—the sun and the moon change. Major earthquakes occur, and there are cataclysmic events on the earth to pressure people on earth to change. Wow.

Meanwhile, back at the ranch, 144,000 Jewish evangelists are being raised up to preach during this timeframe.

THE TRUMPET JUDGMENTS

In Revelation 8, we read of the seventh seal, which begins the trumpet judgments. Everything you have read until now is sobering, but the events that follow are unimaginable and hard to even comprehend. Let me remind you once again that if you are born again, you will not be here.

REVELATION 8:1-7 (NLT)

When the Lamb broke the seventh seal on the scroll, there was silence throughout heaven for about half an hour. I saw the seven angels who stand before God, and they were given seven trumpets. Then another angel with a gold incense burner came and stood at the altar. And a great amount of incense was given to him to mix with the prayers of God's people as an offering on the gold altar before the throne. The smoke of the incense, mixed with the prayers of God's holy people, ascended up to God from the altar where the angel had poured them out. Then the

angel filled the incense burner with fire from the altar and
threw it down upon the earth; and thunder crashed, light-
ning flashed, and there was a terrible earthquake. Then
the seven angels with the seven trumpets prepared to blow
their mighty blasts. The first angel blew his trumpet, and
hail and fire mixed with blood were thrown down on the
earth. One-third of the earth was set on fire, one-third of
the trees were burned, and all the green grass was burned.

When the seventh seal opened, there was silence in heaven
for about 30 minutes. Hebrews 12:1 says those who have gone
on before us are looking over the banister and cheering us on
as we run our race here on earth. So, there's scriptural prece-
dence that those in heaven can see some activity on earth. The
30 minutes of silence may well be to reflect on the catastrophic
events on the earth as the seals are opened. It goes from bad
to worse—from seals to trumpet judgments.

Notice verse 7 that I mentioned earlier. This is where a third
of all the trees are burned up, and there is no more grass. Think
about that for a minute. That significantly injures photosynthesis, the process whereby trees, plants, grass, etc. produce
oxygen. In other words, there will be a weird atmosphere on
earth when the first trumpet judgment starts.

REVELATION 8:8-11

And the second angel sounded, and as it were a great
mountain burning with fire was cast into the sea: and the
third part of the sea became blood; and the third part of
the creatures which were in the sea, and had life, died; and
the third part of the ships were destroyed. And the third

angel sounded, and there fell a great star from heaven, burning as it were a lamp, and it fell upon the third part of the rivers, and upon the fountains of waters; and the name of the star is called Wormwood: and the third part of the waters became wormwood; and many men died of the waters, because they were made bitter.

In verse 8, an asteroid hits the earth and a third of the sea becomes blood. These are some pretty significant changes to the earth. Then in the next few verses, a great star named Wormwood falls from heaven. These signs sound like the worst nightmare from a graphic Hollywood horror movie.

> These signs sound like the worst nightmare from a graphic Hollywood horror movie.

Years ago, I was preaching at a Bible school in the Ukraine, talking about how these two asteroids would hit the earth during the Tribulation. I pointed out that one of them is called Wormwood, and the entire class gasped. I thought, *What's wrong?* The interpreter explained that the word *Wormwood* in the Russian Bible is the word *Chernobyl*. Let that soak in. How many remember the Chernobyl accident in 1986 when a nuclear reactor melted down and killed some 4,000 people? The first time I preached in the Ukraine, a restaurant used a Geiger counter on my potato to make sure it wasn't radioactive. Can you imagine a Geiger counter reading after two asteroids hit?

Maybe you've seen movies like *Armageddon* or *Deep Impact* that tell fictional stories of the world ending because of aster-oids. Truth be told, the movies don't have anything on the terror the earth will see during the Tribulation. But listen to me. The world does not end, but it will go through some serious devastation. We've read that a third of the water will be radio-active. A third of the trees, grass, and plants will be eliminated, affecting the atmosphere. What kind of a mental image does this give you? The grass is toast, and this is only a trumpet judgment. The vials have not even been opened yet.

REVELATION 8:12-13 (NLT)

Then the fourth angel blew his trumpet, and one-third of the sun was struck, and one-third of the moon, and one-third of the stars, and they became dark. And one-third of the day was dark, and also one-third of the night. Then I looked, and I heard a single eagle crying loudly as it flew through the air, "Terror, terror, terror to all who belong to this world because of what will happen when the last three angels blow their trumpets."

Even daylight will be altered. Whoa, whoa, whoa! In Revelation 9, we read of the fifth trumpet.

REVELATION 9:1-3 (NLT)

Then the fifth angel blew his trumpet, and I saw a star that had fallen to earth from the sky, and he was given the key to the shaft of the bottomless pit. When he opened it, smoke poured out as though from a huge furnace, and the sunlight and air turned dark from the smoke. Then locusts came from the smoke and descended on the earth, and they were given power to sting like scorpions.

Notice how supernatural these descriptions are with Lucifer openly killing, stealing, and destroying. Rejoice that you—along with the body of Christ—are in heaven and not on earth for this.

Below we are given more insight about the last trumpet.

REVELATION 9:11-15 (NLT)

Their king is the angel from the bottomless pit; his name in Hebrew is Abaddon, and in Greek, Apollyon—the Destroyer. The first terror is past, but look, two more terrors are coming! Then the sixth angel blew his trumpet, and I heard a voice speaking from the four horns of the gold altar that stands in the presence of God. And the voice said to the sixth angel who held the trumpet, "Release the four angels who are bound at the great Euphrates River." Then the four angels who had been prepared for this hour and day and month and year were turned loose to kill one-third of all the people on earth.

So with that trumpet, a third of the men are killed. Again, this is my conjecture, but let's consider this mathematically to gain more insight. There are almost eight billion people on the planet right now, and I would estimate one billion Christians depart at the Rapture. So, in other words, during this timeframe, demons come out on the earth to kill 2.33 billion people. How horrific is that?

As I said earlier, the purpose of the Tribulation is to apply pressure to hardheaded people. God is doing everything possible to get men and women to call out, "Lord, I call on Your name. I want to be saved." Why? So they don't have to spend eternity in hell.

God will have everyone's attention and make Himself perfectly clear. It won't matter what television channel or streaming service a person watches. It won't matter what news outlet the person follows or what show he or she is watching. People will look on their iPhones and say, "Oh my God, now the Jewish guys are saying, 'Buckle up! Here comes another trumpet!'" It's amazing how God will use all this frustration and pressure to get people to make a change. It's one dramatic rescue mission of epic proportions.

God is so merciful. He told me one day, "The book of Revelation is My *Left Behind* book for the Jews." Maybe you have read the *Left Behind* book that Tim LaHaye wrote. He is predominantly an author of marriage books, but God wanted him to write the end-time series that sold 85 million copies before he passed away in 2016.

Look with me now at the seventh trumpet, which still takes place in the first part of the Tribulation. Still to come is the mid-Tribulation and the Great Tribulation. Giddy up.

REVELATION 11:15 (NLT)

Then the seventh angel blew his trumpet, and there were loud voices shouting in heaven: "The world has now become the Kingdom of our Lord and of his Christ, and he will reign forever and ever."

Interestingly enough, that is exactly what Daniel saw. He saw all these future happenings but was concerned about information Gabriel had given him. Gabriel also told him,

"Don't worry. The Ancient of Days will prevail" (Dan. 7:22). During the midst of all these horrific events, you would think mankind would be toast. But the Bible says the Ancient of Days will prevail.

The overall theme of Revelation is pressure to repent, pressure to repent, pressure to repent, and ultimately, Jesus being revealed. Think of the protocol underway to prepare the earth and hardened hearts to meet King Jesus.

God is in the process of sifting. As I said earlier, at the Second Coming only 50 percent of people have accepted Jesus, so God is smart enough to apply more pressure to these stubborn kids to find out if they will repent or not. In essence, it is a weeding out of people who refuse to be humble.

> The truth is, if you won't humble yourself to hear preaching now, then you will end up wishing you had during this seven-year period called the Tribulation.

The truth is, if you won't humble yourself to hear preaching now, then you will end up wishing you had during this seven-year period called the Tribulation. Thank God someone prayed for all of us who walk with Jesus. Thank God someone prayed for your mother, or your grandmother prayed for you to the point that your heart was soft enough to receive Jesus as your Savior. When someone talked about Jesus, you perked up and said, "Lord, I need to know more about You!" When you heard someone yell, "Repent! Jesus is coming!" you got born again.

OPENING OF THE VIALS

As you have been reading about these shocking and graphic pressures that come to earth, you've probably thought it couldn't get any worse. But you would be wrong. The next event is the opening of the vials, which are absolutely horrendous. You have read of the seven seals and the trumpet judgments, and the majority of them are brought about by a man. Only a couple of them are brought about supernaturally, where demons act out in some way or the heavens are changed.

But now, let's consider the opening of the vials. This is when the events get especially dicey and, in some ways, more challenging to understand. The book of Revelation overall is very much in chronological order, but in a few places, it skips back and forth. For that reason, a lot of people say that it's all difficult to understand. Actually, the book of Daniel skips around a bit too and goes back and forth and back again, so it is also challenging. But this is *End Times Made Easy*, right? So, we're going to do just that.

More specifically, the seals, the trumpets, and the vials are all in chronological order. Actually, I sometimes wonder if people truly don't understand it all, or they just don't like reading it all. I have tons of notes and could go into all kinds of detail, but it's a little overwhelming when you start finding out just how many people get vaporized.

How many of you saw the movie *Raiders of the Lost Ark* that came out in the early 1980s? Do you remember at the very end of the movie, the presence of God came out of the ark of the covenant and people's eyes melted away from their face? That was fiction; this is not. Zechariah 14 gives you a graphic depiction of the end of the Tribulation and the first part of the Second Coming when people will lose flesh. The Bible says the sockets in their eyes will be melted away. It's actually kind of hard to go into too much detail because it's just overwhelming. The earth will definitely experience a season of God's wrath. I almost feel like I need a disclaimer on this book: *For Mature Audiences Only. Graphic Violence. Blood and Gore.*

STAGGERING AUTHORITY

Listen to me clearly! I'm going to say it again: There's *only* good news for the Christian! You will not even be here for these events. But I hear so much confusion on whether Christians are "pre-wrath Rapture" or "Mid-Tribbers." I am what the Bible says, and the Bible says the wrath of God begins when the seals are released. The Antichrist is seal number one, and he cannot come on the scene until you—and the rest of the Church—leave. Thessalonians is very clear and very bold about that point. In fact, the first seal cannot even be opened until the Church leaves. God has given the Church that much authority.

I can just imagine some people thinking, *Well, I know that, Brother Joe, but....* Really, do you know that? Do you confess Scripture over your family daily? Do you decree Scripture over your job? The Church has so much authority that Jesus has to take you off the earth before He can deal with the world. It's staggering, really. Let that sink in.

I realize that far too many Christians don't walk in their authority. I realize that for many years the Church has neglected to use all its authority. But God has given the Church author-ity just the same. It's remarkable! What does God want you to do with all this authority? Use it! Use it for the world. Use it for the kingdom. Use it for yourself. Use it for your loved ones. Use it for your unloved ones. Speak health to your body. Speak to your job. Speak over your family. What do you speak? You agree with God's Word. What can you speak to? Speak to things that you have authority over. My friend, you should be declaring and decreeing God's Word everywhere in your world and beyond.

Someone says, "But God can do whatever He wants when He wants. God is in control." Really? Is He? Then you cannot prosecute a rapist if God's in control because the crime would be God's idea, and that's ridiculous! God is *not* in control. Luci-fer is the god of this world after Adam sinned and handed over his God-given authority to the devil. After Jesus left the cross, He stormed through hell and took back the keys to death, hell, and the grave (Eph. 4:8; Matt. 16:18). What did Jesus do with the keys? He gave them to the Church. Now, God expects *you* to do something about the devil; God expects the Church to pray and use its authority.

Again, the authority of the Church is the whole reason we have to be raptured out of here before the Tribulation can begin. If the Church were on earth during the Tribulation, we would be having prayer meetings to stop asteroids. We would command water to stay blue and stars to remain in the sky. We would decree like Joshua did and command the sun to stand still. And if Joshua did that under the old covenant, imagine what God expects we could do under the new covenant.

Notice the correlation there. All of a sudden, when these vials are opened, mountains will be removed just like Jesus said. At His Word, the earth will be altered because He already put it in His Book. Basically, the earth will be put into a vacuum of God's Word, and it will have no choice but to obey. Just as the heavens do not negotiate with God. They do not argue with God and say, "No, I won't go dark by a third." God's Word is powerful just like your word is powerful. In fact, God's Word is so powerful that He does not need to repeat Himself. God spoke once, and it will all happen just as He declared because God is alert and active, watching over His Word to perform (Jer. 1:12 AMPC).

BETTER THAN ETERNAL HELL

As we have read through events during the Tribulation and the Great Tribulation—the seals, the judgments, and the vials—you recognize how radical it all is. It's literally hell on earth because God is desperately trying to rescue as many people as He can from eternal hell. As bad as hell on earth is for seven years, it's far better than living in hell eternally. These things that we have described sound horrific, but they are still much better than missing out on the presence of God eternally.

> It's literally hell on earth because God is desperately endeavoring to rescue as many people as He can from eternal hell.

We cannot even comprehend eternal separation from God—His love, His goodness, His justice. Even as dark as some circumstances are in the world around us and even with as much sin as exists in the earth, there is still light all around us. God's actions—even His wrath—are to protect you and me.

THE MARK OF THE BEAST

Can you imagine horrendous devils operating outside of a body—the hatred, damnation, and evil in them—blatantly and aggressively leveraging atrocious, hideous, unspeakable acts of evil endorsed by Lucifer and the Antichrist? That's why the Antichrist is called the mark of the beast. A wild animal such as a tiger is bloodthirsty and ready to kill. It feels no remorse because it's a beast, and that is Lucifer's thought pattern. Individuals on earth during the Tribulation and the Great Tribulation will have the opportunity not to take the mark of the beast. People will be forced to choose—allegiance to God or the devil.

THE GREAT TRIBULATION

Everything we've discussed until now has described the first half of the Tribulation. The second half of the Tribulation begins with the opening of the vials. Jesus even pointed out the difference between the Tribulation and the Great Tribulation. What is the demarcation point? Jesus says, "When you see the 'abomination of desolation,' spoken of by Daniel" (Matt. 24:15). In other words, when the vials open and the Antichrist enters the temple and says, "I'm god," the Tribulation will merge into the Great Tribulation.

People who follow Jesus know that the Antichrist is not the Messiah, but there are those who will believe he is because he will bring peace to the world. During the first part of the seal of the Antichrist, the Jews will say, "We finally have our King. The Messiah has come. He's brought peace." From a point of strength, Israel will be ready to annihilate Islam, but the Antichrist will tell them to "just relax!" The Jews will respond, saying,

"Wow! He made us be at peace with Islam because normally we would desire to wipe them off the face of the earth."

Then, all of a sudden, the vials will open. The first three and a half years or 42 months will be the Tribulation, and the second three and a half years or 42 months is the Great Tribulation. Let's begin reading as the vials open and the Great Tribulation begins:

REVELATION 16:1-21 (NLT)

Then I heard a mighty voice from the Temple say to the seven angels, "Go your ways and pour out on the earth the seven bowls [vials] containing God's wrath." So the first angel left the Temple and poured out his bowl on the earth, and horrible, malignant sores broke out on everyone who had the mark of the beast and who worshiped his statue. Then the second angel poured out his bowl on the sea, and it became like the blood of a corpse. And everything in the sea died.

Then the third angel poured out his bowl on the rivers and springs, and they became blood. And I heard the angel who had authority over all water saying, "You are just, O Holy One, who is and who always was, because you have sent these judgments. Since they shed the blood of your holy people and your prophets, you have given them blood to drink. It is their just reward." And I heard a voice from the altar, saying, "Yes, O Lord God, the Almighty, your judgments are true and just."

Then the fourth angel poured out his bowl on the sun, causing it to scorch everyone with its fire. Everyone was burned by this blast of heat, and they cursed the name of God, who had control over all these plagues. They did not repent of their sins and turn to God and give him glory.

Then the fifth angel poured out his bowl on the throne of the beast, and his kingdom was plunged into darkness. His subjects ground their teeth in anguish, and they cursed the God of heaven for their pains and sores. But they did not repent of their evil deeds and turn to God.

Then the sixth angel poured out his bowl on the great Euphrates River, and it dried up so that the kings from the east could march their armies toward the west without hindrance. And I saw three evil spirits that looked like frogs leap from the mouths of the dragon, the beast, and the false prophet. They are demonic spirits who work miracles and go out to all the rulers of the world to gather them for battle against the Lord on that great judgment day of God the Almighty.

"Look, I will come as unexpectedly as a thief! Blessed are all who are watching for me, who keep their clothing ready so they will not have to walk around naked and ashamed." And the demonic spirits gathered all the rulers and their armies to a place with the Hebrew name Armageddon.

Then the seventh angel poured out his bowl into the air. And a mighty shout came from the throne in the Temple, saying, "It is finished!" Then the thunder crashed and rolled, and lightning flashed. And a great earthquake struck—the worst since people were placed on the earth. The great city of Babylon split into three sections, and the cities of many nations fell into heaps of rubble. So God *remembered all of Babylon's sins, and he made her drink the cup that was filled with the wine of his fierce wrath. And every island disappeared, and all the mountains were leveled. There was a terrible hailstorm, and hailstones weighing as much as seventy-five pounds fell from the sky onto the people below. They cursed God because of the terrible plague of the hailstorm.*

In the Great Tribulation, we read about sores, the dying of every living thing in the sea, the water turning to blood—even rivers and fountains become blood. Judgment will have arrived, and verses 5 and 6 explained why. The blood of saints and prophets was shed, and those who are guilty will reap what they have sown. God held off on judgment until this period because He is so righteous, so merciful.

Look again at verses 8 and 9 where the fourth angel poured out his vial upon the sun, causing it to scorch everyone with its fire. Men blasphemed the name of God, who has control over the plagues. Then did not repent and give God glory. It will be like the battle of Moses and Pharaoh all over again. Horrible vials or bowls will be unsealed but people still will not repent.

Finally, in verses 10 to 12, we notice the phrase, "the kings from the east could march their armies toward the west without hindrance." All the nations of the east will come down and attack Israel at the Battle of Armageddon, which is the last vial. Verse 17 says, "And a mighty shout came from the throne in the Temple, saying, 'It is finished!'"

The next few verses tell us that Jerusalem will be divided into three parts. Then, the last vial will include the greatest earthquake the world will ever have seen. Islands will be no more, and mountains will be snapped out of place and leveled. All the cities of the earth and all their buildings will crumble, and hailstones will crush what remains. Whatever people make it through the seals, judgments, and vials will be unbelievably hardheaded.

GREAT WHITE THRONE JUDGMENT

Then, Jesus in the brightness of His glory will lead the charge at the Second Coming. The King of Kings and the Lord of Lords will say, "I've got the earth ready for My kingdom. I have rid the earth of rebellion." Jesus will have removed from the earth all people who thumbed their noses at Him, saying, "Even though You gave your life for me, I don't care." Every knee will bow before Jesus right then and there.

CHAPTER 12

THE SECOND COMING OF JESUS

**THE FIRST TIME** Jesus came to earth, His entrance was as low-key as possible. There was no place for Him at the inn, and the King of Kings was born in a manger—a livestock shack surrounded by hay and animals. King Jesus laid aside all His heavenly privileges and power to humbly take on flesh to rescue you and me. Jesus was not recognized as the Messiah by His own people during His earthly ministry. Instead, He was mocked, beaten, and crucified. But the Second Coming will be a whole different story. This time, Jesus will be welcomed with the pomp and circumstance deserving of a king. Let's put it this way: The Boss is coming back to the planet, and His return will be spectacular—the grand finale event of the universe.

We don't really know the protocol for receiving a heavenly King who comes to earth. How does nature even receive the One who created nature? For thousands of years, man has built edifices to honor himself, but how will we honor Jesus when He returns? Every knee will bow in adoration and every tongue will confess that Jesus Christ is Lord to the glory of God the Father.

Every book in the Bible foretells that Jesus is coming again. Hosea gave you a picture. Malachi gave you a picture. Zephaniah gave you a picture. Joel gave you a picture. All the prophets pointed to the Second Coming, and it's so cool how God gave you different glimpses of just how grand it will be. What a great privilege that we will return with Jesus at the Second Coming—alongside Him on white horses to help the King implement His Kingdom. John described Jesus' return this way, and it's hard to imagine anything cooler.

> The Boss is coming back to the planet, and His return will be spectacular— the grand finale event of the universe.

REVELATION 19:11-14 (MSG)

Then I saw Heaven open wide—and oh! a white horse and its Rider. The Rider, named Faithful and True, judges and makes war in pure righteousness. His eyes are a blaze of fire, on his head many crowns. He has a Name inscribed that's known only to himself. He is dressed in a robe soaked with blood, and he is addressed as "Word of God." The armies of Heaven, mounted on white horses and dressed in dazzling white linen, follow him. A sharp sword comes out of his mouth so he can subdue the nations, then rule them with a rod of iron. He treads the winepress of the raging wrath of God, the Sovereign-Strong. On his robe and thigh is written, King of kings, Lord of lords.

Did you see yourself? You're in verse 14 where it said the "armies of heaven." You will follow Jesus, "mounted on white horses and dressed in dazzling white linen." Maybe you've never ridden a horse before in this life, but you will be riding the coolest horse you've ever seen in the next one.

When I was a kid, my family had an appaloosa that was demon-possessed. I'm kidding, but everybody who got on him got bucked off. I had to climb a tree to get on that horse. I climbed out over the limbs, and the second I got on him, *pshooo*, he shot me back off. But the horses in heaven somehow yield to instruction, and we're going to fly on those horses right along with Jesus. Wow.

> The brightness of His glory will be so magnificent that there will be no need for the sun.

The brightness of His glory will be so magnificent that there will be no need for the sun. The glory will radiate from Jesus' face. Jesus will be wearing crowns on His head and white robes. Talk about pomp and circumstance.

You and I and the Church of Jesus Christ will be right there behind Him, coming from heaven down to earth. There will be no shadows anywhere because He Himself permeates light everywhere as He leads the charge back to earth.

The universe has been expanding at the speed of light for some 13 to 16 billion years. Between Genesis 1 and Genesis 2, there was no time. As far as the universe has spun out, we know there are about 100 billion galaxies with 100 billion stars that are like our sun, but He calls them all by name. The universe and the heavens will bow. All creation is waiting for the Creator to come. And all of a sudden, He comes.

All creation and the hearts of men will bow in adoration. The saints will come marching in. After the Rapture, you will have attended the Reward Seat of Christ and be retrofitted for your future when Jesus reigns for a thousand years. You will have attended the Marriage Supper of the Lamb, the greatest party you've ever been to in your entire life.

Then, all of a sudden, there will be the orders from head-quarters. The regiment of your city and state will be told to rise up on horses, and the excitement will build with every person saying, "Wow! It's time! We're going back to the earth with God! It's time! It's time! We're returning with our King of Kings and Lord of Lords."

Suddenly, we will descend out of heaven on those horses and come reeling down through the universe. We'll see this little spot down there called planet Earth, where the Antichrist is looking stupid and doing evil everywhere evil can be done. As he looks up, he will see Someone brighter than all the 100 billion stars coming right straight at him. It will look like the light on a freight train, and behind that freight train are you and me traveling with *Jesus*.

The Antichrist will think he still can defeat Jesus, but is he in for an epic surprise. You can imagine the Antichrist's staff saying, "What is that coming at us? Is it a missile? No, it's white and blindingly bright. Are those horses?" Talk about a missile—it will be dressed in light hurling toward the planet. My friend, you will be rocketing right from heaven down to earth, and what a view you will have.

The earth will make preparation for that grand entrance of God Himself. The mountains will be leveled. There will be no more islands. There will be great earthquakes. The earth will go through a cataclysmic earthquake and shake like crazy. Jesus will stand at the Mount of Olives and a great earthquake will split apart the mountain with a great valley between the two. King Jesus will stand there with a scepter of righteousness as the scepter of His kingdom, and He will set up His kingdom right then and there. Instantly, He will bring peace into the earth and stop war. Right there, it's eradicated. Wow!

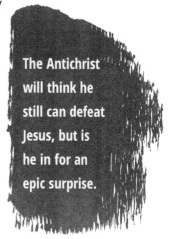

The Antichrist will think he still can defeat Jesus, but is he in for an epic surprise.

Lucifer will say, "I think I messed this deal up." How true—even though it's probably the only truth he's ever told. Can't you hear Lucifer saying, "I'm bailing on this deal. I lose every time. I have been stupid," before Jesus obliterates him with the brightness of His coming? Hallelujah! Amen! Glory to our King of Kings!

It will be the coolest thing ever, and you will be an eyewitness!

Every movie you've ever seen where the hero flies in at the end to save the day comes from right here. Jesus will return and stop a war. There will be no more war because Jesus is the Prince of Peace. Wow.

What a great privilege we will have to return with Jesus to help the King implement His Kingdom. How cool that you will be raised up to be an overseer of His wonderful kingdom for a thousand years. There are great things ahead for all of us. It's an amazing time in history that you and I were chosen to live— right before God physically comes back to the planet.

GRANDDADDY OF EVENTS

There's no question that the Second Coming will be dramatic. Matthew described it this way.

MATTHEW 24:27 (NLT)

For as the lightning flashes in the east and shines to the west, so it will be when the Son of Man comes.

Have you ever seen lightning that was casual? There's no such thing as a casual lightning bolt. While preaching in Virginia a while back, I stood in front of a window in the place where I stayed. This bolt of lightning hit a tree about 20 feet away, and the hair on the back of my head stood straight up. *Kaboom.* Electricity shot out, and the power went out in the entire vicinity. There was nothing casual about it; it got my attention. I didn't go, "Hmmm. What was that?" I knew exactly what it was that almost fried me.

The Second Coming will be the granddaddy of events throughout the universe—throughout all eternity. Skip down a few verses.

MATTHEW 24:29-31 (NLT)

Immediately after the anguish of those days, the sun will be darkened, the moon will give no light, the stars will fall from the sky, and the powers in the heavens will be shaken. And then at last, the sign that the Son of Man is coming will appear in the heavens, and there will be deep mourning among all the peoples of the earth. And they will see the Son of Man coming on the clouds of heaven with power and great glory. And he will send out his angels with the mighty blast of a trumpet, and they will gather his chosen ones from all over the world—from the farthest ends of the earth and heaven.

The Message quotes those verses this way:

Following those hard times, sun will fade out, moon cloud over, stars fall out of the sky, cosmic powers trem-ble. Then, the Arrival of the Son of Man! It will fill the skies—no one will miss it. Unready people all over the world, outsiders to the splendor and power, will raise a huge lament as they watch the Son of Man blaz-ing out of heaven. At that same moment, he'll dispatch his angels with a trumpet-blast summons, pulling in God's chosen from the four winds, from pole to pole.

The Second Coming will be the complete opposite of the Rapture. At the Rapture of the Church, the righteous are taken off the earth and into heaven. At the Second Coming, the wicked are plucked off the earth so Jesus can begin His king-dom on earth with all righteous people.

Remember what He said, "I let the wheat grow with the tares and, at the end of the age, I'll let the angels be the reap-ers" (Matt. 13:37-43). All of a sudden here, Jesus will set up the angels to be the reapers at the end of the Tribulation period. People who have not repented despite all the signs and warn-ings will be separated as the wheat from the chaff.

The righteous natural-bodied people who make it through the latter part of the Tribulation will enter the kingdom of God on the earth. The arrival of these people into the kingdom is a huge deal for you and me because they will be the new kids on the block for a thousand years, and we will be implementing the kingdom and preaching to them. When they reach the age of accountability, they will still have the nature of Adam in them and need to be born again.

You'll be able to say to them, "There's Jesus right there. Get saved!" Christians are sometimes tempted to think our work will be finished at the Rapture, but we have a whole 1,000 years beyond. If you're tasting of the powers of the world to come, you will be operating in much more in the world to come. Going to heaven is not the end of it all—really, it's just the beginning.

ISAIAH'S RENDITION OF THE SECOND COMING

We will return to Matthew 24 shortly, but let's go to Isaiah and look at some Old Testament verses that are very graphic and exact. This is Isaiah's rendition of what the Second Coming will look like.

ISAIAH 2:1-4 (NLT)

This is a vision that Isaiah son of Amoz saw concerning Judah and Jerusalem: In the last days, the mountain of the Lord's house will be the highest of all—the most important place on earth. It will be raised above the other hills, and people from all over the world will stream there to worship. People from many nations will come and say, "Come, let us go up to the mountain of the Lord, to the house of Jacob's God. There he will teach us his ways, and we will walk in his paths." For the Lord's teaching will go out from Zion; his word will go out from Jerusalem. The Lord will mediate between nations and will settle international disputes. They will hammer their swords into plowshares and their spears into pruning hooks. Nation will no longer fight against nation, nor train for war anymore.

Notice the picture of the new earth that Isaiah is creating for us. That's why he wrote this and prophesied this for us. When the Prince of Peace returns, everything is altered. People are deciding, "Let's go up to Jerusalem and worship. This is the event of all events to see the King of Kings and Lord of Lords."

SEVEN STAGES OF THE SECOND COMING

When discussing the Second Coming of the Lord, many people think Jesus will return to the Mount of Olives and that's it, but in reality, there are several stages of the Second Coming.

- **Stage 1:** During the latter part of the Tribulation, allies of the Antichrist assemble for the Battle of Armageddon. Jesus comes back to stop them!

- **Stage 2:** Commercial Babylon is destroyed. There are four or five protocols right here before Jesus sets foot on the earth.

- **Stage 3:** Jerusalem falls and is ravaged.

- **Stage 4:** The Antichrist moves south to attack the remnant because during that time Israel goes down into Bosra to receive protection.

- **Stage 5:** In glory, Jesus returns to the Mount of Olives where He was crucified.

▫ **Stage 6:** Jesus obliterates Lucifer with the brightness of His coming.

▫ **Stage 7:** Jesus instigates cleansing of the temple.

Look with me at Zechariah 13 and 14 to read about these stages of the Second Coming in more detail. It's not good news at all, but it's good to know. Actually, Zechariah 14 is one of the most graphic depictions of the Second Coming in all the Bible, but Zechariah 13 sets the stage for it. We read about stage 3 in Zechariah 13:7-8:

> *Awake, O sword, against my shepherd, and against the man that is my fellow, saith the Lord of hosts: smite the shepherd, and the sheep shall be scattered: and I will turn mine hand upon the little ones. And it shall come to pass, that in all the land, saith the Lord, two parts therein shall be cut off and die; but the third shall be left therein.*

Zechariah is prophesying that right before the Second Coming, two thirds of all of Israel will get killed. In other words, there's another holocaust coming. We don't preach about that very much, but only a third of them will remain through the latter part of the Tribulation. This is sobering!

There are approximately six million Jews living in Israel now. If four million are killed, then two million would remain. Keep in mind that we are seeing the different phases of the Second Coming here and different events are happening in each stage. The Antichrist will be dealt with, Babylon will be dealt with, and Jerusalem will be ravaged. There are actually five or six depictions of that, and it literally says four million Jews will be killed.

In stage four, the Antichrist moves south to attack the remnant because during that time Israel goes down into Bosra to receive protection. When the Antichrist goes down there, stage five takes place, which is pretty radical. Jesus returns in glory to the Mount of Olives, the very mountain where He was crucified. How cool is that? The seventh and final phase that we know is the Battle of Armageddon.

We read earlier in Matthew 24 about Jesus returning at the end of the Battle of Armageddon. The Antichrist thinks he can win, but all of a sudden, Jesus comes back as lightning from heaven. Lucifer is so stupid that he still thinks he can beat Jesus but quickly learns otherwise.

During these different stages of the Second Coming, Jesus rescues the remnant. I really like one of the depictions in Tim LaHaye's *Left Behind* series. It's as cool as it gets. I know it's fiction, but it brings to life Jesus slaying the enemy with the sword of His mouth (Rev. 19:15).

In the *Left Behind* movie, Jesus walks through the valley of Armageddon saying, "I am the root of Jesse. I am He who was and is and is to come." Come on! Jesus begins quoting Himself: "I am Stephen's signs and wonders. I am Peter's shadow. In Genesis, I was the seed of a woman. In Exodus, I was the Passover Lamb. In Leviticus, I was the High Priest. In Numbers, I was the pillar of cloud by day and the pillar of fire by night."

In the depiction, as Jesus is quoting Himself, armies start exploding, and the blood where the Battle of Armageddon takes place is up to the horse's bridle. The Bible says Jesus goes down to Bosra and releases God's wrath.

REVELATION 19:15 (NLT)

From his mouth came a sharp sword to strike down the nations. He will rule them with an iron rod. He will release the fierce wrath of God, the Almighty, like juice flowing from a winepress.

Jesus will walk right into the latter phase of the Second Coming. Before He gets to the Mount of Olives, Jesus will destroy the armies of the Antichrist with His Word. He slays them with the sword of His mouth. Glory! This is God finally bringing recompense to people who were haughty and attacking His kingdom. Look now at Zechariah 14:1-7 (NLT):

Watch, for the day of the Lord is coming when your possessions will be plundered right in front of you! I will gather all the nations to fight against Jerusalem. The city will be taken, the houses looted, and the women raped. Half the population will be taken into captivity, and the rest will be left among the ruins of the city.

Then the Lord will go out to fight against those nations, as he has fought in times past. On that day his feet will stand on the Mount of Olives, east of Jerusalem. And the Mount of Olives will split apart, making a wide valley running from east to west. Half the mountain will move toward the north and half toward the south. You will flee through this valley, for it will reach across to Azal. Yes, you will flee as you did from the earthquake in the days of King Uzziah of Judah. Then the Lord my God will come, and all his holy ones with him.

On that day the sources of light will no longer shine,
yet there will be continuous day! Only the Lord knows
how this could happen. There will be no normal day
and night, for at evening time it will still be light.

Zechariah is physically showing you what will happen when Jesus sets foot on that mountain, and he throws in a number of other details. Bottom line, the Second Coming changes everything. The changes are literally day and night different. In fact, there won't be day or night. I don't know what it will be like, but Jesus will be the only light and the only light needed. He is so bright that there will be no place where shadows can exist. Just imagine Jesus being so radiant that He encompasses everything. Even the sun revolves around Him so brightly that a shadow cannot happen. As in the beginning, life everlasting returns to a planet that has been ruled by a dark angel named Lucifer.

When the Light returns, the earth doesn't even know how to handle it. The earth says, "We don't know whether it's day or night because Jesus' light is so encompassing it lights everything up. What's going on?" What's going on is the King of Kings and the Lord of Lords is back. Whoa!

Continue reading as Zechariah's description grows even more graphic.

ZECHARIAH 14:12-15 (NLT)
And the Lord will send a plague on all the nations that
fought against Jerusalem. Their people will become like
walking corpses, their flesh rotting away. Their eyes will rot
in their sockets, and their tongues will rot in their mouths.

On that day they will be terrified, stricken by the Lord with great panic. They will fight their neighbors hand to hand. Judah, too, will be fighting at Jerusalem. The wealth of all the neighboring nations will be captured—great quantities of gold and silver and fine clothing. This same plague will strike the horses, mules, camels, donkeys, and all the other animals in the enemy camps.

These verses are pretty graphic. Imagine what it would be like to be Zechariah and see this all in a vision. We call Zechariah a minor prophet, but he was seeing some major stuff. What a depiction! Joel saw it and said, "Sound an alarm! Wake everybody up." Joel interpreted it as the Holy Spirit being poured out on everybody, but really he was talking about when God physically comes back to the planet.

SYMBOLIC OF THE SECOND COMING: NOAH AND LOT

Let's re-track a bit more and pick up additional details. Look with me at Matthew chapters 24 and 25.

MATTHEW 24:31-37

And he shall send his angels with a great sound of a trumpet, and they shall gather together his elect from the four winds, from one end of heaven to the other. Now learn a parable of the fig tree; When his branch is yet tender, and putteth forth leaves, ye know that summer is nigh: so likewise ye, when ye shall see all these things, know that it is near, even at the doors. Verily I say unto you, This generation shall not pass, till all these things be fulfilled. Heaven and earth shall pass away, but my words shall not pass away. But of that day and hour knoweth no man, no, not the angels of heaven, but my Father only. But as the days of Noah were, so shall also the coming of the Son of man be.

Jesus is speaking in a parable to His disciples. Notice verse 37 in particular. I like the parallels that Jesus gives us. For example, what happened to Noah? He went through the flood—actually, he rode on top of it. Elsewhere in the Bible, Jesus compares the Second Coming to the days of Lot. What happened to Lot? He escaped judgment. The angel said to Lot, "I can't do anything until I get you out of the city."

In both these types or symbolic representations—Noah and Lot—Jesus is giving you two thought patterns for the Church. Noah didn't get hurt, and Lot escaped. In other words, Jesus is telling us the Church escapes, and the Jews will go through the flood

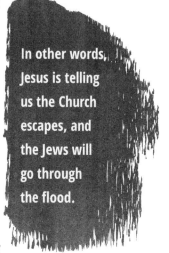

In other words, Jesus is telling us the Church escapes, and the Jews will go through the flood.

Let's look further along in Matthew 24:38-41:

For as in the days that were before the flood they were eating and drinking, marrying and giving in marriage, until the day that Noe entered into the ark, and knew not until the flood came, and took them all away; so shall also the coming of the Son of man be. Then shall two be in the field; the one shall be taken, and the other left. Two women shall be grinding at the mill; the one shall be taken, and the other left.

Now remember, Jesus is not talking about the Rapture here as people often misconstrue; He's talking about the Second Coming.

I was preaching in France a while back, and we talked about this. In France, one percent of the population is saved. In Germany, three percent is saved. Still, from the scripture we read that ultimately there will be revival where about 50 percent get saved. It's just unacceptable to me that a nation could have only one or three percent born again. Then again, during the end times even sign after sign after sign after pressure after seal after trumpet judgment after vial judgment, only half the people turn to God. You would think the percentage would be totally different as people think, *Man, I've never seen fireworks like this in all my life. I better repent!* It's absolutely absurd that the other half is saying, "It's not worth it to repent."

Nevertheless, Jesus removes the unrighteous off the earth and leaves the righteous. Again, this text does not refer to the Rapture but the Second Coming. In fact, all the accounts in Matthew refer to the Second Coming, even though I hear preachers all over the world mistakenly explain it otherwise. Jesus is very, very clear in Matthew 24.

SHEEP AND GOAT JUDGMENT

In Matthew 25, we read more about Jesus sitting on the throne of His kingdom, and the Sheep and Goat Judgment or "the Judgment of the Nations."

MATTHEW 25:31-34

When the Son of man shall come in his glory, and all the holy angels with him, then shall he sit upon the throne of his glory: And before him shall be gathered all nations: and he shall separate them one from another, as a shepherd divideth his sheep from the goats: And he shall set the sheep on his right hand, but the goats on the left. Then shall the King say unto them on his right hand, Come, ye blessed of my Father, inherit the kingdom prepared for you from the foundation of the world.

Notice it doesn't say in verse 31 when Jesus comes back to catch the Church away and receive it unto Himself. No. That's a whole different event that was seven years earlier. At the Rapture we go up to meet Jesus in the air. At the Second Coming, Jesus physically comes back and puts His foot on the Mount of Olives. These are two completely and totally separate events.

These scriptures above speak of the Second Coming when Jesus wants natural-bodied, righteous people to "inherit the kingdom prepared for you from the foundation of the world." When Adam sinned, Jesus didn't say, "Oops. He messed up. Too bad. It won't happen now." No, it was simply an interruption in God's plan. Yet right here, Jesus is returning to God's plan. Even though they're not glorious like Adam and Eve were before the Fall, He likes a natural kingdom, a natural earth. Too often people have this weird thinking that heaven is ethereal, but the truth is, heaven is more real than the earth.

God wants natural man to have a natural kingdom, and He's going to reign in that natural kingdom for a thousand years. Jesus will reign on David's throne. Talk about humility—Jesus will sit on a man's throne. I believe that Jesus' humility will be the one thing that shocks us the most when we see

Him face to face. His mercy, kindness, and humility will impact you unbelievably.

There's a lot of erroneous teaching about the Sheep and Goat Judgment because people misunderstand who Jesus is talking to and what He means in Matthew 7.

MATTHEW 7:21-23 (NLT)

Not everyone who calls out to me, "Lord! Lord!" will enter the Kingdom of Heaven. Only those who actually do the will of my Father in heaven will enter. On judgment day many will say to me, "Lord! Lord! We prophesied in your name and cast out demons in your name and performed many miracles in your name." But I will reply, "I never knew you. Get away from me, you who break God's laws."

On Judgment Day people say to Jesus, "Lord! Lord! We prophesied in Your name, cast out demons in Your name, and performed miracles in Your name." Jesus responds, "I never knew you. Get away from Me." That is not Jesus talking to the Church. It refers to people in the latter part of the Tribulation who try to work their way into the Second Coming. Sadly, people misdirect the whole passage by directing this scene toward the Church to scare people into salvation. It's disgusting to promote fear in people.

You will see here that Jesus judges the nations based on how they treat Israel during that time. I believe Iran and Iraq probably won't be here, but there will be people from those nations who are there. A nation as a whole that doesn't treat Israel correctly will not enter the Millennial Kingdom.

Egypt will be there, although over the years Egypt has been horrible to Israel. But one president of Egypt, Anwar Sadaat, made peace with Israel, and it blesses the whole nation for a thousand years. He paid a price for it. His plan was to be a friend to Israel, but he was assassinated. He was shot during a parade the day after he made peace with Israel.

God's Kingdom

God's kingdom is a very physical thing. You will notice that the land will be partitioned based on tribe—tribe of Judah, tribe of Benjamin. The whole land will be opened and be much larger than Israel is today.

Someone might ask, "Aren't some of the wars that are happening in the Middle East kind of Israel's fault because they took the land?" No. Israel received its land by proclamation in the Balfour Declaration. As we discussed in Chapter 4, Chaim Weizmann invented a way of producing acetone that helped England win World War I.[1] England was so grateful, they asked him what he wanted as a reward. He said, "I want a homeland for my people." So, the Balfour Declaration was a public statement issued by the British government in 1917 during World War I, announcing a "national home for the Jewish people" in Palestine, which was then an Ottoman region with a small minority of Jewish people.

Through the United Nations, U.S. President Harry Truman put forth the very first vote to pass a declaration saying Israel had a right to their land because they were there thousands of years before. So, let's be clear. Every war from then until now is not because Palestine is defending their nation from Israel who took their land. Israel didn't take anything. Their nation was to them by proclamation of God, England, and the United States.

People often say, "But Israel is occupying Palestinian land." Wrong. They are not "occupying" anything. It's theirs! It would be like someone from Canada coming to America and saying, "We're taking Colorado."

"No, you're not taking Colorado. It's part of the U.S.A.," you would respond.

"You're occupying Colorado."

"Well, you're not occupying Colorado."

Wouldn't that be crazy? It makes no sense whatsoever. When it comes to Israel, Lucifer has deceived the whole world into thinking Israel is to blame for war in the Middle East. The Palestinians continually stab, bomb, and aggressively and violently attack Israel. Jews must be continually on guard against these acts of violence round the clock. We have no conception of this kind of Luciferic mentality the Jews encounter on a daily basis.

But what we do know is that you and I will have a front-row seat for the battle of the ages. A rebel angel named Lucifer dared say, "I'll be like the Most High." After a six-day period when the angel tried to destroy God's creation, God said, "No you won't. I'll send the seed that will bruise you." Hallelujah. And Jesus came and redeemed us from Adam's fall, and this whole plan is playing out while we're alive on the earth.

If you were here 500 years ago, you would say, "Wow. Well, I have no idea what's going on." But you are watching the battle of the ages unfold where Lucifer is saying, "I'm going to kill Israel." He can't get to the Father, so He tries to get what's on the Father's heart. He wants to annihilate them. But the devil cannot kill Israel. He's tried, but he just can't get it done. In the midst of it all, God raised up the Church, so for the past 2,000-year period God has had the believer on Earth with the keys to the kingdom. Come on now!

During the Millennium, God will tout you and show you off. It's amazing how He will brag on His kids who first trusted in Him. God will show forth His glory because you trusted in Him when you couldn't see Him. He's proud of you, believer!

Amazingly enough, however, Jesus will reign right here on earth for a thousand years, and people still will reject Him. Not you—you trusted Him when some guy preached the Bible, so God will say, "Look at my Church. They took Me at My Word." *Wow.*

> God will show forth His glory because you trusted in Him when you couldn't see Him. He's proud of you, believer!

We are viewing this battle unfold right this minute, and right after we exit the planet via the Rapture, God will physically deal with Lucifer. He defeated him 2,000 years ago, and the bully has been under our feet ever since. But it won't be long before Jesus tosses him in a deep, dark pit.

PHYSICAL CHANGES

The Sheep and Goat Judgment happens immediately, but after that, there's not a lot written about the physical changes implemented as the Millennial Reign begins. The Bible talks about a 75-day interval period, and there will be about 25 days for something else to happen.

There will also be about 45 days to cleanse the Temple that will be rebuilt. For God to be here, even the dirt has to go through natural purifications. Even the dirt has to get ready for Him to come back. There will be 45 days of physical purification to get ready for God to be there. There will still be natural people there who have the stain of Adam on them, and God will be like, "I can't have that stain near Me." Think about it. The Temple area has to be cleaned for 45 days, and yet God lives in you. Whoooo! He who knew no sin was made sin that I'd be made the righteousness of God in Him (2 Cor. 5:21). He didn't deserve sin, but He was made sin. I didn't deserve righteousness, but He made me righteous. This gives you a picture of what He thinks about you.

The book of Ezekiel spends four to eight chapters discussing the particulars of the Temple where Jesus will dwell. There are all kinds of natural and spiritual things that he outlines.

Above it all, you will see Jesus smile like you've never seen before. He will say, "I get to come back, but I won't have to get beat up this time!" He's so normal. He'll be thinking, *Isn't this cool? I get to come back as proper as it ought to be.* The first time He came, He realized, "I am separated from My Father." But this time, Jesus will say, "At last, all creation will see what My Dad is really like. I'll be able to implement the mercy of My Father for a thousand years."

Jesus raised you up to help Him implement that mercy, which is the whole point during that thousand years. Mercy will reign. Kindness will reign. Goodness will reign. We are all in preparation for implementing that thousand-year kingdom.

Jesus, we bow our hearts in adoration to You even now. We recognize that the earth is just about to prepare for all these traumatic events, but we are so thankful and blessed that we get to focus on the Reward Seat of Christ and the Marriage Supper of the Lamb. We get to focus on this grand event where You physically return to be seen by all and receive the honor due Your name. Every knee will bow, every tongue will confess and bless Your wonderful name, dear Jesus. Honor and dominion and power unto You who was and is and is to come. Hallelujah.

It's been said that the book of Revelation is a book of worship because the entire book is about Jesus being revealed and how we worship Him as King. The book is also about His love for us and His return for us. The Lord prompts me over and over and over to make sure His people know how much He loves them.

> The purpose of end-time teaching is to convey to you how excited Jesus is to see you, and He wants you excited to see Him as well.

The purpose of end-time teaching is to convey to *you* how excited Jesus is to see *you*, and He wants you excited to see Him as well.

Think how much you love some of the people in your life. That's only a fraction of His love for you. You can multiply that many times over, and you still wouldn't be able to wrap your head around His great love for you. But God is planning to express that love to bless you throughout eternity. What He has planned for you is beyond amazing.

CHAPTER 13

LET'S MAX IT OUT BEFORE WE GO

THE CHURCH HAD a powerful beginning. The book of Acts records an outpouring of power—signs, wonders, and miracles all through the first six chapters. Yet the Word of God promises us even more explosive power as the Church Age wraps up. As the Author and Finisher of our faith, Jesus has already given us a glimpse of what the last-days Church will look like. In fact, He demonstrated it for us, and He's waiting for the Church to pick up where He left off and do even greater works!

Christians often ask, "What am I supposed to be like?" Look at Jesus. You're supposed to be just like Him. Jesus said, "I tell you the truth, anyone who believes in me will do the same works I have done, and even greater works, because I am going to be with the Father" (John 14:12 NLT). The Greek word for *same* is the word *parallel*. In other words, your works will be identical to His. Your whole life should be a total expression of Jesus the way Jesus is an expression of the Father.

A Picture of the Last Days

Look with me at James 5, which is actually an end-time chapter. It doesn't paint a very pretty picture of the end-time climate, but it does show how we are to respond to it. Verse 3 sums up a lot, saying, "Your gold and silver are corroded. The very wealth you were counting on will eat away your flesh like fire. This corroded treasure you have hoarded will testify against you on the day of judgment" (NLT). So how do we counter this bleak picture?

Patience can prevent us from missing something important, and stability prevents us from floundering.

James 5:7-8

Be patient therefore, brethren, unto the coming of the Lord. Behold, the husband-man waiteth for the precious fruit of the earth, and hath long patience for it, until he receive the early and latter rain. Be ye also patient; stablish your hearts: for the coming of the Lord draweth nigh.

James tells us right here that when we look at the Church, we should see patience and stability and stability and patience. God wants us to be just as patient as He is and stabilize or establish our hearts for the Lord's coming. Face it—we humans don't like patience, but it keeps us in position. Patience can prevent us from missing something important, and stability prevents us from floundering. James tells us why Jesus is looking for both these elements before He returns.

JAMES 5:10-11 (MSG)

Take the old prophets as your mentors. They put up with anything, went through everything, and never once quit, all the time honoring God. What a gift life is to those who stay the course! You've heard, of course, of Job's staying power, and you know how God brought it all together for him at the end. That's because God cares, cares right down to the last detail.

James says if you stay the course, you will have something to get excited about in the end. It worked that way for Job. What he greatly feared came upon him, but Job ended up with double what he lost. In other words, James is showing you that there's a purpose for being patient and stable. The end-time outpouring will see double what the early church saw. That's righteous!

James does not just say, "Be patient. Be stable. Be patient. Be stable." No, he tells you to be patient and stable so you remain in position to finish off the Church Age like it should be finished. Why is it even necessary to say this? Because we all know friends and acquaintances who are not in church like they were 20 years ago. Somewhere along the way they decided it wasn't worth it.

That won't be me. I haven't come this far to back up at the end. Some people have gotten weary in well doing, but I refuse to be one of them. This is it! The grand finale is coming! Everything you've ever heard and been taught about Jesus Christ is for *right now!*

JAMES 5:16

Confess your faults one to another, and pray one for another, that ye may be healed. The effectual fervent prayer of a righteous man availeth much.

James is showing us that despite the frailties of the flesh, we must respond with the supernatural: we confess our faults and pray one for another. In other words, despite your frailty and humanness, do something *supernatural.* Elijah did.

JAMES 5:17-18

Elias [Elijah] *was a man subject to like passions as we are, and he prayed earnestly that it might not rain: and it rained not on the earth by the space of three years and six months. And he prayed again, and the heaven gave rain, and the earth brought forth her fruit.*

This *is* a picture of what the last-day Church should look like. Elijah dictated the natural atmosphere for three and a half years—just as we should be dictating the spiritual atmosphere now.

Elijah's ministry was not known for great preaching. The Bible doesn't mention one word about his preaching, but people knew God was with him. They didn't understand him, but they recognized the power and presence of God with him. Maybe you're in the same situation. Maybe your friends think you are crazy. No matter, they should be able to see God at work in your life.

I like what that one preacher said, "Preach Jesus. Use words if necessary." Your life preaches for you just as Elijah's life preached for him. Even in the ministry of Jesus, people didn't say, "Whoa, He's a great orator." No, people said, "Listen to the authority of His words. There's power when He speaks."

James is making the point that authority backed Elijah's words. Elijah said, "Oh, by the way, it will not rain for three and a half years," and it did not. Elijah walked in so much God-given authority that even nature obeyed him. What does that say about the Church? It says we should be walking in so much authority that the flesh, the devil, the weather, and everything else is subject to us because we're walking like the sons and daughters of God we are.

God is not looking for you to be weird or crazy—just powerful. The last thing Jesus said before He left this earth was that He would send the Holy Spirit to "[fill] you with power from heaven" (Luke 24:49 NLT). Jesus expects you to walk in the power He gave you—walking through this natural world supernaturally to finish spectacularly.

Too many people hear sermon after sermon after sermon and still don't take hold of their God-given power.

MAX OUT

Too many people hear sermon after sermon after sermon and still don't take hold of their God-given power. They still don't look like Jesus or do His works. Paul had something to say about this.

1 THESSALONIANS 1:5-6 (NLT)

For when we brought you the Good News, it was not only with words but also with power, for the Holy Spirit gave you full assurance that what we said was true. And you

257

know of our concern for you from the way we lived when we were with you. So you received the message with joy from the Holy Spirit in spite of the severe suffering it brought you. In this way, you imitated both us and the Lord.

The Greek word for *imitated* is *mimicked.* Paul is saying that the believers began to imitate them and Jesus. They did not listen to 25 years or even five years of messages to form this conclusion. They heard one message and *immediately began* to imitate Paul and Jesus. Now that's pretty radical!

A lot of times you hear, "If I could travel with the right minister, it would be different. If I could be around this or that famous preacher, then the anointing will come on me." But what about being around Jesus like these guys in the Thessalonian church? They heard one message and said, "I can act like Paul. I can act like Jesus."

What moved them so powerfully? *Simple authorization.* Jesus said, "I'm not here. You are here for Me. Be Me." And they simply took Jesus at His word and did it! The message is so simple it almost bores some Christians, and yet it's the very instruction that ignited the early church to action.

The early church wasn't based on an abundance of teaching like today where we are surrounded by it day and night on every media platform. They didn't have a gazillion electronically archived messages or libraries of books. They had one message: "I can be just like Jesus." There's something about authorization that produces liberty and boldness.

Let me ask you this. Before you got your driver's license, did you ever drive a little? If yes, I bet you weren't as bold circling your neighborhood when you saw a police officer drive by. In my case, I grew up on a farm. Let's call it Hillbillyville, Louisiana, U.S.A., and I drove an Impala out on the farm when I was seven and drove a truck when I was ten. I remember driving the truck down the highway hauling hay at age 13 with a policeman behind me. I thought, *Oh dear, Lord, I don't even have my license.* I couldn't wait until I was a legal driver so when an officer passed, I could confidently say to myself, *No problem here. I'm authorized!*

Let me give you another example. For a time, my sister and brother-in-law lived as missionaries in Heidelberg, Germany, and when I visited I could travel on the Autobahn. It's just the coolest, classiest highway on earth with absolutely no speed limit. You can max it out! You are authorized to go as fast as you want to go. Come on.

When they drove me to Brussels, there was a sticker in their car that read *155 MPH LIMIT.* The car wasn't rated for more, but that was plenty. It seemed we were flying down the road, but even then, plenty of cars passed us. I thought, *This thought pattern to max it out is the coolest thing on the planet!*

One time, a German pastor drove me from Frankfurt to Zurich, with the speedometer at the redline limit the whole time. "Don't you ever want to take it off redline and let the motor rest?" I asked.

"Why would I want to do that?" he said, looking at me like something was wrong with me. I thought his motor would blow up, but his thought pattern was to max it out.

On the other hand, it would be weird to be cruising on the Autobahn at 80 kilometers per hour when the speed limit is

300 kilometers per hour. Would you want to drive a Porsche or a Ferrari on the Autobahn going 60 miles per hour in first gear? People would pass you wondering, *What's wrong with that driver? With 500 horsepower, the driver should be doing 300 kilometers, so why is he crawling?*

Friend, that's a picture of the Church today. We've been authorized to be just like Jesus, so there's no way we should be satisfied in first gear. We Christians should think like Autobahn drivers: *We're authorized! Let's get going! Let's max it out!* Those Autobahn drivers are a different breed. They floor it up to a stop sign—varoom, varoom—and then slam on the brakes. There are two speeds—varoom and errrrt—because the drivers are on authorized overdrive, max-it-out-all-the-time speed. It's wonderful! If you need to get somewhere, drive like a plane. Do it. Get there.

> We Christians should think like Autobahn drivers: We're authorized! Let's get going! Let's max it out!

Church! That's what we need to do! We need to max out what we're authorized to do in these last days. We've settled for such subpar performance when we should be excelling for Jesus.

YOU ARE AUTHORIZED

Look what Jesus said when the time came that He needed to duplicate His ministry to reach farther and faster.

LUKE 9:1-2 (NLT)

One day Jesus called together his twelve disciples and gave them power and authority to cast out all demons and to heal all diseases. Then he sent them out to tell everyone about the Kingdom of God and to heal the sick.

Guess how long it took them to get results? *Instantly!* Let that soak in. Did they wait five or six years for results? No. Someone might say, "But those were the twelve around Jesus for three and a half years. Of course, they would get instant results. They traveled with Him." Really? Keep reading.

LUKE 10:1 (NLT)

The Lord now chose seventy-two other disciples and sent them ahead in pairs to all the towns and places he planned to visit.

How long did it take the 70 to duplicate Jesus' ministry? *Instantly.* Did it take them one to five years of preparation? No. Don't misunderstand me, preparation time is not lost time. My point is that too often Christians don't think they qualify to do the works of Jesus, but Jesus Himself qualified us! In Luke 9:49, John tells Jesus:

LUKE 9:49-50 (NLT)

"Master, we saw someone using your name to cast out demons, but we told him to stop because he isn't in our group." But Jesus said, "Don't stop him! Anyone who is not against you is for you."

The guy got results, and he was not even authorized. The guy had enough brains to see what worked. He did what Jesus did and got the same results Jesus got. It freaked out the disciples. "When the seventy-two disciples returned, they joyfully reported to Him, 'Lord, even the demons obey us when we use your name!'" (Luke 10:17 NLT). Notice how Jesus responded.

Luke 10:18-20 (TLB)

"Yes," he told them, "I saw Satan falling from heaven as a flash of lightning! And I have given you authority over all the power of the Enemy, and to walk among serpents and scorpions and to crush them. Nothing shall injure you! However, the important thing is not that demons obey you, but that your names are registered as citizens of heaven."

Jesus was saying to the disciples, "Obviously devils bow to you because I authorized you." The demons were even more freaked out when they were ordered around and began screaming at him, "What do you want with us, O Son of God? You have no right to torment us yet" (Matt. 8:29 TLB). They knew exactly what was going on. The King of Kings and Lord of Lords encased in flesh was all of a sudden authorized and operating in Adam's authority.

> **They just went, used the name, and did the works. You can too!**

Jesus authorized His followers to do the same, and they did. It didn't take long, and it was not hard for them. They didn't wait until they learned to flow. They just went, used the name, and did the works. *You can too!*

NINE FINGERS GROW

Years ago, I was invited to be a guest on the God Channel in Newcastle, England, after teaching on the gifts of the Spirit in a Bible school there. An actor who was not born again was hired to host the show and interview me. With a strong English accent, he asked, "Now, Joe, in one of your services, a person with no fingers grew fingers. Is that correct?"

"Yes, that's right," I said. "I was preaching in a youth service, but one of the youth wouldn't stop talking while I was preaching. I walked back toward him, but they continued talking. 'You guys need to be hearing the Word,' I said, but they still talked. 'Everybody under 21 stand up,' I said, but the talking continued. I tried to explain how the Lord wanted to use them, but even standing up, they continued talking.

"Suddenly, the Lord gave me a word of knowledge that somebody had damaged their knuckles. A woman who had only one finger came down front; her other fingers were cut off. I said to Jesus, 'Lord, I was thinking You meant arthritis—not fingers.'

> Boom. Pop. Nine fingers grew out instantly!

"But we serve a great big God. I prayed, 'Lord, thank You for new fingers for this woman.' *Boom. Pop.* Nine fingers grew out instantly! Even the talking youth went silent as they watched her fingers grow."

Meanwhile, the English actor interviewing me totally freaked out. "Oh, my God! Oh, my God!" he kept saying while the show cut to break.

What built a platform for this kind of supernatural demonstration? Being authorized by Jesus to do the works of Jesus. It's simply faith in the Name.

KNOW YOUR LINES

Matthew 28 tells us all about what we believers should look like before we leave this earth. It's not weird. It's not strange. It's looking like *Jesus*.

Matthew 28:18-19 (NLT)

Jesus came and told his disciples, "I have been given all authority in heaven and on earth. Therefore, go and make disciples of all the nations, baptizing them in the name of the Father and the Son and the Holy Spirit."

This is the Great Commission, which in the original Greek says: "I'm giving you freedom of action. I'm giving you the right to act on My behalf." That's radical! We recognize this level of authority as power of attorney. But Jesus took it one step further and said, "You take My place. I'm not here, but you are here for Me."

For some odd reason, that reminds me of Clint Eastwood movies. When I was a kid, my dad took me to see *Magnum Force* and *Dirty Harry* movies while my mom, thank God, took to me to church.

In the classic *Dirty Harry* movie, Clint Eastwood holds a .44 magnum and says the line, "Go ahead. Make my day." That's the most iconic Eastwood line ever! But it's not real. It's just a movie. I've read that he doesn't even like guns.

The director told Clint, "We'll get you a fake gun, and you follow my lead. Walk over to the guy on the ground and make us think you're going to blow his head off." As a professional actor, Clint learned his lines. All the cameras were ready and focused. The assistant yelled, "Quiet on the set!"

The director said, "Action!" and Clint said his famous line, "In all the confusion, I can't remember if I've shot five times or six times. Do you feel lucky, punk? Go ahead and make my day."

The guy on the ground thought his brains would get blown out, but the whole thing was fake. Clint read a script. He was acting.

How could he be so bold? Because he knew his lines.

You've also got lines and a holy script! That Hollywood script didn't count for anything except box office tickets, but your script is eternal. The problem is most Christians aren't bold because they don't know their lines. Wouldn't it be weird if all of a sudden the director hollered "Action!" and Clint said in a monotone voice, "Go ahead. Make my day." That would be a horrible box office flop.

> **You've also got lines and a holy script!**

Even worse, most Christians are confused and think they are the guy on the ground about to get shot. Then they hear a little Word and think, *Well, maybe I'm Clint Eastwood*. Listen! If your Christian walk were a movie, you are not the guy on the ground or Dirty Harry. You are Jesus, acting out His part on the earth.

Your script is called the Bible, and it's 66 books full of your lines. The more of these lines you get in you, the bolder you will be. When the devil comes at you, you say, "It is written!" I'm not talking about you using some fake monotone, "It, it, is, uh, written...." No! Know your lines!

You have the holy script that gives you freedom of action. You don't have to wait for an unction or a special command to do what the Word says. Just do it!

'GET UP IN JESUS' NAME'

Colleen and I were living in California a few years back and went to a friend's house to visit. As we pulled in the circle drive,

I suggested Colleen and Lauren get out and wait for me to park since there were so many cars. I looked behind me, and it was clear. But as I backed up the van, God help me, I ran over my wife.

Colleen screeched bloody murder! I pulled the van forward and hurried back to her as she lay on the ground screaming in agony. People gasped and came running in panic.

> "My God! My God! This is real!" she shrieked as she was instantly made whole.

I walked up to Colleen and said, "I command your ankle and leg to be healed right now in the name of Jesus. Get up!" Colleen looked at me like I was crazy. I said, "Get up in Jesus' name!" and stood her on her feet. The power of God coursed up and down her body like heat!

"My God! My God! This is real!" she shrieked as she was instantly made whole. Colleen had no pain—not during the party, not the next day, not ever. Did some special gift of the Spirit operate? No. The name of Jesus operated because He authorized me. I have freedom of action, and so do you.

This is how Jesus wants us to finish the Church Age. You do it with your authority. Too often we wait on somebody else to do it, but Jesus is waiting on *you!*

TWO ANGELS DELIVER NEW HEART

Let me give you one more example. Years ago, I was ushering in a church in Tulsa and working for a couple of ministries. I really wanted to help, but I did not want to preach. About that time, my buddy Ross Roberts was preaching at a camp meeting and made me go preach with him. As we got off the plane, a camera crew met us because the church had put posters all over the town saying, *Jesus is your Healer.*

My minister friend screamed into the camera, "I dare you to bring the sick! Bring the lame, the halt, and the withered to the meetings. God will heal them!" I thought, *Can't you just ask them to come to the meetings?* I ducked my head and freaked out.

I preached Sunday morning, and my sermon was horrible—hideous, even, and dry as corn shucks. A lady even came up afterward and said, "Don't try to do this for a living!" I'm serious.

My buddy was to preach Sunday night, but he was delayed going in. I headed on out to my seat and sat waiting for him to come in. All of a sudden, I had discerning of spirits operate. I looked up, and two angels stood right in front of me. They were huge—nine or ten feet tall—and looked like linebackers. The two angels looked very purposeful. They didn't change their expression at all, but just stared right at me. I thought, *I'm not sure what angel protocol is, but I'm going to keep my mouth shut. I won't bother them if they don't bother me.* I was freaked out.

Ross came in and asked, "Joe, you got something?"

"No, I don't have a thing," I said. "You preach."

He got up and started preaching for a few minutes, and the Holy Ghost said to me, "Those angels have come to deliver a woman a new heart."

How cool! I thought. *My buddy will call that out.* But he didn't call that out. He looked at me again and said, "Joe, have you got something?"

"Yes!" I said, "There's somebody here who has heart trouble." A lady came walking down the aisle. I said to her, "You need a brand-new heart because the Lord sent two angels to deliver it to you." We prayed for her, and she fell out under the power.

On the way down, she had congestive heart failure and looked like she might die before we could pray for her. After we prayed, she jumped up saying, "Whooo, glory!" She went back to her seat a vibrant picture of health.

When my buddy gave an altar call, the woman and her whole family got saved. The next day, the woman returned to her cardiologist who said, "Wow! What happened to you? You seem like you have energy today."

"I went to this crazy church service and got healed," she excitedly explained.

"I'll be the judge of that!" the doctor said. He did an EKG, another EKG, and yet another EKG. Finally, he said, "I don't get it, but you have a perfectly flawless heart muscle like that of a 17-year-old." The doctor was so freaked out that he called the news media, and they came to cover the story.

That night the news media came to the service, and it was a circus. It was the craziest church service I've ever been in. I was even scared, and I'm not scared of anything. After that, the service was packed out with a variety of people. Some people had candles, some had incense, some had crystals.

The headline in the afternoon newspaper read: *Angels Bring Woman New Heart. Christ Redeemed Her from the Curse of the Law.* The place packed out again, and all the people came forward to give their lives to the Lord.

Was it great preaching that brought those miracles? No. More than one person told me not to preach for a living. Ross set the tone for the meeting when he said, "I dare you to come! God will heal you!"

Jesus pictures the last-days Church like the ministry of Elijah—bold, daring, miraculous, and powerful. Connect the ministry of Jesus to that, and you've got mercy, kindness, goodness, and grace. Hear and speak the Word like never before, pray in tongues like never before, and get out where the people are and do the works of Jesus. This is what Jesus wants to see right before He comes back. The 12 and the 70 just went, and it's time we do the same. It's time we do the works of Jesus before we take off to meet Him in the air.

> The headline in the afternoon newspaper read: *Angels Bring Woman New Heart. Christ Redeemed Her from the Curse of the Law.*

CHAPTER 14

THE MILLENNIAL REIGN OF CHRIST

WHEN THE GLORIFIED Church comes back with Jesus at the Second Coming, there will be a dual group of people who live on planet Earth. There will be the body of Christ and natural righteous people whom Jesus welcomes to the kingdom. You will be overseeing these natural people and be a sphere of influence in their lives. Jesus will assume His throne, and the new order in the Millennial Reign of Christ will be supernaturally natural and cooler than anything and everything you can possibly imagine.

When Jesus arrives, blazing in beauty and surrounded by His angels, He will take His place on His throne. You will hear these words: "Come, you who are blessed by my Father, inherit the Kingdom prepared for you from the creation of the world" (Matt. 25:34 NLT). Israel will be the head of all nations. Jesus will rule from His throne in Jerusalem, and you will implement His kingdom.

Best yet, during the Millennial Reign of Christ the devil will be locked up and get everything he deserves.

REVELATION 20:1-3

And I saw an angel come down from heaven, having the key of the bottomless pit and a great chain in his hand. And he laid hold on the dragon, that old serpent, which is the Devil, and Satan, and bound him a thousand years, and cast him into the bottomless pit, and shut him up, and set a seal upon him, that he should deceive the nations no more, till the thousand years should be fulfilled: and after that he must be loosed a little season.

NATURALLY SUPERNATURAL

Jesus begins this wonderful Millennial Reign with righteous, natural-bodied people to rebuild the scorched and damaged earth. Don't you love verse 3 where it says regarding the devil, "and shut him up"?

During the Millennial Reign, life will be natural and glorious, all at the same time. Jesus will let natural man rebuild the earth. Creations and inventions will soar and technology will go ballistically cool with God Himself living on the planet. Creativity will be off the charts with access to some really cool inventions. Jesus will permeate the land with peace—even the lamb and the lion will be pals. Your glorified body will transport you from heaven to earth and right through walls. You will be the emergency glory police or spiritual peace-keeping force empowered and skilled in the gifts of the Spirit to implement the kingdom among natural-bodied people on earth.

On television you might see the apostle Paul being interviewed. Or maybe Paul will have his own show called *What Life Was Really Like in the Church Age* where he calls your pastor for an interview. I can just imagine Paul asking his guests, "Did you rise up in dominion and walk in authority and victory?" You'll probably hear the whole audience shout, "Hallelujah! Glory to God!" and give a standing ovation.

Movies will probably be made about John the Baptist, Elijah, and David defeating Goliath. Jesus will be on Fox News and maybe even CNN. You will see Jesus on Skype, Facebook, Instagram, and Twitter. He will permeate everything!

During the Millennial Reign, life will be natural and glorious, all at the same time.

As I've said before, at the Second Coming, there will be a great earthquake and the Mount of Olives will split in two. There's a great valley there, and the water will come from the Dead Sea right by Jesus as it flows outward and heals all the waters in the earth. There's so much life in Jesus; everything about Him is life everlasting. Jesus will quicken the whole earth. He also said out of your belly will flow living water.

Jesus will be on Fox News and maybe even CNN.

So what a wonderful start for this thousand years. The minute Jesus assumes the throne, peace is instituted, and we will enjoy a thousand years of rest. The earth has been getting ready for this for a long time after enduring a 6,000-year curse that's about to be lifted off. The Bible says that creation groans and travails, waiting for that day to come. It's just about here!

CHANGES IN NATURE

Nature itself is in for dramatic changes during the Millennial Reign. We see in Isaiah 11 some of the specific elements instantly altered:

ISAIAH 11:4-7 (NLT)

He will give justice to the poor and make fair decisions for the exploited. The earth will shake at the force of his word, and one breath from his mouth will destroy the wicked. He will wear righteousness like a belt and truth like an undergarment. In that day the wolf and the lamb will live together; the leopard will lie down with the baby goat. The calf and the yearling will be safe with the lion, and a little child will lead them all. The cow will graze near the bear. The cub and the calf will lie down together. The lion will eat hay like a cow.

Especially notice verse 6—that is a radical change from life as we know it now. Can you imagine a little kid with a lion on a leash? You might take your kids to the park to walk your lion instead of your dog. It will be crazy cool when a tiny kid walks a great big lion around the park. The minute Jesus arrives on the planet, even beasts will be different. I plan on having a pet lion. What will you have?

Maybe you'll have a tiger or an alligator in your backyard. You can tell the alligator what to do, and he will obey. "Hey, alligator, don't go over here. Sit, alligator, sit." We will have complete dominion, and it will boggle your mind. It is almost hard for our brains to comprehend these changes. They seem bizarre right now, but during the Millennium you will be in a glorified body and live as never before! What an incredible place we will enjoy!

ISAIAH 11:8-9 (NLT)

The baby will play safely near the hole of a cobra. Yes, a little child will put its hand in a nest of deadly snakes without harm. Nothing will hurt or destroy in all my holy mountain, for as the waters fill the sea, so the earth will be filled with people who know the Lord.

> Maybe you'll have a tiger or an alligator in your backyard.

ISAIAH 30:26 (NLT)

The moon will be as bright as the sun, and the sun will be seven times brighter—like the light of seven days in one!

Whoa—that's some kind of sunlight!

There will be plenty of time for enjoying life. As I mentioned earlier, I plan to play golf for the first six months of the Millennium. I will play golf at St. Andrews, then Augusta, then Hawaii. I will be translated to Pebble Beach, head to Hawaii, and come right back around to St. Andrews. Come on now! They will have tee boxes for the mortals and tee boxes for the saints.

It's amazing how some people think we won't want to do natural things like sports or music. Some people think we will only do spiritual things or work once we're in glorified bodies. No, friend, the Millennium will be a thousand years of rest. We will have some duties, but whatever we do, it will be joyous not laborious. Our thinking can be way too religious sometimes.

Obviously, the changes in nature will include a change in photosynthesis. The earth will probably have a more oxygen-rich environment. In fact, I believe life will be like it was before the flood, when people lived a thousand years, and the air was so much richer and more vibrant. It will be easy for natural people to live a thousand years—no big deal. How cool is that? What a wonderful time to be on the planet when Satan is bound, and the glory of the Lord is all over the earth.

ATTENDING CHURCH

Will there still be church during the Millennium? Absolutely. Actually, we don't hear a lot of teaching about the Millennium because people think, *Why do we need that?* Only because you will be living here a thousand years or so. Notice how concentrated church will be.

ZECHARIAH 14:16-19

And it shall come to pass, that every one that is left of all the nations which came against Jerusalem shall even go up from year to year to worship the King, the Lord of hosts, and to keep the feast of tabernacles. And it shall be, that whoso will not come up of all the families of the earth unto Jerusalem to worship the King, the Lord of hosts, even upon them shall be no rain. And if the family of Egypt go not up, and come not, that have no rain; there shall be the plague, wherewith the Lord will smite the heathen that come not up to keep the feast of tabernacles. This shall be the

punishment of Egypt, and the punishment of all nations
that come not up to keep the feast of tabernacles.

You just read how we will be required to attend church and the Feast of Tabernacles once a year. Right now, we need to hear the Word daily to sustain us, but Jesus is so powerful that hearing Him personally once a year will sustain us during the Millennium. Imagine that! In Jesus' presence, once a year will carry you the whole year.

The passage above says people who don't go church will be heathen. Even though everyone is born again at the beginning of the Millennium, when the natural people have children who reach the age of accountability, they will need to be born again. They will need to hear preaching and go to Jerusalem once a year to worship. You will say to them, "You might want to get born again. Jesus is sitting right over there!"

Some may revolt, although I don't know how anyone could reject Jesus. How could anyone not like Jesus with nothing but wonderful all over the earth? Nevertheless, people will reject Him. That's why the Bible says in the ages to come He'll show forth His goodness and kindness to those who first trusted in Him (Eph. 2:7). That's us, praise God, the Church!

SACRIFICES REINSTITUTED

During the Millennial Reign, sacrifices will be reinstituted. The Temple will be rebuilt right after we're raptured, and all throughout the thousand years, the Jews will offer sacrifices in Israel. It seems bizarre in a way that they will still be killing animals, but the sacrificial act will symbolically look back at what Jesus accomplished on the cross. Of course, in the sacrifices recorded in the Old Testament, the Jews looked forward to what Jesus would accomplish in the future.

These sacrifices will be a picture of the hideousness of sin and how Jesus gave His flesh to be beaten and His blood poured out to redeem mankind. Jesus will do this for those who don't want to get born again. He will show them what He did for them: "I gave My life for you! I ransomed you!"

REBUILDING THE EARTH

As we mentioned earlier, the earth will be so damaged from the Great Tribulation that God will have man rebuild the earth.

ISAIAH 61:4 (NLT)

They will rebuild the ancient ruins, repairing cities
destroyed long ago. They will revive them, though they
have been deserted for many generations.

I have preached in the Ukraine many times, and I remember on one of the trips noticing how sadly dilapidated just about everything was. The power went out every day. The gas went out every day. The water went out every day. Frankly, most people don't own anything, so they don't respect anything. That's the work of communism.

For the first 100 years of the Millennium, many of these former communist countries will be using super soakers filled with Clorox, spraying their whole country. There will be brooms and mops and super soakers cleaning with bleach from one end of the country to the other.

The Lord will let them do it, too. You may think He will just twitch His nose like some fictionalized *Bewitched* show of the

1960s, but not so. Jesus loves man giving expression to the creativity God put in him, and it will forever be that way. Forever man will be bringing little trinkets into the New Jerusalem, saying, "Hey, Dad, look what I made!"

God will say, "That's so good, son! You whittled out a little chair for me. That's so sweet of you. I've got a throne, but that's wonderful. Good job!" You know how our kids give us pictures, and we put them up on the refrigerator? God will say, "Isn't that great! Good job!" God loves His kids doing things that bring them joy.

We can read about details of the Temple in Ezekiel 46 and see that it will be so cool and elaborate. God is really particular about the whole thousand years, and He's looking forward to dwelling with man in glory. It's exciting!

This next passage points out how naturally the earth will be rebuilt and how we're involved.

Isaiah 65:20-22 (NLT)

No longer will babies die when only a few days old. No longer will adults die before they have lived a full life. No longer will people be considered old at one hundred! Only the cursed will die that young! In those days people will live in the houses they build and eat the fruit of their own vineyards. Unlike the past, invaders will not take their houses and confiscate their vineyards. For my people will live as long as trees, and my chosen ones will have time to enjoy their hard-won gains.

You also see that longevity will be restored when a 100-year-old person isn't even considered old. Hallelujah to that! "But,

Joe, what does 'only the cursed will die that young' mean? That doesn't sound good." It may sound complicated, but it's really not. Here's what it means. If a 100-year-old sinner refuses to receive Jesus as Savior even while He reigns in Jerusalem and the person refuses to worship at the Feast of Tabernacles, he will go to hell accursed when he dies. It's sad! The person could have lived a thousand years enjoying every provision of God—including fellowship with the King of Kings.

JESUS WILL BRAG ON THE CHURCH

During the Millennium, Jesus will promote you and tout you. There will be natural-bodied people who might get frustrated and whine, but Jesus will say, "Look at My Church. They defeated the devil while he was physically on earth. What are you complaining about?" Come on!

"It's just so hard!" the natural-bodied people might say about something or other.

Jesus will answer, "*Hooold* on now. My Church dealt with Lucifer on the planet and put him under their feet. They stood on My Word and walked in their authority. My Church told Lucifer, 'You're not running over me! You're under my feet!'" Jesus will show you off.

It's important to realize that we are living for eternity. The Church Age drawing to a close is not the end; the Rapture is the beginning. God has deposited so much in your spirit, and you have such radical dreams for the future because you will live forever. Hallelujah!

ISAIAH 60:21-22 (NLT)

All your people will be righteous. They will possess their land forever, for I will plant them there with my own hands in order to bring myself glory. The smallest family will become a thousand people, and the tiniest group will become a mighty nation. At the right time, I, the Lord, will make it happen.

Jesus will want you to pursue the desires of your heart. If you like to do videos, maybe you will make movies. If you like to write songs, do it prolifically. I don't know why we think we will float around on clouds with harps all day. You will pursue the passions you have in your heart with a complete expression of wholeness in your life. You will live with zero frustration. Come on! That makes me want to shout!

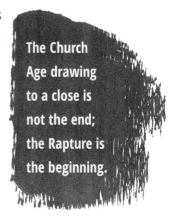

The Church Age drawing to a close is not the end; the Rapture is the beginning.

RULERSHIP

There will be rulership during the Millennium, and you and I will help implement the kingdom. We will not simply taste of the powers to come or the gifts of the Spirit but fully function in them—all nine.

"What will rulership be like?" someone might ask. The rulership we have now in the Church Age is principalities, powers, rulers of the darkness of this world, and wicked spirits in heavenly places. Lucifer has a sphere of influence over regions. In this current dispensation, Lucifer has a right to be here because

Adam surrendered his authority. Jesus took back that authority and handed it to the Church. Now the keys are in our hands.

During the Millennium, you will rule over a city, cities, or even a region. Based on what you did while in this dispensation, the Lord will assign you rulership. As we said earlier, you are writing your resume right now.

This is conjecture, but I think Jesus will set you up over a region and say, "Here's your jurisdiction." The Bible says you will be judging angels (1 Cor. 6:3). That word *judge* means *"rule over."* All of a sudden, angels will be subject to you. During the thousand years, Jesus will rule the world from Jerusalem, and you will implement His kingdom. Natural people will still have accidents and make mistakes because normal-bodied people can do wild and crazy things from time to time. I don't say that with disrespect—just awareness of humankind. But guess who will be assigned to show up and get them set free? *You!*

> **During the Millennium, you will rule over a city, cities, or even a region.**

GLORY POLICE

You will have seen the accident in a vision called a word of wisdom, and you will arrive in time for the guy's motorcycle mishap. Maybe he doesn't hit the jump just right and breaks his neck. You will walk right over to him, saying, "Rise. Take up your bed and walk!"

During the Church Age, many of us labored to operate more in the gifts of the Spirit and got frustrated about not doing more, but you are not done! During the Millennium, you and every other glorified believer will function mightily in the gifts of the Spirit—a thousand years of continuing to move in the gifts.

If a guy on the top of a ladder falls off and hurts his shoulder, you will walk through the wall just like Jesus and lay hands on him. The glory of the Lord will shoot into his bones and sinews, and he will say, "Wow! All the pain is gone!"

"Of course, you don't hurt anymore!" you answer. "Jesus reigns from Jerusalem, and I'm just implementing His healing power all over the earth." You might as well know how to function with God now because you will be doing a whole lot more of it for a very long time to come.

During the Millennium, God will give man a whole thousand years to make correct choices. Yet even with the devil bound, people will still say, "The devil made me do it." No, the devil did not make them do it. Even with Lucifer not around to tempt them, some people will still choose evil. God gives every man an opportunity to make good choices.

You and I will be like the emergency police, the emergency glory people, the emergency judges. If someone tries to rob a bank or do something stupid, that troublemaker will be messing with the wrong person in the wrong dispensation. You will walk right through the wall and nab the thief.

> You and I will be like the emergency police, the emergency glory people, the emergency judges.

"How did you know I was going to rob the place?" the thief might ask.

"I had a word of wisdom," you will answer. "Don't be trying this stuff in the Millennium." It will almost be like some of these movies you've watched where the hero sees in the future. You will have a word of wisdom to see the future plan and purpose of God before it happens.

That's tasting of the power of the world to come, and that is the way we will function for a whole thousand years. Natural man may seem limited during that thousand years, but you will have oversight and function in God's glory.

Whatever comes along, your attitude will be, "No problem!" Word of knowledge and word of wisdom will be how you will deal with it all. Won't it be amazing to have a group of people who can handle every problem that comes up? That will be *you!* Jesus will have you infiltrated into the whole earth with supernatural equipment for a thousand years. You will be fulfilled spiritually and physically. You will lack nothing and live to the fullest!

GOD WILL RADIATE THROUGH YOU

God knows the end from the beginning, and He will raise you up to implement a thousand years of influence over the whole earth to where the glory of God will be literally manifested through you. This is what Lucifer had before he fell from heaven. He was the anointed cherub who covered the throne of God as glory radiated through his pipes, tabrets, and stones. The trouble was, he got to thinking, *Check it out! I'm so cool! Hear that? It's coming from me.* But it wasn't coming *from* him—it was coming from *behind* him. It was coming from God.

During the whole thousand years, you will be in a glorified body with the full expression of God's goodness as He will radiate through you. Natural-bodied people will be in awe of the power of God you demonstrate. They will think, *Wow! I should receive Jesus. He's glowing and all these saints are glowing to help me live my life.* You will be instrumental in getting people to accept Jesus as their Savior during the Millennium.

That means your work to evangelize and witness won't end with the Church Age. We think, *Wow, during the Millennium, I will have a thousand years for golf or whatever.* Yes, you'll have plenty of time for golf or your hobby, but you will also have plenty of resurrection time. You'll have some good lake time and good throne time. You'll enjoy a joyful, normal, peaceful life full of strength.

You will enjoy every facet of Jesus. Life with Jesus will be normal. The world tries to portray Jesus as some weird religious freak. Not so. Bless His heart! Jesus is supernatural all right, but He's also normal. He's supernaturally normal. Jesus is not weird, ghost-like, woo-woo, or eerie. He's really very normal and everything good.

MORNING COMMUTE FROM HEAVEN

Believer, there are such great things ahead for you! In fact, let me give you a little conjecture. In John 14, Jesus said He was going to prepare a place for us. It will be a mansion, not just a tent. I personally believe we will live in heaven—commuting back and forth to the earth just like angels do. Your commute between heaven and earth would be no big deal as you travel at the speed of thought!

> I personally believe we will live in heaven—commuting back and forth to the earth just like angels do.

Angels do it all the time. The Bible says, "For I tell you that in heaven their angels are always in the presence of my heavenly Father" (Matt. 18:10 NLT). They're also back and forth on earth protecting the children they are assigned to guard.

We might have mansions in heaven and commute for work or even a cruise here on earth. You will see star cruisers raised up and rocket ships made by the mortals. You will enjoy the benefits of creativity everywhere you look all the while thinking, *Bless their little hearts! Those toys are cool, but I don't need a rocket. Instantly, I can be wherever I need to be. Hallelujah! Bless you little mortals having to do things like in the olden days.*

THE LAST REBELLION

It's really intriguing to read what happens at the end of the thousand years when Satan will get out of jail. He will cause trouble again as usual and be defeated again as usual.

REVELATION 20:7-9 (NLT)

When the thousand years come to an end, Satan will be let out of his prison. He will go out to deceive the nations—called Gog and Magog—in every corner of the earth. He will gather them together for battle—a mighty army, as numberless as sand along the seashore. And I saw them as they went up on the broad plain of the earth and surrounded God's people and the beloved city. But fire from heaven came down on the attacking armies and consumed them.

These scriptures freak me out considering we will live in a perfect society during the Millennial Reign. As mentioned earlier. Jesus will be on television, radio, and everything you can imagine, but there will still be people who rebel. It's not just a few rebels either. Verse 9 above said they will be "numberless as sand along the seashore." It blows my mind!

Verse 9 also said that Satan will surround God's people. In the Greek, it literally says Satan and his cohorts will be "airborne." Technology will have developed to the point that Satan's army thinks if they send flying saucers over Jerusalem, they will conquer Jesus. Bless their darlin' hearts and stupid heads, as Brother Hagin used to say. What happens? Fire from heaven consumes them! And that's that. That's the last rebellion. Period. End of story.

God gives man a whole thousand years to make correct choices, but even without the devil there to tempt and harass them, some still choose darkness. So, Satan will be released to gather them up, and then the rebellion will be squashed. But God in His great mercy will give man every opportunity to turn to Him.

If man can be creative after the Fall of man and while enduring the curse on the earth, imagine how glorious the thousand years will be without all that trouble! There will be joy unspeakable and full of glory. There are many, many verses about the Millennium.

GREAT WHITE THRONE JUDGMENT

As the Millennium draws to a close, we will see the Great White Throne Judgment when the earth will be renovated by fire, and God will move heaven down to earth. God will move a whole planet down to this planet, and the new Jerusalem will be here on earth.

During the Great White Throne Judgment, the Book of Works will be opened, and God will say, "You have accepted My Son's works or you wouldn't be here, but you thought on your own merits you could be pure as Me." I guarantee you that it will function like a court of law. The case will be presented against an individual like this, "Even during that seven-year period when you had more fireworks than you could even imagine, you determined not to ever repent. I gave you opportunity after opportunity after opportunity." He will show them all the opportunities because God is so merciful, so just, and so fair.

TREE OF LIFE REINTRODUCED

In Revelation 21, the word *Jerusalem*, according to *Strong's Concordance*, is actually *plural*—referring to the earthly Jerusalem and the heavenly Jerusalem. There will be a highway between the two, and that is when the Tree of Life will be reintroduced.

Natural man will live on the earth forever, eating of the Tree of Life to sustain a natural life. You and I won't need to eat even the Tree of Life because, "He that hath the Son hath life" (1 John 5:12). Essentially, life will revert back to what it was when Adam and Eve were here. If they had eaten of the Tree of Life in a sinful state, they would have lived sinfully forever. But the natural-bodied people who make it to that point will eat of the Tree of Life to sustain them. On either side of the pure river coming out of the Throne of God will be a Tree of Life, and the leaves will be for the healing of the nations (Rev. 22:2). The word *healing* is actually translated *preservations*—referring to the Tree of Life.

It is hard to even imagine how natural and supernatural it will be all at the same time. It's hard to wrap your brain around how cool it will be. Imagine a gorgeous sunset you have seen in times past, and then realize that the beauty you saw was through a filter of the curse currently on earth. Imagine a sunset with no curse. Imagine life on this earth with no devil. Imagine a new heaven and new earth and all the joy that will flood your soul.

Begin to say aloud even now: "My future is bright. I will run my race and sweep souls into the kingdom. I will do God's will." The implementation of all this Word you've heard will not be pushed aside. You will function in all that authority and power and of the powers of the world to come.

> It is hard to even imagine how natural and supernatural it will be all at the same time.

You will comprehend and judge with a merciful heart because you knew what it was like living on earth during the Church Age. Just watch! God will have you rule with such insight, and it will be marvelous. If you like to build furniture, you might be the coolest furniture builder in the whole thousand years. If you like to paint, you might paint for a thousand years, and people will go, "Check out that incredible painting!" It will be a wonderful expression of joy and gratitude toward our Father and His Son.

So get it in your heart right now. Great, great, great things are ahead as Jesus comes back to the planet. The King of Kings and the Lord of Lords is about to step over the banister and say, "Come up hither! Come up to the throne of God." With a shout of the voice of the archangel, we shall be changed and so shall we ever be with the Lord.

There is a lot more that could be said about the Millennium, but my friend, you have nothing but wonderful things ahead. Yes, there is darkness on the horizon. National and international affairs don't look good. We live in perilous times—no question about it. The Tribulation is coming for those who don't believe, and the horrific reports only go from bad to worse. But while there is plenty of bad news swirling around you, there is no bad news for the Christian. You have only a glorious future ahead because Jesus loves you more than life itself, and He can hardly wait to see you face to face.

> You have only a glorious future ahead because Jesus loves you more than life itself, and He can hardly wait to see you face to face.

CLARENCE LARKIN ESCHATOLOGY CHARTS

MILLIONS HAVE GAINED visual insight and a greater understanding of Bible history, Bible prophecies, and dispensational timelines as they study the eschatology charts created by the late Clarence Larkin (1850–1924). We've reprinted a few primary ones here for you to enjoy.

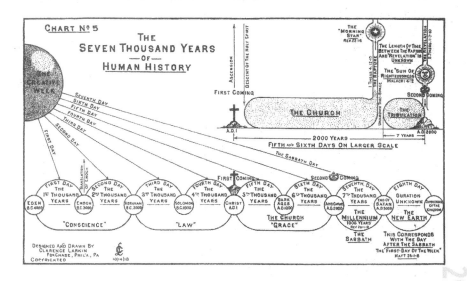

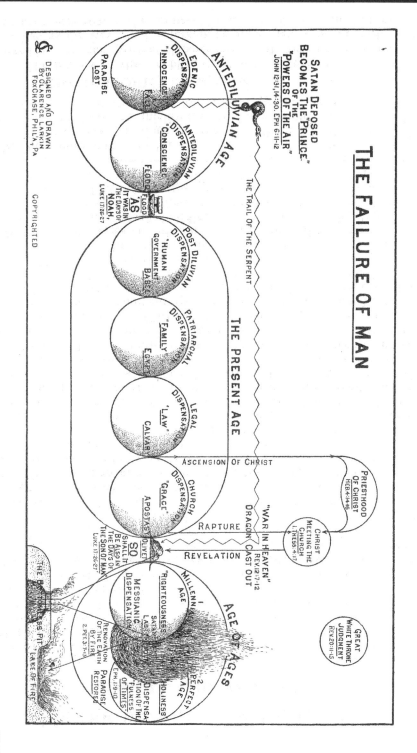

THE FAILURE OF MAN

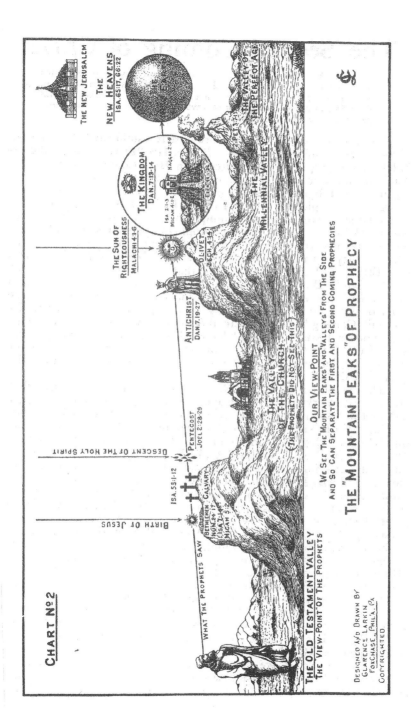

CHART № 2

THE OLD TESTAMENT VALLEY
THE VIEW-POINT OF THE PROPHETS

THE "MOUNTAIN PEAKS" OF PROPHECY

OUR VIEW-POINT
WE SEE THE "MOUNTAIN PEAKS" AND "VALLEYS" FROM THE SIDE
AND SO CAN SEPARATE THE FIRST AND SECOND COMING PROPHECIES
(THE PROPHETS DID NOT SEE THIS)

DESIGNED AND DRAWN BY
CLARENCE LARKIN
FOXCHASE, PHILA., PA.
COPYRIGHTED

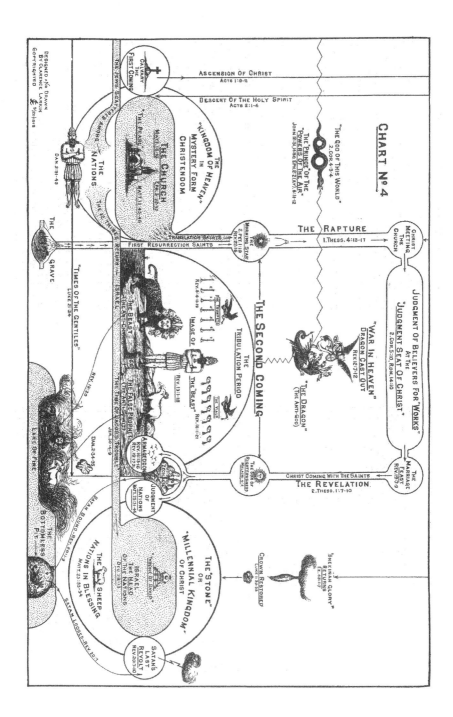

HOW TO LIVE WITH JESUS FOREVER

TO MEET JESUS in the air when the trumpet blasts at the Rapture and return with Jesus at the Second Coming to live with Him forever, there's one important thing you must do. You must receive Jesus Christ as your Savior and Lord. It's the most important decision you'll ever make, and it's as easy as believing and praying the prayer below aloud.

Dear heavenly Father:

Your Word says, "Whosoever shall call on the name of the Lord shall be saved" (Acts 2:21). I call on You right now!

The Bible says if I confess with my mouth that Jesus is Lord and believe in my heart that You have raised Him from the dead, I will be saved (Romans 10:9-10).

Jesus, I believe in my heart and confess with my mouth that You were raised from the dead. I ask You now to be my Savior and Lord. Thank You for forgiving me of sin.

Second Corinthians 5:17 says this means I now belong to You and have become a new person on the inside. The old life is gone; a new life has begun in Jesus' name. Amen.

NOTES

CHAPTER 3 // THE FUTURE BEFORE IT HAPPENS

1. The Hebrew word *moed* reflects times and seasons God appoints.

CHAPTER 4 // 75+ SIGNS OF JESUS' RETURN...AND COUNTING

1. In Leviticus 25, God commanded Israel to observe a year of Jubilee every 50 years. It was a year of rest, debt forgiveness, slave liberation, restitution, and liberty.

2. "10 Glorious Photos of Israel's Fruit and Vegetable Bounty," Touchpoint Israel, May 29, 2018, https://www.touchpointisrael .com/2018/05/29/10-glorious-photos-of-israels-fruit-and -vegetable-bounty.

3. Michael Freemantle, "The Weizmann Contribution," *ChemistryWorld*, July 5, 2017, https://www.chemistryworld.com/ opinion/the-weizmann-contribution/3007435.article.

4. Michelle Ule, "The Taking of Jerusalem: December 11, 1917," https://www.michelleule.com/2018/12/14/jerusalem.

5. Reuben Lewis, "Israeli Inventions That Changed the World," The Culture Trip, April 12, 2021, https://theculturetrip.com/middle -east/israel/articles/11-israeli-innovations-that-changed-the -world.

6. "Black Gold Under the Golan," *The Economist,* November 7, 2015, https://www.economist.com/middle-east-and-africa/2015/11/07/ black-gold-under-the-golan.

7. Grant R. Jeffrey, *The New Temple and the Second Coming* (Colorado Springs, CO: WaterBrook Press, 2007).

8. "Foxes seen walking near the Western Wall, fulfilling biblical promise," *The Jerusalem Post,* August 8, 2019, https://www.jpost.com/israel-news/foxes-seen-walking-near-the-western-wall-fulfilling-biblical-promise-598053.

9. Rossella Tercatin, "Ancient Judean ritual baths fill with water following intense winter rains," *The Jerusalem Post,* February 19, 2020, https://www.jpost.com/israel-news/winter-rains-fill-up-ritual-baths-used-by-pilgrims-2000-years-ago-617997.

10. Andrew Ackerman, "Fed Prepares to Launch Review of Possible Central Bank Digital Currency," *The Wall Street Journal*, October 4, 2021, https://www.wsj.com/articles/fed-prepares-to-launch-review-of-possible-central-bank-digital-currency-11633339800.

11. James T. Areddy, "China Creates Its Own Digital Currency, a First for Major Economy," *The Wall Street Journal*, April 5, 2021, https://www.wsj.com/articles/china-creates-its-own-digital-currency-a-first-for-major-economy-11617634118.

12. Eugene Bach, "One World Religion Headquarters Set to Open Next Year," Back to Jerusalem, https://backtojerusalem.com/one-world-religion-headquarters-set-to-open-next-year.

13. Stephen M. Miller, "Valley of Armageddon," https://stephenmillerbooks.com/2013/01/valley-of-armageddon.

14. "How China's one-child policy created massive gender gap in country," February 23, 2021, https://www.wionews.com/world/how-chinas-one-child-policy-created-massive-gender-gap-in-country-365759.

15. Eliana Rudee, "Ezekiel's End-of-Days Vision Revealed: Dead Sea Coming to Life," Israel365 News, October 4, 2018, https://www.israel365news.com/114621/ezekiels-vision-revealed-dead-sea-life.

16. Hadassah Brenner, "Is the Sea of Galilee's recent water level rise dangerous?" *The Jerusalem Post,* March 29, 2021, https://www.jpost.com/israel-news/is-the-sea-of-galilees-recent-water-level-rise-dangerous-663520.

17. New World Encyclopedia, s.v. "Talmud," https://www.newworldencyclopedia.org/entry/Talmud.

18. Tzvi Joffre, "Was Netanyahu-Gantz impasse predicted in mystic's hidden manuscript?" *The Jerusalem Post,* September 24, 2019, https://www.jpost.com/israel-news/netanyahu-gantz-impasse -predicted-in-hidden-manuscript-of-leading-mystic-602670.

19. Bill Perkins, "Petra: Prepared by God?" https://compass.org/wp -content/uploads/2017/08/Petra-Prepared-by-God.pdf.

20. Mary Bufe, "Ancient Nabataeans Used Sophisticated Water Technologies to Create a Thriving Desert City," February 18, 2019, https://news.wef.org/ancient-nabataeans-used-sophisticated -water-technologies-to-create-a-thriving-dessert-city.

21. Matthias Williams and Robin Emmott, "Ukraine Says Russia Will Soon Have Over 120,000 Troops on Its Borders," *USNews,* April 20, 2021, https://www.usnews.com/news/world/articles/2021-04-20/ russia-to-reach-over-120-000-troops-on-ukraines-border-in-a -week-ukraine-says.

22. NATO, "Joint press conference," November 25, 2021, https://www .nato.int/cps/en/natohq/opinions_188958.htm.

23. "Russian troops rush to fill void left by U.S. troops in northern Syria," CBS, October 15, 2019, https://www.cbsnews.com/news/ russia-in-syria-russian-troops-fill-void-left-by-trumps-troop -withdrawal-in-northern-syria.

24. Amos Harel, "Israeli Satellite Images Reveal: Iran Builds Military Base Near Damascus," Haaretz, February 28, 2018, https://www .haaretz.com/middle-east-news/syria/israeli-satellite-images -reveal-iran-builds-military-base-near-syria-1.5863736.

25. Alon Ben-Meir, "'Army of Islam': Erdogan's Plot Against Israel," *The Globalist,* March 26, 2018, https://www.theglobalist.com/turkey -erdogan-democracy-media-israel-united-states-europe.

26. Oren Dorell, "Iran calls Israel 'rabid dog' amid nuclear talks," *USA Today,* November 20, 2013, https://www.usatoday.com/ story/news/world/2013/11/20/iran-nuclear-talks-geneva -israel/3649815.

27. Zvi Bar'el, "Behind Erdogan's Remarkable Claim," Haaretz, October 9, 2020, https://www.haaretz.com/israel-news/.premium-erdogan -jerusalem-is-ours-what-really-stands-behind-turkey-hagia -sophia-church-of-the-holy-sepulchre-1.9207465.

28. Adam Eliyahu Berkowitz, "Latest 'Palestinian' Claim: Big Ben Is Ours and We Want It Back," Israel365 News, January 25, 2021, https://www.israel365news.com/164450/latest-palestinian -claim-big-ben-is-ours-and-we-want-it-back.

29. Animal Planet, March 2009.

30. Zafrir Rinat, "Israel's 500 Million Birds: The World's Eighth Wonder," Haaretz, January 13, 2017, https://www.haaretz.com/israel-news/ .premium.MAGAZINE-israels-500-million-birds-the-worlds-eighth -wonder-1.5485176.

31. Harvey Sullivan, "First 'red heifer' born in Israel for 2,000 years," *The Sun,* September 10, 2018, https://www.thesun.co.uk/news/ 7217719/bible-prophecy-apocalypse-firs-red-heifer-born-israel.

32. "Another Red Heifer Born in Israel," March 21, 2019, https://www .thekingiscoming.com/blog/2019/3/21/another-red-heifer-born -in-israel.

33. "Can a Chip Be Implanted in Humans?" August 10, 2020, https:// gpstrackerreviews.net/are-chips-being-implanted-in-humans.

34. "World Hunger: Key Facts And Statistics 2021," Action Against Hunger, https://www.actionagainsthunger.org/world-hunger-facts -statistics.

35. Ryan P. Mulligan and Andy Take, "The world's biggest waves: How climate change could trigger large landslides and 'mega- tsunamis,'" The Conversation, https://theconversation.com/the -worlds-biggest-waves-how-climate-change-could-trigger-large -landslides-and-mega-tsunamis-115882.

36. Alexandra Witze, "The tides they are a-changin'—and it's not just from climate change," *Knowable Magazine,* April 22, 2020, https:// knowablemagazine.org/article/physical-world/2020/tides-they -are-changin-and-its-not-just-climate-change.

37. Alexis Madrigal, "Mysteriously High Tides on East Coast Perplex Scientists," *WIRED*, July 30, 2009, https://www.wired.com/2009/07/ hightides.

38. "More than 500 hospitalized from scorpion stings after storm in Egypt," NBC News, November 16, 2021, https://www.nbcnews .com/news/world/500-hospitalized-scorpion-stings-storm-egypt -rcna5659.

39. Jay Michaelson, "Extreme Weather? Blame the End Times," The Daily Beast, April 14, 2017, https://www.thedailybeast.com/extreme-weather-blame-the-end-times.

40. Peter White, "Late-Nights Hosts Come Together to Tackle Climate Change," Deadline.com, September 15, 2021, https://deadline.com/2021/09/late-nights-hosts-come-together-to-tackle-climate-change-1234834059.

41. Tony Phillips, "A Tetrad of Lunar Eclipses," NASA Science, March 27, 2014, https://science.nasa.gov/science-news/science-at-nasa/2014/27mar_tetrad.

42. "How rare is the Revelation 12 Heavenly sign?" October 20, 2014, http://www.christiantalkzone.net/forum/index.php?threads/how-rare-is-the-revelation-12-heavenly-sign-23-september-2017-once-in-7000-years.3276.

43. Hyonhee Shin, "S.Korea scrambles fighter jets as China, Russia aircraft enter air defense zone," Reuters, November 19, 2021, https://www.reuters.com/world/skorea-scrambles-fighter-jets-china-russia-aircraft-enter-air-defense-zone-2021-11-19.

44. "China surprises U.S. with nuclear-capable hypersonic missile test, FT reports," CNBC, Ocober 17, 2021, https://www.cnbc.com/2021/10/17/china-surprises-us-with-nuclear-capable-hypersonic-missile-test-ft-reports.html.

45. "Thriving in a World of 'Knowledge Half-Life,'" CIO.com, April 5, 2019, https://www.cio.com/article/3387637/thriving-in-a-world-of-knowledge-half-life.html.

46. Amitabh Ray, "Human knowledge is doubling every 12 hours," October 22, 2020, https://www.linkedin.com/pulse/human-knowledge-doubling-every-12-hours-amitabh-ray.

47. "Issue brief: Nation's drug-related overdose and death epidemic continues to worsen," American Medical Association, https://www.ama-assn.org/system/files/issue-brief-increases-in-opioid-related-overdose.pdf.

48. Wide-ranging online data for epidemiologic research (WONDER), Atlanta, GA: CDC, National Center for Health Statistics, 2020, available at http://wonder.cdc.gov.

49. Nicola Stow, "Fit for a Tyrant," The US Sun, December 3, 2019, https://www.the-sun.com/news/us-news/116748/inside-abandoned-babylon-built-by-saddam-hussein-who-thought-he-was-reincarnation-of-ancient-king-nebuchadnezzar.

50. "Criminal Justice Facts," The Sentencing Project, https://www.sentencingproject.org/criminal-justice-facts.

51. Ryan Lucas, "FBI Data Shows an Unprecedented Spike in Murders Nationwide in 2020," NPR.org, September 27, 2021, https://www.npr.org/2021/09/27/1040904770/fbi-data-murder-increase-2020.

52. David Dickinson, "Is This Month's Jupiter-Venus Pair Really a Star of Bethlehem Stand In?" Universe Today, October 14, 2015, https://www.universetoday.com/122738/is-this-months-jupiter-venus-pair-really-a-star-of-bethlehem-stand-in.

53. "Macron's overtures to Catholic Church make waves in secular France," Reuters, April 10, 2018, https://www.reuters.com/article/uk-france-religion/macrons-overtures-to-catholic-church-make-waves-in-secular-france-idUKKBN1HH2L3.

54. Avi Mayer, "Hate is on the rise: Antisemitism surges on America's far left and far right," USA Today, October 26, 2021, https://www.usatoday.com/story/opinion/2021/10/26/antisemitism-rises-far-left-and-right/6138796001/?gnt-cfr=1.

55. "Israel and Hamas May Reach Cease-Fire Soon, Officials Say," The New York Times, May 19, 2021, https://www.nytimes.com/live/2021/05/19/world/israel-palestine-gaza.

56. "What is the significance of the Eastern Gate of Jerusalem?" GotQuestions.org, https://www.gotquestions.org/eastern-gate-Jerusalem.html.

57. "The Reforestation of Israel," Aardvark Israel, https://aardvarkisrael.com/the-reforestation-of-israel.

58. "Global Terrorism Database," UMD, https://www.start.umd.edu/research-projects/global-terrorism-database-gtd.

59. "Israel Advances Plan for New Settlement Homes, in First for Bennett Era," The New York Times, October 27, 2021, https://www.nytimes.com/2021/10/27/world/middleeast/israel-settlements-west-bank.html.

60. "St. Malachy," https://catholicprophecy.org/st-malachy.

61. Khaled al-Khateb, "Russia begins restoration of Arch of Triumph in Syria's Palmyra," Al-Monitor, November 14, 2021, https://www .al-monitor.com/originals/2021/11/russia-begins-restoration-arc -triumph-syrias-palmyra.

62. Adam Eliyahu Berkowitz, "Russians Rebuilding Pagan Arch of Palmyra: Preparation for Messiah?" Israel365 News, April 12, 2021, https://www.israel365news.com/189320/russians-rebuilding -pagan-arch-of-palmyra-preparation-for-messiah.

63. Adam Eliyahu Berkowitz, "Jewish Prophecy Predicts Temple of Ba'al Arch in London Will Bring Messiah," Israel365 News, April 14, 2016, https://www.israel365news.com/65680/could-model -baal-temple-arch-bring-messiah-talmud-says-yes-jewish-world.

64. Hananya Naftali, "Water Turns BLOOD Red Near Dead Sea During Jewish Holiest Season," YouTube, September 18, 2021, https:// www.youtube.com/watch?v=MQEVDYmakjl.

65. Tzvi Joffre, "Pool of water near Dead Sea turns blood red, authorities investigating," *The Jerusalem Post,* September 13, 2021, https://www.jpost.com/middle-east/pool-of-water-near-dead -sea-turns-blood-red-authorities-investigating-679278.

66. Rohit Ranjan, "Spain: Hundreds of Birds Rain Down on Ferrol Streets, Authorities Probe Mystery Death," Republic World, December 3, 2021, https://www.republicworld.com/world-news/ europe/spain-hundreds-of-birds-rain-down-on-ferrol-streets -authorities-probe-mystery-death.html.

67. "Science and the Bible," Facts About Israel, https://www .factsaboutisrael.uk/science-and-the-bible.

68. Margaret Davis, "Solar Storm Warning: NASA Prepares for Swirling Debris That May Hit Earth This Week and Cause Mild Disturbance," *The Science Times,* December 9, 2021, https://www .sciencetimes.com/articles/34955/20211209/nasa-released-solar -storm-warning-swirling-sun-debris-hit-earth.htm.

69. Tariq Malik, "Huge solar flare could supercharge northern lights on Halloween," Space.com, October 29, 2021, https://www.space .com/northern-lights-on-halloween-from-solar-flare-october -2021.

70. Megan Marples and Ashley Strickland, "Massive X-class solar flare erupted from sun," CNN, July 7, 2021, https://www.cnn.com/2021/07/07/world/solar-flare-cycle-25-scn/index.html.

71. Rasha Aridi, "For the First Time Ever, a NASA Spacecraft Has 'Touched' the Sun," *Smithsonian*, December 15, 2021, https://www.smithsonianmag.com/smart-news/nasa-spacecraft-just-touched-the-sun-heres-what-we-learned-180979227.

72. Michael Snyder, "Donald Trump Was Born Exactly 700 Days Before Israel Became a Nation," Charisma News, January 4, 2017, https://www.charismanews.com/opinion/62169-donald-trump-was-born-exactly-700-days-before-israel-became-a-nation.

73. Richard Stone, "Russia, China, United States Race to Build Hypersonic Weapons," Science.org, January 8, 2020, https://www.science.org/content/article/national-pride-stake-russia-china-united-states-race-build-hypersonic-weapons.

74. "Russia deploys Avangard hypersonic missile system," BBC News, December 27 2019, https://www.bbc.com/news/world-europe-50927648.

75. Blake Stilwell, "Why Russia's Hypersonic Missiles Can't Be Seen on Radar," Military.com, https://www.military.com/equipment/weapons/why-russias-hypersonic-missiles-cant-be-seen-radar.html.

76. "Russia leads the world in hypersonic missiles tech, Putin says," Reuters, December 12, 2021, https://www.reuters.com/world/russia-leads-world-hypersonic-missiles-tech-putin-says-2021-12-12.

CHAPTER 5 // A GREAT TRANSITION OF DISPENSATIONS

1. "Climate Change Indicators: Wildfires," EPA, Environmental Protection Agency, May 19 2021, www.epa.gov/climate-indicators/climate-change-indicators-wildfires.

2. John G. Lake: His Life, His Sermons, His Boldness of Faith (Harrison House Publishers, first edition and printing, 2013).

3. "The seven dispensations: What are they?" Compelling Truth, https://www.compellingtruth.org/seven-dispensations.html.

CHAPTER 6 // THE RAPTURE

1. Strong's #726: harpazo (pronounced har-pad'-zo) from a derivative of 138; to seize (in various applications): catch (away, up), pluck, pull, take (by force). Thayer's Greek Lexicon: harpazō: to snatch out or away.

CHAPTER 7 // NATIONS LINING UP FOR THE EZEKIEL 38 WAR

1. Zvi Bar'el, "Behind Erdogan's Remarkable Claim," Haaretz, October 9, 2020, https://www.haaretz.com/israel-news/.premium-erdogan-jerusalem-is-ours-what-really-stands-behind-turkey-hagia-sophia-church-of-the-holy-sepulchre-1.9207465.

2. Adam Eliyahu Berkowitz, "Latest 'Palestinian' Claim: Big Ben Is Ours and We Want It Back," Israel365 News, January 25, 2021, https://www.israel365news.com/164450/latest-palestinian-claim-big-ben-is-ours-and-we-want-it-back.

3. Ray Locker, "Pentagon 2008 study claims Putin has Asperger's syndrome," *USA Today*, February 4, 2015, https://www.usatoday.com/story/news/politics/2015/02/04/putin-aspergers-syndrome-study-pentagon/22855927.

CHAPTER 11 // THE TRIBULATION AND THE GREAT TRIBULATON

1 Celine Cantar, "Palestinians in Syria Struggle for Bread and Agency," December 2014, https://www.opendemocracy.net/en/north-africa-west-asia/palestinians-in-syria-struggle-for-bread-and-agency.

CHAPTER 12 // THE SECOND COMING OF JESUS

1. Michael Freemantle, "The Weizmann Contribution," ChemistryWorld, July 5, 2017, https://www.chemistryworld.com/opinion/the-weizmann-contribution/3007435.article.

END OF DAYS UPDATES

Weekly updates where Bible prophecy meets headline news...
UNTIL JESUS RETURNS!

OUR VISION

Proclaiming the truth and the power of the Gospel of Jesus Christ with excellence. Challenging Christians to live victoriously, grow spiritually, know God intimately.

Connect with us on

Facebook @ HarrisonHousePublishers

and Instagram @ HarrisonHousePublishing

so you can stay up to date with news

about our books and our authors.

Visit us at **www.harrisonhouse.com**

for a complete product listing as well as

monthly specials for wholesale distribution.